QGIS 2 Cookbook

Become a QGIS power user and master QGIS
data management, visualization, and spatial
analysis techniques

Alex Mandel

Víctor Olaya Ferrero

Anita Graser

Alexander Bruy

[PACKT] open source*
PUBLISHING   community experience distilled

BIRMINGHAM - MUMBAI

QGIS 2 Cookbook

First published: April 2016

Production reference: 1250416

Published by Packt Publishing Ltd.
Livery Place
35 Livery Street
Birmingham B3 2PB, UK.

ISBN 978-1-78398-496-1

www.packtpub.com

Credits

Authors

Alex Mandel

Víctor Olaya Ferrero

Anita Graser

Alexander Bruy

Reviewers

Jorge Arévalo

Olivier Dalang

Ben Mearns

Commissioning Editor

Pramila Balan

Acquisition Editor

Vinay Argekar

Content Development Editor

Amey Varangaonkar

Merint Mathew

Technical Editor

Dhiraj Chandanshive

Copy Editor

Priyanka Ravi

Project Coordinator

Suzanne Coutinho

Proofreader

Safis Editing

Indexer

Rekha Nair

Production Coordinator

Aparna Bhagat

Cover Work

Aparna Bhagat

About the Authors

Alex Mandel is a geospatial scientist who has a PhD in geography and more than 12 years of experience in applying GIS to a variety of projects. He has also taught courses on GIS, geospatial programming, and Geoweb.

Víctor Olaya Ferrero is a GIS developer. He is the creator and main developer of the QGIS Processing Framework. He is also the author of *Sistemas de Información Geográfica*, a free book about the fundamentals of GIS.

I would like to thank my co-authors and everyone else in the QGIS community.

Anita Graser studied geomatics at the University of Applied Sciences Wiener Neustadt, Austria, from where she graduated with a master's degree in 2010. During her study, she gained hands-on experience in the fields of geo-marketing and transportation research. Since 2007, she has been working as a **geographic information system** (**GIS**) expert with the dynamic transportation systems group at the **Austrian Institute of Technology** (**AIT**), where she focuses on analyzing and visualizing spatio-temporal data.

Anita serves on the OSGeo board of directors and the QGIS project steering committee. She has been working with GIS since 2005, provides QGIS training courses, and writes a popular blog on open source GIS at `anitagraser.com`.

I would like to thank my family, partner, and coworkers for their support and encouragement. Of course, I also want to thank the whole QGIS community for their continued efforts to provide the best open source GIS experience possible.

Alexander Bruy is a GFOSS advocate and open source developer working on the QGIS project. He has also maintained a collection of his own open source projects. He has been working with QGIS since 2006, and now he is an OSGeo charter member and QGIS core developer. He is also the author of *QGIS By Example, Packt Publishing*.

Alexander is currently a freelance GIS developer and works for various companies worldwide.

About the Reviewers

Jorge Arévalo is a computer engineer from Universidad Autónoma de Madrid, UAM. He started developing web applications with JS, PHP, and Python in 2007. In 2010, he began collaborating with PostGIS and GDAL projects after participating in GSoC 2009, creating the PostGIS Raster GDAL driver. He currently works as a technology trainer and Python/Django developer. He also organizes hackathons with others at `http://hackathonlovers.com/`.

Jorge Arévalo has co-written the book *Instant Zurb Foundation 4* for Packt Publishing. He has also worked as reviewer for the books *PostGIS Cookbook*, *OpenLayers 3 Beginner's Guide*, and *Getting Started with Memcached*, all of them for Packt Publishing.

> I want to thank my wife Elena for her continuous love and support while reviewing this book.

Olivier Dalang completed his master's degree in architecture and urban planning from EPFL, Switzerland. He then worked as an urban planner at Team+ as a volunteer for the NGO urbaMonde, which is active in Senegal, and as a researcher and lecturer at EPFL on the Venice Time Machine project. He got more and more acquainted with QGIS through the different positions he worked in. Being a programmer, he developed a few plugins, of which a few are now in the core.

Ben Mearns lives in Philly, PA, where he consults, teaches, advises, speaks, and creates geographical information. In private practice, he has previously been the lead geospatial information consultant and instructor on GIS for natural resource management at the University of Delaware. He has held other GIS and data positions at the Cartographic Modeling Lab at the University of Pennsylvania, Princeton University, and Macalester College. He is currently writing *QGIS Blueprints* with Packt Publishing, which will soon be available in the market.

I would like to thank my girlfriend, Catherine Moore, and mother, Raiana Mearns, for their support during the review of this book.

www.PacktPub.com

eBooks, discount offers, and more

Did you know that Packt offers eBook versions of every book published, with PDF and ePub files available? You can upgrade to the eBook version at www.PacktPub.com and as a print book customer, you are entitled to a discount on the eBook copy. Get in touch with us at customercare@packtpub.com for more details.

At www.PacktPub.com, you can also read a collection of free technical articles, sign up for a range of free newsletters and receive exclusive discounts and offers on Packt books and eBooks.

https://www2.packtpub.com/books/subscription/packtlib

Do you need instant solutions to your IT questions? PacktLib is Packt's online digital book library. Here, you can search, access, and read Packt's entire library of books.

Why Subscribe?

- ▶ Fully searchable across every book published by Packt
- ▶ Copy and paste, print, and bookmark content
- ▶ On demand and accessible via a web browser

Table of Contents

Preface

Location-based technology is the latest buzzword to explain tools related to spatial knowledge and analysis. For those who work on map making, geospatial science, or any number of other things with spatial data, **Geographic Information Systems** (**GIS**), which is the more traditional name for such tools, is a field of study with decades of innovation.

QGIS (previously known as **Quantum GIS**), a cross-platform, free, and open source software, provides a traditional desktop-based geographic information system. Unlike a traditional system though, it is highly customizable, extendable, and, by design, works in tandem with a ton of other GIS-related tools (more are added all the time).

QGIS is a crossing point of the free and open source geospatial world. While there are a great many tools in QGIS, it is not one massive application that does everything, and it was never really designed to be that from the beginning. It is rather a visual interface to much of the open source geospatial world. You can load data from proprietary and open formats into spatial databases of various flavors and then analyze the data with well-known analytical backends before creating a printed or web-based map to display and interact with your results. What's QGIS's role in all this? It's the place where you check your data along the way, build and queue the analysis, visualize the results, and develop cartographic end products.

If you need to test modify one layer before doing a batch of 1000, use QGIS. Want to make sure the results of that SQL query or script make sense, use QGIS. Need to tinker with alternative methods of displaying your data to find the right colors, lines, and layers to convey your message, use QGIS. Find something QGIS can't do, look at other tools it works with, search the plugin list, write a plugin, or submit a new feature request. With such a mentality, everything is possible—it just takes an understanding of how to get there.

This book is all about showing you how to do all these great things and all the new cool things you didn't know you wanted to do. When QGIS doesn't do what you need or doesn't work with the tools you want to use, we'll show you where to go and who to talk to about making your dream of new functionality a reality.

What this book covers

Over the course of 12 chapters, this book will take you from data input and output, through data management and analysis, to creating print and web output, as well as extending QGIS.

Chapter 1, Data Input and Output, covers loading and saving data with special instructions for trickier formats, batch conversions, and databases.

Chapter 2, Data Management, describes the basic manipulation of attributes, indexes, and queries to make the use of your data more efficient.

Chapter 3, Common Data Preprocessing Steps, deals with converting data into the formats you need for analysis, including vector to and from raster, transitioning through different types of vectors, and cutting your data to just the important areas.

Chapter 4, Data Exploration, explores methods for visualizing and understanding the information in your data.

Chapter 5, Classic Vector Analysis, shows the QGIS way of performing traditional analysis methods of vector layers.

Chapter 6, Network Analysis, dives into the methods for analyzing routes and networks.

Chapter 7, Raster Analysis I, covers raster analysis that is primarily related to topography and hydrology.

Chapter 8, Raster Analysis II, covers common raster analysis methods and introduces more advanced multispectral and classification data handling.

Chapter 9, QGIS and the Web, explores the use of live data from the Web and how to put up your own web map based on a QGIS project.

Chapter 10, Cartography Tips, reveals advanced tips and tricks to get the most out of the cartographic tools in QGIS.

Chapter 11, Extending QGIS, shows you how to take QGIS beyond the out-of-the-box features with plugins, customization, and add-on tools.

Chapter 12, Up and Coming, hints at the future with cutting-edge plugins and how to participate in the future development of QGIS.

What you need for this book

We recommend installing QGIS 2.8 or later; you will need at least QGIS 2.4. During the writing of this book, several new versions were released, approximately every 4 months, and most recently, 2.14 was released. Most of the recipes will work on older versions, but some may require 2.6 or newer. In general, if you can, upgrade to the latest stable release or **Long Term Support (LTS)** version.

There are also a lot of side interactions with other software throughout many of these recipes, including—but not limited to—Postgis 2+, GRASS 6.4+, SAGA 2.0.8+, and Spatialite 4+. On Windows, most of these can be installed using OSGeo4W; on Mac, you may need some additional frameworks from Kyngchaos, or if you're familiar with Brew, you can use the OSGeo4Mac Tap. For Linux users, in particular Ubuntu and Debian, refer to the UbuntuGIS PPA and the DebianGIS blend.

Does all of this sound a little too complicated? If yes, then consider using a virtual machine that runs OSGeo-Live (http://live.osgeo.org). All the software is preinstalled for you and is known to work together.

Lastly, you will need data. For the most part, we've provided a lot of free and open data from a variety of sources, including the OSGeo Educational dataset (North Carolina), Natural Earth Data, OpenFlights, Wake County, City of Davis, and **Armed Conflict Location & Event Data Project (ACLED)**. A full list of our data sources is provided here if you would like additional data.

We recommend that you try methods with the sample data first, only because we tested it. Feel free to try using your own data to test many of the recipes; however, just remember that you might need to alter the structure to make it work. After all, that's what you'll be working with normally.

The following are the data sources for this book:

- OSGeo Educational Data: http://grass.osgeo.org/download/sample-data/
- Wake County, USA: http://www.wakegov.com/gis/services/pages/data.aspx
- Natural Earth Data: http://www.naturalearthdata.com/
- City of Davis, USA: http://maps.cityofdavis.org/library
- Stamen Designs: http://stamen.com/
- Armed Conflict Location & Event Data Project: http://www.acleddata.com/

Who this book is for

This book is for anyone who wants to do more with QGIS. It's aimed at an intermediate to advanced audience that already has some experience using GIS (any). The goal is to master the fundamentals of QGIS and launch you, the reader, to the next level of being a QGIS power user and community member.

Whatever your current level of experience with QGIS, you will find a lot of new ways to put your skills to good use. For those who are new to GIS, this book shows you many of the things that are possible with GIS. For those of you who are new to QGIS, this book is a guide on how to do the things you know from elsewhere with QGIS. For advanced users, this book is a reference and cheat sheet to the common tools you use often but can't quite remember how they work. And for all users, this book is filled with unknown and barely documented aspects of QGIS that you didn't think possible but likely want to use.

Sections

In this book, you will find several headings that appear frequently (Getting ready, How to do it, How it works, There's more, and See also).

To give clear instructions on how to complete a recipe, we use these sections as follows:

Getting ready

This section tells you what to expect in the recipe, and describes how to set up any software or any preliminary settings required for the recipe.

How to do it...

This section contains the steps required to follow the recipe.

How it works...

This section usually consists of a detailed explanation of what happened in the previous section.

There's more...

This section consists of additional information about the recipe in order to make the reader more knowledgeable about the recipe.

See also

This section provides helpful links to other useful information for the recipe.

Conventions

In this book, you will find a number of text styles that distinguish between different kinds of information. Here are some examples of these styles and an explanation of their meaning.

Code words in text, database table names, folder names, filenames, file extensions, pathnames, dummy URLs, user input, and Twitter handles are shown as follows: "Create a Spatialite database if you don't already have one and name it cookbook.db."

A block of code is set as follows:

```
geom,id,elevation
LINESTRING(0 1, 0 2, 1 3),1,50
LINESTRING(0 -1, 0 -2, 1 -3),2,60
LINESTRING(0 1, 0 3, 5 4),3,70
```

When we wish to draw your attention to a particular part of a code block, the relevant lines or items are set in bold:

```
geom,id,elevation
LINESTRING(0 1, 0 2, 1 3),1,50
LINESTRING(0 -1, 0 -2, 1 -3),2,60
LINESTRING(0 1, 0 3, 5 4),3,70
```

Any command-line input or output is written as follows:

```
-gcp sourceX sourceY destinationX destinationY
```

New terms and **important words** are shown in bold. Words that you see on the screen, for example, in menus or dialog boxes, appear in the text like this: "Check the **Use visible raster layers** checkbox or choose **SELECT**."

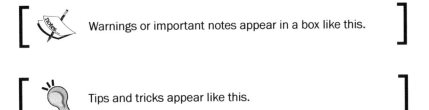

> Warnings or important notes appear in a box like this.

> Tips and tricks appear like this.

Reader feedback

Feedback from our readers is always welcome. Let us know what you think about this book—what you liked or disliked. Reader feedback is important for us as it helps us develop titles that you will really get the most out of.

To send us general feedback, simply e-mail `feedback@packtpub.com`, and mention the book's title in the subject of your message.

If there is a topic that you have expertise in and you are interested in either writing or contributing to a book, see our author guide at `www.packtpub.com/authors`.

Customer support

Now that you are the proud owner of a Packt book, we have a number of things to help you to get the most from your purchase.

Downloading the example code

You can download the example code files for this book from your account at `http://www.packtpub.com`. If you purchased this book elsewhere, you can visit `http://www.packtpub.com/support` and register to have the files e-mailed directly to you.

You can download the code files by following these steps:

1. Log in or register to our website using your e-mail address and password.
2. Hover the mouse pointer on the **SUPPORT** tab at the top.
3. Click on **Code Downloads & Errata**.
4. Enter the name of the book in the **Search** box.
5. Select the book for which you're looking to download the code files.
6. Choose from the drop-down menu where you purchased this book from.
7. Click on **Code Download**.

Once the file is downloaded, please make sure that you unzip or extract the folder using the latest version of:

- WinRAR / 7-Zip for Windows
- Zipeg / iZip / UnRarX for Mac
- 7-Zip / PeaZip for Linux

Downloading the color images of this book

We also provide you with a PDF file that has color images of the screenshots/diagrams used in this book. The color images will help you better understand the changes in the output. You can download this file from http://www.packtpub.com/sites/default/files/downloads/QGIS2Cookbook_ColorImages.pdf.

Errata

Although we have taken every care to ensure the accuracy of our content, mistakes do happen. If you find a mistake in one of our books—maybe a mistake in the text or the code—we would be grateful if you could report this to us. By doing so, you can save other readers from frustration and help us improve subsequent versions of this book. If you find any errata, please report them by visiting http://www.packtpub.com/submit-errata, selecting your book, clicking on the **Errata Submission Form** link, and entering the details of your errata. Once your errata are verified, your submission will be accepted and the errata will be uploaded to our website or added to any list of existing errata under the Errata section of that title.

To view the previously submitted errata, go to https://www.packtpub.com/books/content/support and enter the name of the book in the search field. The required information will appear under the **Errata** section.

Piracy

Piracy of copyrighted material on the Internet is an ongoing problem across all media. At Packt, we take the protection of our copyright and licenses very seriously. If you come across any illegal copies of our works in any form on the Internet, please provide us with the location address or website name immediately so that we can pursue a remedy.

Please contact us at copyright@packtpub.com with a link to the suspected pirated material.

We appreciate your help in protecting our authors and our ability to bring you valuable content.

Questions

If you have a problem with any aspect of this book, you can contact us at questions@packtpub.com, and we will do our best to address the problem.

Data Input and Output

1

In this chapter, we will cover the following recipes:

- Finding geospatial data on your computer
- Describing data sources
- Importing data from text files
- Importing KML/KMZ files
- Importing DXF/DWG files
- Opening a NetCDF file
- Saving a vector layer
- Saving a raster layer
- Reprojecting a layer
- Batch format conversion
- Batch reprojection
- Loading vector layers into SpatiaLite
- Loading vector layers into PostGIS

Introduction

If you want to work with QGIS, the first thing you need is spatial data. Whether you want to prepare a nice-looking map layout or perform spatial analysis, you need to open some data to work with. This chapter deals with the basic input and output commands, which will allow you to use data in several different formats and also export to the most convenient format in case you want to use it in different applications or share with others.

Automation is possible for many of the operations that you will see in this cookbook. This chapter contains some recipes that use automation to process a set of input files.

Finding geospatial data on your computer

This recipe shows you how to use the QGIS browser to locate and open spatial data.

Getting ready

Before you start working, make sure that you have copied the sample dataset to your filesystem and you have it located.

How to do it...

There are several ways of locating and opening a data file to open it in QGIS, but the most convenient of these is the QGIS browser:

1. To enable this, go to the **View | Panels** menu and enable the **Browser** checkbox in it. The browser will be shown by default in the left-hand side of the QGIS window, as shown in the following screenshot:

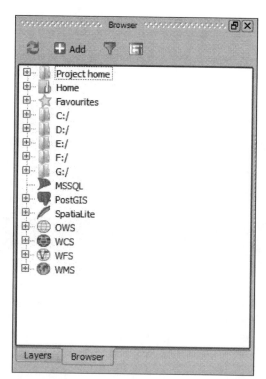

Browser contains a tree with all the available sources of spatial data. This includes data files in your filesystem, databases, and remote services.

2. Navigate to the folder where you copied the sample dataset, and you will see a list of available data files, as shown in the following screenshot:

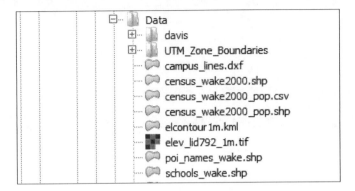

 Not all files are shown but just the ones that are identified as valid data sources.

3. To add a file to your project, just right-click on it and select **Add Layer**:

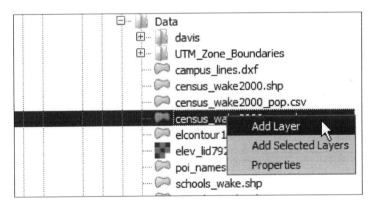

4. Multiple selections are allowed. In that case, select the **Add selected layer** menu.

Another way of opening a file is by just dragging it and dropping it into the QGIS canvas. Dragging multiple files is allowed, as well, as shown in the following screenshot:

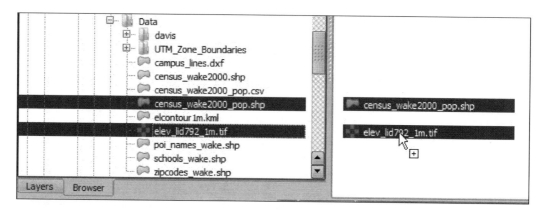

How it works...

The browser acts as a file explorer that is directly linked to QGIS, which only shows valid data files and can be used to easily add them to a QGIS project.

There's more...

There are a few more things that you need to know that are related to this recipe. They are explained in the following sections.

Adding layers with the Layer menu

As an alternative to the browser, the **Layer** menu contains a set of entries. Each of them deals with a different type of data. They give you some additional options, and they might allow you to work with formats that are not directly supported by the browser.

Adding a folder to Favorites

Navigating to the folder where your data is located can be tedious. If you use a given folder regularly, you can right-click on it and select **Add as favorite**. The folder will appear on the **Favorites** section at the top of the browser tree.

Nonfile data sources

The browser also shows non-file data, such as remote services. Services have to be defined before they appear on the corresponding section in the browser. To add a service, right-click on the service name and select **New connection...**. A dialog will appear to define the service connection parameters.

As an example, try adding the following WMS service, using the WMS entry in the browser, as shown in the following screenshot:

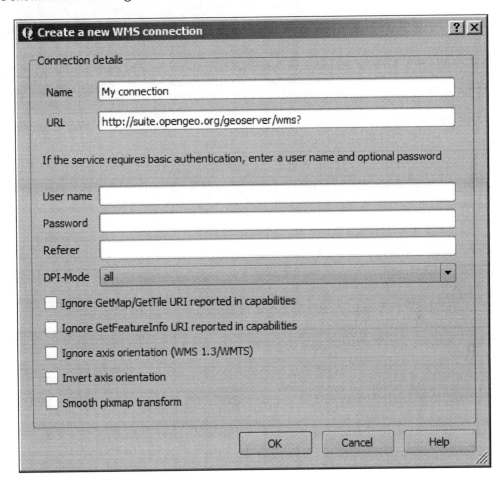

A new entry will appear, containing the layers offered by the service, as shown in the following screenshot:

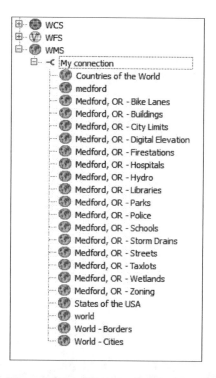

Describing data sources

You can get additional information about a data file before opening it. This recipe shows you how to explore the properties of a data origin.

Getting ready

Before you start working, make sure that you have copied the sample dataset to your filesystem and that you have it located.

How to do it...

1. In the QGIS browser, navigate to the folder with your sample dataset. Select the `elev_lid792_1m` file and right-click on it. In the context menu, select **Properties**. A dialog like the one in the following screenshot will appear:

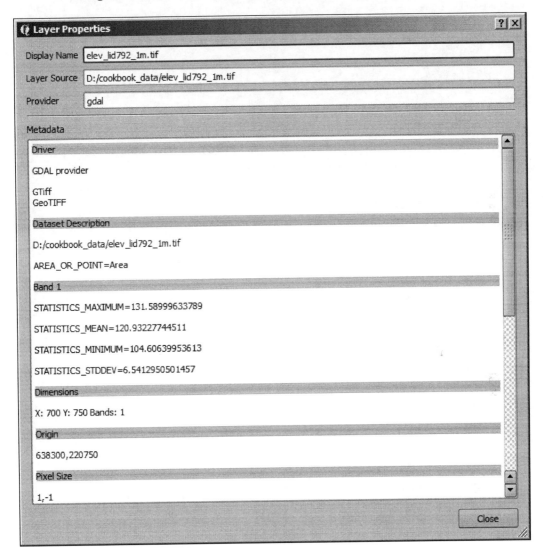

This dialog displays the properties of a raster layer.

2. Now, let's select a vector layer instead. Select the `elev_lid792_randpts.shp` file, right-click on it, and select **Properties**. The information dialog will look like the following:

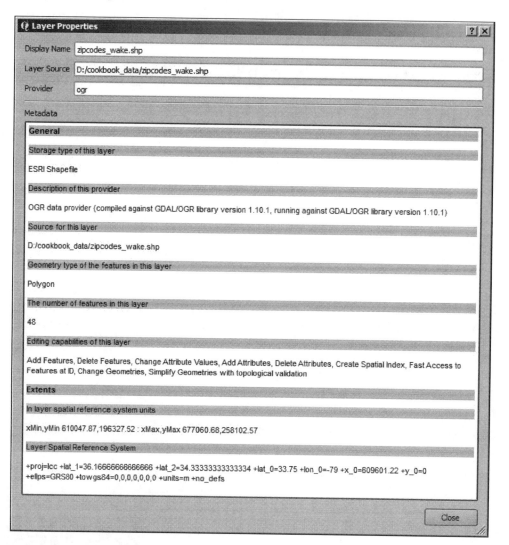

How it works...

In the upper part of the description window, you will see a field named **Provider**. **Provider** defines the type or data origin and who takes care of reading the data and passing it to QGIS. For raster layers, you will see `gdal` as **Provider**. For most file-based vector layers, `ogr` will be the provider that will appear. They refer to the GDAL and OGR libraries, two open-source libraries that are used by many GIS programs to access both raster and vector data.

There's more...

If the data is already loaded in QGIS, you can access the information about it in the **Properties** section of the layer (right-click on the layer name to select the **Properties** entry in the context menu). In the sections displayed in the left-hand side, select the **Metadata** section. You will see a box containing all the information corresponding to the layer data origin:

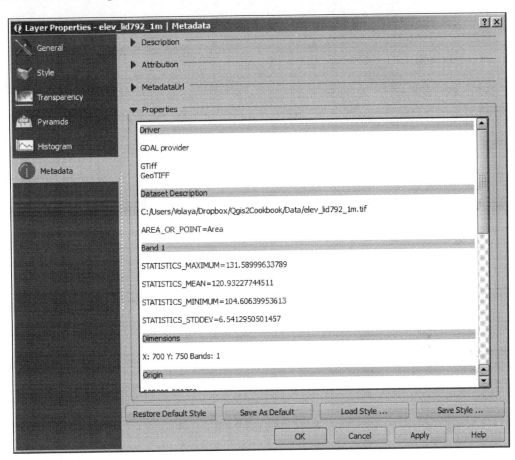

Functionality provided by the GDAL library, which (mentioned earlier) acts as a provider for raster layers, is also available in the **Raster** menu. This includes processing and data analysis methods, but it also includes the information tool that is used to describe a raster data source. You will find it by navigating to **Raster | Miscellaneous | Info**:

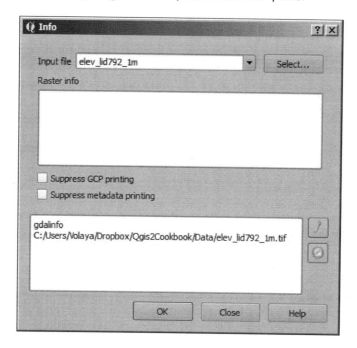

See also

▸ This is a more complex way to retrieve properties as you can call the tool by adjusting the parameters with more details to get additional information. To know more, check the gdalinfo help page at `http://www.gdal.org/gdalinfo.htm`.

Importing data from text files

Data can be imported from text files, providing some additional about how the geometry information is stored in the text. This recipe shows you how to create a new points layer, based on a text file.

How to do it...

1. Select the **Add delimited text layer** menu entry from the **Layer** menu. You will see a dialog like the following one:

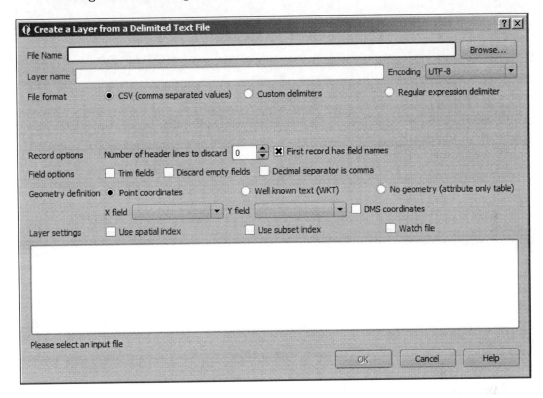

2. In the upper field, enter the path to the `elev_lid792_randpts.csv` file in the sample dataset. That file contains a points layer as text.

3. Once you enter the file path or select it in the file browser that can be opened by clicking on the **Browse** button, the fields in the lower part of the dialog will be filled, as shown in the following screenshot:

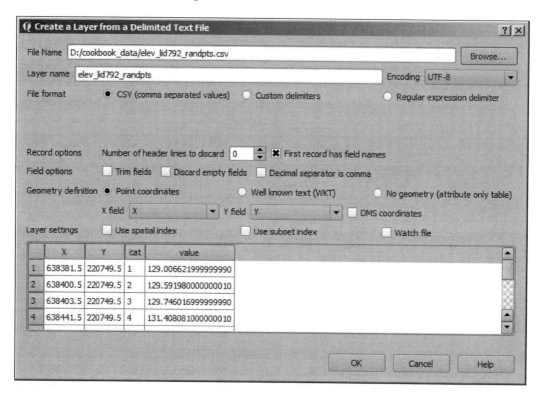

 We are using a CSV file that has values separated by commas, so you must select the **CSV** option in the **Format** field.

The **X field** and **Y field** drop-down lists will be populated with the fields that are available, which are described in the first line of the text file. Select **X** for **X field** and **Y** for **Y field**. Now, QGIS knows how to create the geometries and has enough information to create a new layer from the text file.

4. Enter a name for the layer in the **Layer name** field and click on **OK**. The layer will be added to the QGIS project, as shown in the following screenshot:

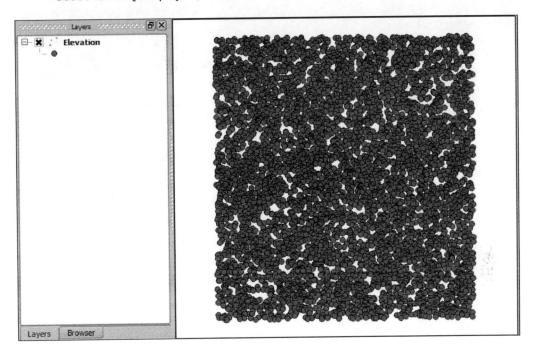

5. No information about the CRS is contained in the text file or entered in the parameters dialog, so it must be added manually. In this case, the CRS used is EPSG:3358. To set this as the CRS of the layer, right-click on the layer name and select **Set layer CRS**:

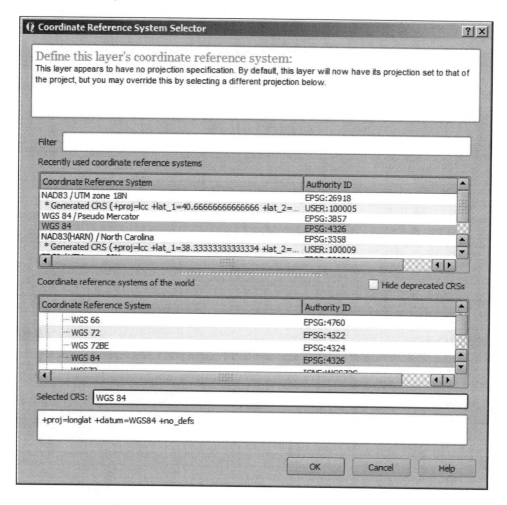

6. In the CRS selection dialog, select the EPSG:3358 CRS and click on **OK.** The layer now has the correct CRS.

How it works...

Data is read from the text file and processed to create geometries. All the fields in the table (all data in a row in the text file) are also added, including the ones used to create the geometries, as you will see by right-clicking on the layer and selecting **Open attribute table**, as shown in the following screenshot:

	X ▽	Y	cat	value	
0	638381.5	220749.5	1	129.006622	
1	638400.5	220749.5	2	129.59198	
2	638403.5	220749.5	3	129.746017	
3	638441.5	220749.5	4	131.408081	
4	638469.5	220749.5	5	131.441025	
5	638495.5	220749.5	6	130.65657	
6	638535.5	220749.5	7	128.474167	
7	638591.5	220749.5	8	124.363976	
8	638689.5	220749.5	9	124.692833	
9	638752.5	220749.5	10	124.022858	
10	638935.5	220749.5	11	112.479012	

Along with the CSV file, this file may contains a CSVT file, which describes the types of the fields. This is used by QGIS to set the appropriate type for the attributes table of the layer. If the CSVT file is missing, as in our example's case, QGIS will try to figure out the type based on the values for each field.

There's more...

Layers created from text files are not restricted to point files. Any geometry can be created from the text data. However, if it is not a point, instead of selecting two columns, you must place all the geometry information in a single one and enter a text representation of the geometry. QGIS uses the **Well-Known Text (WKT)** format, which is a text markup language for vector geometries, to describe geometries as strings. Here is an example of a very simple CSV file with line features and two attributes:

```
geom,id,elevation
LINESTRING(0 1, 0 2, 1 3),1,50
LINESTRING(0 -1, 0 -2, 1 -3),2,60
LINESTRING(0 1, 0 3, 5 4),3,70
```

See also

► To know more about the WKT format, you can go to http://en.wikipedia.org/wiki/Well-known_text

Importing KML/KMZ files

KML and KMZ files are used and produced by Google Earth and are a popular format. This recipe shows you how to open them with QGIS.

How to do it...

1. To open a KML layer, select **Layer/Add vector layer...**. In the dialog that opens, click on the **Browse** button to open the file selector dialog. Select the **Keyhole Markup Language** (**KML**) format and then select the file that you want to load. In the example dataset, you can find several KML files. Select the `elcontour1m.kml` file. Click on **OK** in the vector layer selector dialog, and the layer will be added to your project, as shown in the following screenshot:

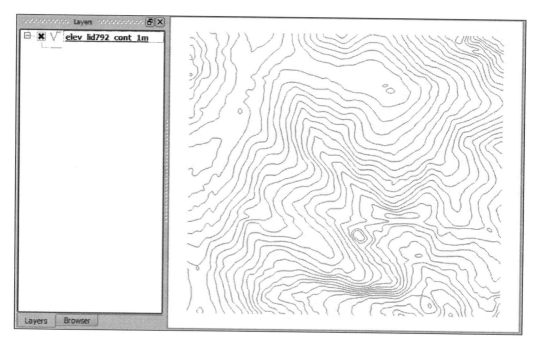

 KMZ files can also be opened in QGIS.

2. Go to **Layer | Add vector layer....** In the dialog that opens, click on the **Browse** button to open the file selector dialog. Select the **All files** option to view all the files and then select the `elcontour1m.kmz` file. There is not a KMZ file type defined in QGIS, but QGIS supports it because the underlying OGR library can read KMZ files as well.

3. Click on **OK** on the open layer dialog to open the selected layer.

From the layers contained in the KMZ file, you must select one of them. In this case, only a layer is contained in the `elcontour1m.kmz` file, so it is loaded automatically. The layer will be added to your QGIS project.

How it works...

KMZ files are compressed files that contain a set of layers. When you select it, the OGR library will unzip the content of this file and then open the layers that it contains.

If just a single layer is contained, you will not see the layer selection dialog. QGIS will automatically open the only layer in the KMZ file.

There's more...

As KMZ is not recognized as a supported format, the KMZ file will not appear in the QGIS browser. However, the browser supports zipped files, and a KMZ file is actually a zipped file with KML files inside it. Unzip it in a folder and then you will be able to use the QGIS Browser to open the layers it contains.

Importing DXF/DWG files

CAD files, such as DXF and DWG files, can be opened with QGIS. This recipe shows you how to do this.

How to do it...

1. To open a DXF layer, select **Add vector layer...** in the **Layer** menu. In the dialog that opens, click on the **Browse** button to open the file selector dialog. Select the **Autocad DXF** format and then the file that you want to load.

2. In the example dataset, you can find several DXF files. Select the `Wake_ApproxContour_100.dxf` file. Click on **OK** in the vector layer selector dialog and the layer will be added to your project, as shown in the following screenshot:

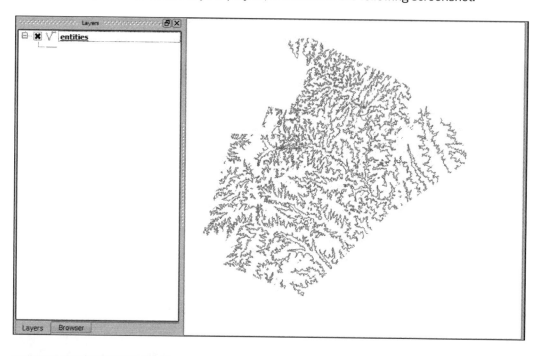

How it works...

DXF files are read as normal vector layers although they do not have the same structure as a regular vector layer as they do not allow adding arbitrary attributes to each geometry.

There's more...

The example DXF file that you opened contained just one type of geometry. DXF files can, however, contain several of them: in this case, they cannot be added to QGIS in one layer. When this happens, QGIS will ask you to select the type of geometry that you want to open.

In the sample dataset, you will find a file named `CSS-SITE-CIV.dxf`. Open it and you will see the following dialog:

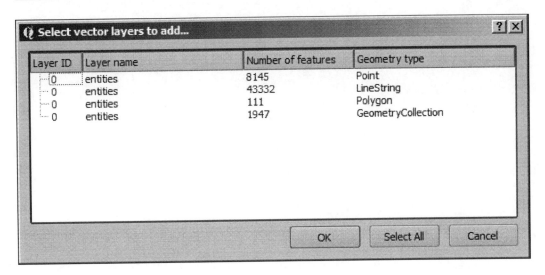

Select one of the available geometries, and a layer will be added to your QGIS project.

Opening DWG files

DWG is a closed format of Autodesk. This means that the specification of the format is not available. For this reason, QGIS, like other open source applications, does not support DWG files. To open a DWG file in QGIS, you need to convert it. Converting it to a DXF file is a good option as this will let you open your file in QGIS without any problem. There are many tools to do this. The Teigha converter can be found at `http://opendesign.com/guestfiles/TeighaFileConverter` and is a popular and reliable option.

Another option is using the free service offered by Autodesk, called Autocad 360, which can be found at `https://www.autocad360.com/`.

Opening a NetCDF file

The NetCDF data is a data format, which is designed to be used with array-oriented scientific data, and it is frequently used for climate or ocean data, among others. This recipe shows you how to open a NetCDF file in QGIS.

How to do it...

NetCDF files are raster files, and they can be opened using the **Add raster layer** menu. Select `NGMT NetCDF Grid` for CDF as the file format in the file selection dialog that you will see, and select the `rx5dayETCCDI_yr_MIROC5_rcp45_r2i1p1_2006-2100.nc` file from the example dataset. Click on **OK**.

How it works...

The proposed NetCDF file contains a single variable, which is opened as a regular raster layer.

There's more...

A NetCDF file can contain contain multiple layers. In this case, QGIS will prompt you to select the one that you want to add from the ones contained in the specified file.

When only one layer is available, it is opened directly, as in the previously described example.

The NetCDF Browser plugin

Another way of opening NetCDF files is using the NetCDF Browser plugin. Select the **Manage and install plugins...** menu to open the plugin manager. Go to the **Not installed** section and type `netcdf` in the search field to filter the list of available plugins. Select the **NetCDF Browser** plugin and click on **Install plugin** to install it. Close the plugin manager.

The plugin is now installed, and you can open it by selecting **NetCDF Browser** in the **Plugins** menu:

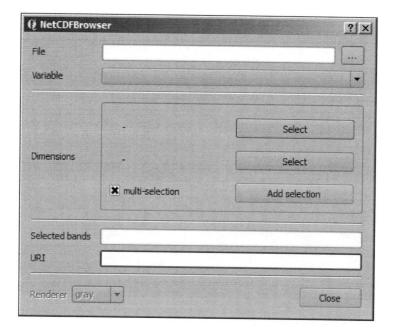

Select the **NetCDF** file in the upper field. The other fields will be updated with the content of the selected file. Select a layer from the available ones and click on **Add** to add the layer to your QGIS project.

Saving a vector layer

QGIS supports multiple formats, not just to read vector layers but to also save them. This recipe shows you how to export a vector layer, converting it to a different format.

Getting ready

You will use the layer named `poi_names_wake.shp` in this recipe. Make sure that it is loaded in your QGIS project.

How to do it...

1. Right-click on the name of the points layer in the QGIS table of contents and select the **Save as...** menu. You will see the following window:

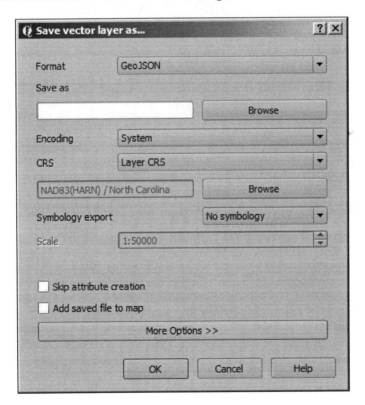

2. Let's suppose that you want to use this layer to create a web map. A popular format supported by libraries, such as Leaflet of OpenLayers 3, is the GeoJSON format. Select **GeoJSON** in the format field and enter a path and filename in the **Save as** field.

3. In the **Save as** dialog, click on **OK**. The GeoJSON file will be created.

How it works...

The OGR library, which is used by QGIS to read and open files, is also used to write them. Not all of the formats that are supported for reading purposes are also supported for writing purposes.

You can export even the layers that are not originally file-based to a file, such as a layer coming from a PostGIS database or a WFS connection. Just select the layer in the table of contents and proceed as just explained.

There's more...

The **Save as** dialog allows additional configuration beyond what you have seen in the example in this recipe.

Fine-tuning the export operation

Depending on the format that you select to export your layer, different options are available to configure how the layer is exported.

The options are shown by clicking on the **More options** button. Select **GeoJSON** as the export format and then display the options for that particular format. The **COORDINATE PRECISION** option controls the number of decimal places to write in the output GeoJSON file. The default precision is too high for almost all cases, and most of the time, having three or four decimal places is more than enough. Set the precision to 4, enter a valid path and filename, and export the layer by clicking on **OK**. Your points layer will now be saved in a smaller GeoJSON file. You can open this with a text editor to verify that the coordinates are expressed with the selected precision or compare its size with the one created without specifying a precision value.

Opening the layer after creating it

If you want to work with the layer after it is created, check the **Add saved file to map** box. The output layer will be opened and added to your current QGIS project.

Saving a raster layer

Raster layers can be exported to a different file. The export process can be used to crop the layer or perform resampling, creating a modified layer. This recipe shows you how to do this.

Getting ready

Open the `elev_lid792_1m` layer in your QGIS project.

How to do it...

1. Right-click on the name of the raster layer in the QGIS table of contents and select the **Save as...** menu. You will see the following window:

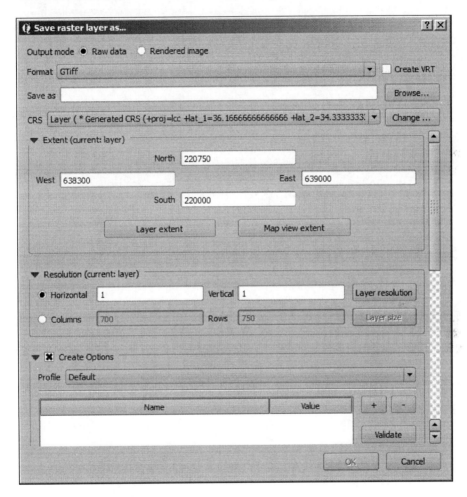

2. In the **Resolution** fields, replace both of them with a value of 2. The original resolution (the size of the cell) is 1, as you saw in a previous recipe.

3. Enter an output file path in the **Save as** field.

4. Click on **OK**. The layer will be saved with a coarser resolution than the original one.

How it works...

The GDAL library is used to save the file. Not all formats supported for input are also supported for output, but the most common ones are supported for both operations.

There's more...

The layer can be exported with a reduced extent. In the QGIS canvas, zoom to a small part of the raster layer. Then open the **Save as** dialog. In the **Extent** section, click on the **Map view extent** button. The bounding coordinates of the current map view will be placed in the four coordinate fields.

Enter a file path to save the file to and click on **OK**. A layer with a reduced extent covering only the region shown in the map view will be exported.

Reprojecting a layer

Layers may be in a CRS other than the one that is best for a given task. Although QGIS supports on-the-fly reprojection when rendering, other tasks, such as performing spatial analysis, may require using a given CRS or having all input layers in the same one. This recipe shows you how to reproject a vector layer.

Getting ready

Open the layer named `Davis_DBO_centerline.shp` from the sample dataset.

How to do it...

The `Davis_DBO_centerline.shp` layer uses a CRS with feet as the unit, which makes this unsuitable for certain operations. We plan to use this layer in future recipes to calculate routes and work in metric units, so including this in a CRS that uses them is then a much better option:

1. Right-click on the layer name in the table of contents and select **Save as...**.
2. Select **Selected CRS** in the drop-down list to specify a different output CRS. Click on the **Browse** button to select a CRS. You will see the **CRS selector** dialog.

3. You will be converting the point to the EPSG:26911 CRS. Use the filter box to find it among the list of available CRSs and select it. Then click on **OK**.

4. Click on **OK** in the **Save as** dialog to create the layer. A new shapefile will be created with the projected lines.

How it works...

Reprojecting is done by the OGR library when it saves the file because this is one of the options that it supports.

There's more...

Raster layers can be reprojected in a similar way:

1. In the **Save as** dialog, for raster layers, you can find a CRS field with a **Browse** button.

2. Click on it to open the CRS selector, and select the destination CRS.

3. When you click on **OK**, the raster layer will be exported using the selected CRS instead of its original one.

Batch format conversion

The **Save as** dialog can be used to convert the format of a single layer. When several layers have to be converted, it is a better idea to use some automation. This recipe shows you how to easily convert an arbitrary number of layers.

Getting ready

No previous preparation is needed. Batch conversion is not performed based on open layers but performed directly on files, so there is no need to open layers in QGIS before converting them.

How to do it...

1. Open the **Processing Toolbox** menu by selecting **Toolbox** in the **Processing** menu. The **Processing Toolbox** menu is the main element of the QGIS Processing framework, and it is used to call its algorithms:

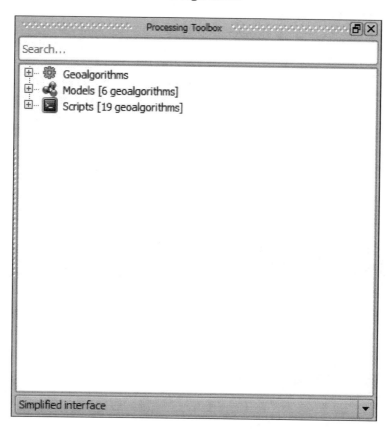

2. In the filter box of the **Processing Toolbox** menu, type `save` to filter the list of available algorithms. Locate the **Save selected features** algorithm, right-click on it, and select **Execute as batch process**. The batch processing interface will be displayed, as shown in the following screenshot:

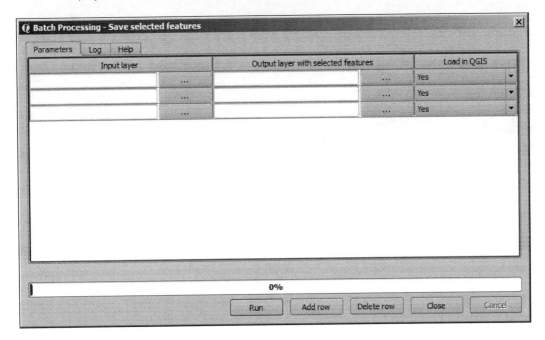

3. In the upper cell in the **Input layer** column, click on the **...** button and select **Select from filesystem**. A file selector dialog will appear. Select the content of the `batch_conversion` folder in the dataset. It should have a total of three files. Click on **OK** on the file selection dialog. The batch processing interface should now have all these selected files, one in each row in the parameters table.

4. In the **Output layer** column, click on the button in the first row. A dialog for saving the file will be opened. Select a file path in your filesystem where you want to save the output files and type `converted.geojson` as the output filename. Click on **OK** and a new dialog like the one shown in the following screenshot will appear:

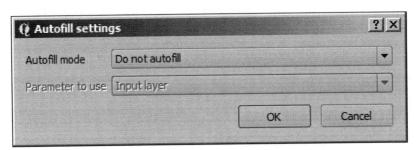

5. Select **Fill with parameter values** in the first field and **Input layer** in the second one. Click on **OK**. All the rows in the table will now have an output value, which was created using the entered filename as a prefix, followed by the name of the input layer.

6. To avoid layers being loaded after they are created, set the first cell in the **Load into QGIS** column to **No**. Then, double-click on the column header to automatically copy this value to all the rows below.

7. With the table already complete, you can launch the batch conversion process by clicking on **Run**. The GeoJSON files will be created in the specified paths.

How it works...

The conversion is performed by an algorithm from the QGIS Processing framework. Processing algorithms can be run either as individual algorithms or, in this case, in a batch process.

Outputs of Processing algorithms can be created in all formats supported by QGIS. The format is selected using the corresponding extension in the filename and, unlike in the case of saving a single layer, does not have to be selected in a field or list. Using geojson as the extension for your output files, you tell processing that you want to generate a file in this format.

Although the algorithm saves only the selected features of the layer, if there is no selection, it will use all the layer features. This is the default behavior of all algorithms in processing. As there is no selection in the layers that you have converted, all of their features will have been used.

When converting files this way, the additional options from the **Save as** dialog are not available, and the default configuration values are used.

There's more...

You can also convert vector layers with another more complex algorithm from the **Processing Toolbox** menu, which allows you to enter the configuration parameters used by the underlying OGR library that takes care of the process. It's called **Export vector**. Find it in the toolbox, right-click on it, and select **Execute as batch process**:

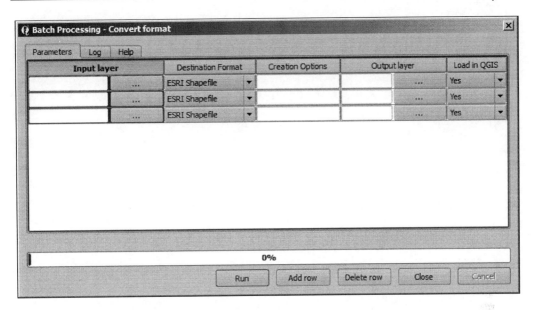

In this case, the output format is not controlled by the extension of the output filename as it happens with other processing algorithms according to what has been already explained.

Batch reprojection

Layers can be reprojected in a batch operation without having to enter parameters individually on the **Save as** dialog. This recipe shows you how to reproject a set of layers to a different CRS using an algorithm from the **Processing Toolbox** menu. You will see how to reproject all the files accompanying the Davis_DBO_centerline.shp file that you reprojected in the *Reprojecting a layer* recipe.

How to do it...

1. In the filter box of the **Processing Toolbox** menu, type `Reproject` to filter the list of available algorithms. Locate the **Reproject layer** algorithm, right-click on it, and select **Execute as batch process**. The batch processing interface will be shown, as follows:

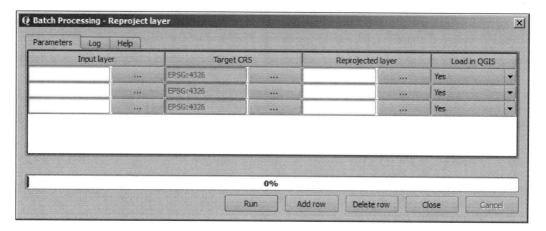

2. In the upper cell of the **Input layer** column, click on the **...** button and select **Select from filesystem**. A file selector dialog will appear. Select the content of the `davis` folder in the dataset and add the files to the table.

3. In the first cell in the **Target CRS** column, click on the **...** button. A CRS selector will appear. Select the `EPSG:26911` CRS, as you did in a previous recipe when converting a single layer. Copy the value to the rest of rows in the column by double-clicking on the column header.

4. Set all the values in the **Reprojected layer** column. Select a file in the first cell, and then use the **Fill with parameter value** option to automatically fill the rest of rows.

5. Once the table is complete, click on **Run** to reproject the layers.

How it works...

The reprojection algorithm is a part of the Processing framework, so you can select the output format by changing the output file extension. You can use this to not only reproject a set of input layers but to also convert their format, all in a single step.

There's more...

Raster layers can also be reprojected with another algorithm from the **Processing Toolbox** menu named **Warp (reproject)**. These inputs are rather similar to the ones in the reprojection tool for vector layers with some additional parameters that are specific to raster layers. Select the algorithm, right-click on it, and select **Execute as batch process** to run it and convert a set of raster layers.

Loading vector layers into SpatiaLite

SpatiaLite is a single file relational database that is built on top of the well-known SQLite database. It can store many layers of various types, including nonspatial tables. Interfaces to the format also allow the ability to run spatial queries of various kinds. It's a highly-flexible and portable format that is great for everyday use, especially when working on standalone projects or with only one user at a time. SpatiaLite works in a similar manner to PostGIS without the need to configure or run a database server.

Getting ready

Pick a vector layer and load it up in QGIS. This step is optional, as you can pick the source layer from the filesystem in a later dialog.

How to do it...

1. Create a SpatiaLite database if you don't already have one and name it cookbook.db. The easiest way to do this is with the **Browser** tab, as shown in the following screenshot:

2. Then, pick one of the following methods to import your data. The first option is faster, but the second option gives you more control over the import settings:

   □ Import method 1—the fast method

   1. In the QGIS **Browser** tab, find the layer that you want to copy to the database.

   2. Drag and drop this layer on the **Spatialite DB** entry.

> If you have a lot of files listed, this will be quite difficult as the browser doesn't scroll during the drag operation. You can optionally open a second browser window and drag the layer across. Also, note that this defaults to multi-type geometry. If you need to control the options, use the next method.

   □ Import method 2—the standard method

   1. Open **DB Manager** from the **Database** menu.

   2. Expand the **Spatialite** item to list your databases. Expand the database that you want to connect to.

   3. Click on the following import layer icon:

   4. A dialog will pop up, providing you with import options.

> SQL databases are usually case insensitive, so you can use all lower case characters. Also, never use spaces or special characters in table names; this can just lead to headaches later. An occasional underscore is okay.

   5. Select the layer to import from the drop-down list.

   6. Fill in a name for the new table.

   7. In most cases, the only thing left to do is check the **Create spatial index** checkbox.

   8. If this works, great. Now, you can load the layer to the map and verify that it's identical to the input.

> This method is more similar to traditional database import and very similar to the *PostGIS* recipe next in this chapter.

How it works...

QGIS converts your geometry to a format that is compatible with SpatiaLite and inserts it, along with the attribute table. Afterwards, it updates the metadata tables in SpatiaLite to register the geometry column and build the spatial index on it. These two postprocesses make the database table appear as a spatial layer to QGIS and speed up the loading of data from the table when panning and zooming.

There's more...

The import dialog contained a few other features that are often useful. You can reproject data as part of the import process if you want, or you can specify the projection if QGIS didn't detect it properly. You can also name the geometry column something different than the default, geom; for example, utmz10n83 (this is normally not recommended). You can specify the character encoding of the text in the event that it's not handled correctly.

You can even use the dialog to append data to an existing table; for example, you have multiple counties with the same data structure that come as two separate files, but you want them all in one layer.

If, for some reason, the layer didn't import the way that you want, delete it and redo the import. If you delete layers, make sure to learn how to vacuum the database to recover the now empty space in the file and shrink its total size (this is not automatic).

 Look for the **Vacuum** option as a button in many graphical tools. If you don't see it, no worries, just run the SQL, VACUUM;.

What happens if this fails? Databases can be really picky sometimes. Here are some common issues and solutions:

- It could be character encoding (accents, non-Latin languages), which requires that you specify the encoding.

- It could be picky about mixing multilayers with regular layers. Multilayers is when you have several separate geometries that are part of one record. For example, Hawaii is actually many islands. So, if you only have one row representing Hawaii, you need to cram all the island polygons into one geometry field. However, if you mix this with North Dakota, which is just a polygon, the import will fail. If you have this problem, you'll need to perform the import on the command-line using ogr2ogr and its newish feature, -nlt PROMOTE_TO_MULTI, which converts all single items to multi-items to fix this.

- Depending on your original source, you may have a mix of points, lines, and polygons. You'll either need to convert this to a Geometry Collection, or you need to split each type of geometry into a separate layer. Geometry Collections are currently poorly-supported in many GIS viewers, so this is only recommended for advanced users.

See also

If you need more advanced settings or can't get the QGIS tool to work, you may need to use the QspatiaLite Plugin (install this with **Manage Python Plugins** under the **Plugins** menu), the spatialite-gui (download this from `https://www.gaia-gis.it/fossil/spatialite_gui/index`) application, or the ogr2ogr command line (this comes with QGIS, which is part of OSGeo4w shell on Windows, or the terminal on Mac or Linux).

Loading vector layers into PostGIS

PostGIS is the spatial add-on to the popular PostgreSQL database. It's a server-style database with authentication, permissions, schemas, and handling of simultaneous users. When you want to store large amounts of vector data and query them efficiently, especially in a multicomputer networked environment, consider PostGIS. This works fine for small data too, but many users find its configuration too much work when SpatiaLite may be better suited.

Getting ready

Pick a vector layer and load it in QGIS. You will also need to have a working copy of Postgres/PostGIS running, a PostGIS database created, and an account that allows table creation.

 BostonGIS maintains a decent tutorial on installation for Windows, and getting a PostGIS set up for everyone. You can find this at `http://www.bostongis.com/?content_name=postgis_tut01#316`.

You should configure QGIS to be aware of your database and its connection parameters by creating a new database item in the PostGIS load dialog or by right-clicking on **PostGIS** in the **Browser** tab and selecting **New Connection**:

You can find more information about PostGIS at `http://docs.qgis.org/2.8/en/docs/user_manual/working_with_vector/supported_data.html#postgis-layers`.

How to do it...

Now that you can connect to a PostGIS database, you are ready to try importing data:

1. Open **DB Manager** from the **Database** menu.

2. Expand the **PostGIS** item to list your databases. Expand the database that you want to connect to, and you should be prompted to authenticate (if you haven't saved your password in the settings).

3. Expand the list and select the **Public** schema.

In general, unless you are performing advanced work and understand how Postgres schemas work, place your layers in the **Public** schema. This is the default that everyone expects.

4. Click on the following import layer icon:

5. A dialog will pop up, providing you with import options.

 SQL databases are usually case insensitive, so you can use all lowercase. Also, never use spaces or special characters in table names; this can just lead to headaches later. An occasional underscore is okay.

6. Select the layer to import from the drop-down list.

7. Fill in a name for the new table.

8. Check whether **schema** is set to **public**.

9. In most cases, the only thing left to do is check the **Create spatial index** checkbox:

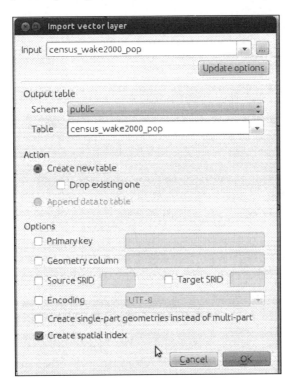

How it works...

QGIS converts your geometries to a format that is compatible with PostGIS, and inserts it, along with importing the attributes. Afterwards, it updates the metadata views in PostGIS to register the geometry column and build the spatial index on it. These two post-processes make the database table appear as a spatial layer to QGIS and speed up the loading of data from the table when panning and zooming.

There's more...

The options presented in the dialog are not all the options that are available. If you need more control or advanced options present, you'll likely be looking at the command-line tools: shp2pgsql (a graphical plugin for pgadmin3 is available on some platforms) and ogr2ogr. The shp2pgsql tool generally only handles shapefiles. If you have other formats, ogr2ogr can handle everything that QGIS is capable of loading. You can also use these tools to develop batch import scripts.

To import large or complicated CSV or text files, you sometimes will need to use the pgadmin3 or psql command-line interface to Postgres.

Need even more control? Then, consider scripting. OGR and Postgres both have very capable Python libraries.

Another option is using the OpenGeo Suite plugin, which has some additional options, such as allowing importing multiple layers into a single table or into one table per layer. To learn more about this, including how to install it, refer to `http://qgis.boundlessgeo.com/static/docs/intro.html`.

What happens if this fails? Databases can be really picky sometimes:

- It could be character encoding (accents, non-Latin languages), which requires specifying the encoding.

- It could be picky about mixing multilayers with regular layers. Multilayers is when you have several separate geometries that are part of one record. For example, Hawaii is actually many islands. So, if you only have one row representing Hawaii, you need to cram all the island polygons into one geometry field. However, if you mix this with North Dakota that is just a polygon, the import will fail. If you have this problem, you'll need to perform the import on the command-line using ogr2ogr and its new feature, `-nlt PROMOTE_TO_MULTI`, which converts all single items to multi-items, to fix this.

- Depending on your original source, you may have a mix of points, lines, and polygons. You'll either need to convert this to a Geometry Collection, or you need to split each type of geometry into a separate layer. Geometry Collections are currently poorly supported in many GIS viewers, so this is only recommended for advanced users.

See also

For more information on PostGIS installation and setup, refer to `http://postgis.net/install`.

For a more in-depth text on using PostGIS, there are many books available, including Packt Publishing's *PostGIS Cookbook*.

2
Data Management

In this chapter, we will cover the following recipes:

- ▶ Joining layer data
- ▶ Cleaning up the attribute table
- ▶ Configuring relations
- ▶ Joining tables in databases
- ▶ Creating views in SpatiaLite
- ▶ Creating views in PostGIS
- ▶ Creating spatial indexes
- ▶ Georeferencing rasters
- ▶ Georeferencing vector layers
- ▶ Creating raster overviews (pyramids)
- ▶ Building virtual rasters (catalogs)

Introduction

One of the reasons to use QGIS is its many features that enable management and analysis preparation of spatial data in a visual manner. This chapter focuses on common operations that users need to perform to get data ready for other uses, such as analysis, cartography, or input into other programs.

In this chapter, you will find recipes to manage vector as well as raster data. These recipes cover the handling of data from both file and database sources.

Joining layer data

We often get data in different formats and information spread over multiple files. Therefore, one important skill to know is how to join attribute data from different layers. Joining data is a way to combine data from multiple tables based on common values, such as IDs or categories.

This exercise shows you how to use the join functionality in **Layer Properties** to join geographic census tract data to tabular population data and how to save the results to a new file.

Getting ready

To follow this exercise, load the census tracts in `census_wake2000.shp` using **Add Vector Layer** (you can also drag and drop the shapefile from the file browser to QGIS) and population data in `census_wake2000_pop.csv` using **Add Delimited Text Layer**.

 You can also load the `.csv` text file using **Add Vector Layer**, but this will load all data as text columns because the `.csv` file does not come with a `.csvt` file to specify data types. Instead, the **Add Delimited Text Layer** tool will scan the data and determine the most suitable data type for each column.

How to do it...

To join two layers, there has to be a column with values/IDs that both layers have in common. If we check the attribute tables of the two layers that we just loaded, we will see that both have the `STFID` field in common. So, to join the population data to the census tracts, use the following steps:

1. Open the **Layer Properties** option of the `census_wake2000` layer (for example, by double-clicking on the layer name in the **Layers** list) and go to **Joins**.

2. To set up a new join action, press the green **+** button in the lower-left corner of the dialog.

3. The following screenshot shows the **Add vector join** dialog, which allows you to configure the join by selecting **Join layer**, which you want to use to join the census tracts and the columns containing the common values/IDs (**Join field** and **Target field**):

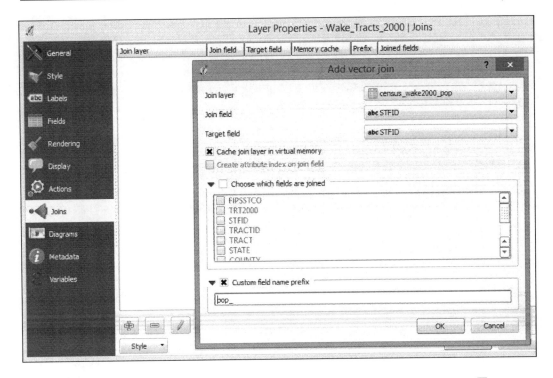

 If you want to change a join, you just need to select the join definition from the list and then press the edit button with the pencil icon, which you find below the list. This will reopen the join definition dialog, and you can make your changes.

4. When you press **OK**, the join definition will be added to the list of joins, as shown in the following screenshot.

5. To verify that you set up the join correctly, close **Layer Properties** and open attribute table to see whether the population columns have been added and are filled with data.

How it works...

Joins can be used to join vector layers and tabular layers from many different file and database sources, including (but not limited to) Shapefiles, PostGIS, CSV, Excel sheets, and more.

When two layers are joined, the attributes of **Join layer** are appended to the original layer's attribute table. If you want, you can use the **Choose which fields are joined** option to select which of the fields from the population layer should be joined to the census tracts. Otherwise, by default, all fields will be added. The number of features in the original layer is not changed. Whenever there is a match between the values in the join and the target field, the new attribute values will be filled; otherwise, there will be NULL values in the new columns.

By default, the names of the new columns are constructed from join layer name with underscore followed by join layer column name. For example, the STATE column of census_wake2000_pop becomes census_wake2000_pop_STATE. You can change this default behavior by enabling the **Custom field name prefix** option, as shown in the previous screenshot. With these settings, the STATE column becomes pop_STATE, which is considerably shorter and, thus, easier to handle.

There's more...

The join that you've created now only exists in memory. None of the original files have been altered. However, it's possible to create a new file from the joined layers. To do this, just use **Save as ...** from the **Layer** menu or **Context** menu. You can choose between a variety of data formats, including the ESRI shapefile, Mapinfo MIF, or GML.

Shapefiles are a very common choice as they are still the de facto standard GIS data exchange format, but if you are familiar with GIS data formats, you will have noticed that the names of the joined columns are too long for the 10 character-name length limit of the shapefile format. QGIS ensures that all columns in the exported shapefiles have unique names even after the names have been shortened to only 10 characters. To do this, QGIS adds incrementing numbers to the end of, otherwise, duplicate column names. If you save the join from this example as a shapefile, you will see that the column names are altered to census_w_1, census_w_2, and so on. Of course, these names are less than optimal to continue working with the data. As described in *How it works...* in this recipe, the names for the joined columns are a combination of joined layer name and column name. Therefore, we can use the following trick if we want to create a shapefile from the join: we can shorten the layer name. Just rename the layer in the layer list. You can even have a completely empty layer name! If you change the joined layer name to an empty string, the joined column names will be _STATE, _COUNTY, and so on instead of census_wake2000_pop_STATE and census_wake2000_pop_COUNTY. In any case, it is good practice to document your data and provide a description of the attribute table columns in the metadata.

In any case, it is very likely that you will want to clean up the attribute table of the new dataset, and this is exactly what we are going to do in the next exercise.

Cleaning up the attribute table

There are many reasons why we need to clean up attribute tables every now and then. These may be because we receive badly structured or named data from external sources, or because data processing, such as the layer joins that we performed in the previous exercise, require some post processing. This recipe shows us how to use attribute table and the **Table Manager** plugin to rename, delete, and reorder columns, as well as how to convert between different data types using **Field Calculator**.

Getting ready

If you performed the previous recipe, just save the joined layer to a new shapefile; otherwise, load census_wake2000_pop.shp. In any case, you will notice that the dataset contains a lot of duplicate information, and the column names could use some love as well. To follow this recipe, you should also install and enable the **Table Manager** plugin by navigating to **Plugins | Manage and Install Plugins**.

How to do it...

1. Our first step to clean up this dataset is to delete duplicated information. From all available columns, we only want to keep _STATE, _COUNTY, _TRACT, FIPSSTCO, TRT2000, STFID, _POP2000, AREA, and PERIMETER.

2. To delete the other columns, enable editing using the **Toggle editing mode** button in the upper-left corner of the attribute table or by pressing *Ctrl + E*. This activates the **Delete column** button.

3. Alternatively, you can also press *Ctrl + L* to open the **Delete attributes** dialog. This dialog allows us to delete multiple columns at once. Just select all the columns that you want to be deleted, press **OK**, and QGIS will display the reduced attribute table.

 It's worth noting that the changes will only be permanent once you use the **Save edits** button or disable the editing mode and confirm that you want to save the changes.

4. Next, we will rename columns to remove the leading underscores in some of the column names. This can be done using the **Table Manager** plugin.

5. When you start the plugin (edit mode should be disabled), you will see a list of the layer columns. The plugin allows you to change the order of columns, as well as rename, insert, clone, and delete columns.

6. To rename a column, just select it in the list and press the **Rename** button. You'll then be asked to provide a new name. Go ahead and remove the leading underscores from _STATE, _COUNTY, _TRACT, and _POP2000.

7. Finally, using the **Move up** and **Move down** buttons, you can also rearrange the column order to something more intuitive. We'd suggest moving STFID to the first position and AREA and PERIMETER to the last.

8. If you press **Save**, the changes will be saved back to the layer source file. Alternatively, you can also create a new file using **Save as...**.

How it works...

The steps provided in this exercise are mostly limited to layers with shapefile sources. If you use other input data formats, such as MIF, GML, or GeoJSON files, you will notice that the **Toggle editing** button is grayed out because these files cannot be edited in QGIS. Whether a certain format can be edited in QGIS or not depends on which functionality has been implemented in the respective GDAL/OGR driver.

> The GDAL/OGR version that is used by QGIS is either part of the QGIS package (as in the case of the Windows installers) or QGIS uses the GDAL library existing in your system (on Linux and Mac). To get access to specific drivers that are not supported by the provided GDAL/OGR version, it is possible to compile custom versions of GDAL/OGR, but the details of doing this are out of the scope of this cookbook.

There's more...

Another common task while dealing with attribute table management is changing column data types. Currently, it is not possible to simply change the data type directly. Instead, we have to use **Field Calculator** (which is directly accessible through the corresponding button in the **Attributes** toolbar or from the attribute table dialog) to perform conversions and create a new column for the result.

In our `census_wake2000_pop.shp` file, for example, the tract ID, TRACT, is stored in a REAL type column with a precision of 15 digits even though it may be preferable to simply have it in a STRING column and formatted to two digits after the decimal separator. To create such a column using **Field Calculator**, we can use the following expression:

```
format_number("TRACT",2)
```

Compared to a simple conversion (which would be simple, use `tostring("TRACT")`, `format_number("TRACT",2)` offers the advantage that all values will be formatted to display two digits after the decimal separator, while a simple conversion would drop these digits if they are zeros.

Of course, it's also common to convert from text to numerical. In this case, you can chose between `toint()` and `toreal()`.

See also

► Have a look through the conversion functions in the **Field Calculator Function** list to see the other available functions that can deal with date and time data types. Usage of all these functions is explained in **Selected function help** directly in the calculator dialog.

Configuring relations

In the *Joining layer data* recipe, we discussed that joins only append additional columns to existing features (1:1 or n:1 relationships). Using joins, it is, therefore, not possible to model 1:n relationships, such as "one zip code area containing n schools". These kinds of relationships can instead be modeled using relations. This recipe introduces the concept of relations and shows how you can put them to use.

Getting ready

To follow this exercise, load zip code areas and schools from `zipcodes_wake.shp` and `schools_wake.shp`.

How to do it...

Relations are configured in **Project Properties**. The dialog is very similar to the join dialog:

1. Define the two layers (**Referencing/Child** and **Referenced/Parent**), as well as the fields containing the common values/IDs. As you want to model "one zip code area contains n schools," the zip code dataset is the parent layer and the school dataset is the child layer. The connection between both datasets is established based on the zip code fields (**ADDRZIPCOD** and **ZIPNUM**), as shown in the following screenshot:

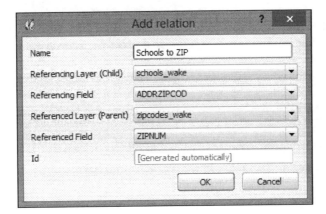

2. To verify that the relation is set up and working, you can either check the attribute table in form view (button in the lower-right corner), as shown in the following screenshot, or open an individual feature form. You will find that the relation information has been appended at the end of the form:

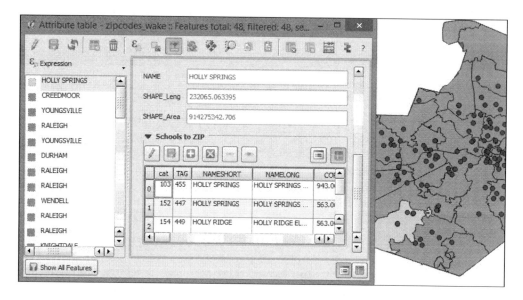

As the preceding screenshot shows, setting up this relation enables you to get access to all schools within a certain zip code in a very convenient way. As the edit button suggests, it is even possible to edit the school data from this view. You can simply edit the values in the table view. You can add and delete schools from the dataset using the **+** and **X** buttons. The next two buttons enable you to quickly add new entries to the relation or to remove them.

How it works...

In this example, removing a school from the dataset works just fine, but adding a school via this dialog makes less sense because you cannot create a point geometry through this process.

If you press the button to add to the relation, you will get a dialog that allows you to choose which existing school you want to add. In the background, the school's ADDRZIPCOD value is updated to match the zip code we just assigned it to.

Similarly, if you select a school and press the button to remove the relation, what actually happens is that the school's ADDRZIPCOD value is set to NULL.

Joining tables in databases

If you use a database (SpatiaLite or PostGIS) to store your data, vector and nonspatial, then you also have the option of using the database and SQL to perform tables joins. The primary advantages of this method include being able to filter data before loading in the map, perform multitable joins (three or more), and have full control over the details of the join via queries.

Getting ready

You'll need at least two layers in either a SpatiaLite or PostGIS database. These two layers need at least one column in common, and the column in common should contain unique values in at least one table. In this case, our example uses the census_wake_2000 polygon layer and census_wake_2000_pop.csv.

How to do it...

1. Open the **DB Manager** plugin that comes with QGIS. You can find this in the **Database** menu.

2. Select your database from the tree on the left-hand side, use cookbook.db in **SpatiaLite** (which was created in *Chapter 1, Data Input and Output*).

 If you don't see this database listed, use **Add SpatiaLite Layer** (the icon or the menu item), or right-click on **SpatiaLite** in the **Browser** window to make a new connection and add it to an existing database.

3. Now, open the SQL window (the second icon from the left in top toolbar of the plugin window).

4. Put in the following SQL code to query and JOIN the tables:

```
SELECT *
FROM census_wake2000 Sas a
JOIN census_wake2000_pop AS b
ON a.stfid = b.stfid;
```

How it works...

SELECT lists all the columns that you want from the source tables; in this case, * means everything. FROM is the first (left) table, as a is an alias, which is used so that there's less typing later. JOIN is the second (right) table, and ON indicates which columns to should be matched between the two tables. The rest of how this works in relational database theory is best explained in other texts.

There's more...

In databases, there's more than one type of join. You can perform a join where you retain only the matches in both tables, or you can retain all content from the left (first table) and any matches from the right. You can also control how a one-to-many relationship is summarized or select specific records instead of aggregating.

If you want to save the results of a query you have two options. You can make a view or a new table. A view is a saved copy of your query. Every time you open it, the query will be rerun. This is great if your data changes because it will always be up-to-date, and this doesn't use any additional disk space. On the other hand, a table is like saving a new file; it becomes a static new copy of the results. This is good to repeatedly access the same answer, and it is usually faster to use, especially for large tables.

See also

▶ Refer to the *Creating views in SpatiaLite* and *Creating views in PostGIS* sections in this chapter to learn how to make views of the query results.

▶ For more general information on writing SQL queries refer to http://sqlzoo.net/

▶ Refer to *Chapter 1, Data Input and Output*, about using the cookbook.db database

Creating views in SpatiaLite

In a database, view is a stored query. Every time you open it, the query is run and fresh results are generated. To use views as layers in QGIS takes a couple of steps.

Getting ready

For this recipe, you'll need a query that returns results containing a geometry. The example that we'll use is the query from the *Joining tables in databases* recipe (the previous recipe) where attributes were joined 1:1 between the census polygons and the population CSV. The QSpatiaLite plugin is recommended for this recipe.

How to do it...

The GUI method is described as follows:

1. Using the **QspatiaLite** plugin (which is in the **Database** menu, if you've activated it) place the following in the query:

```
SELECT *
FROM census_wake2000 as a
```

```
JOIN census_wake2000_pop as b
ON a.stfid = b.stfid;
```

2. From the **Option** dropdown, select the last choice, **Create Spatial View & Load in QGIS**, and set the **Geometry field** box value to the name of your geometry field from your spatial layer. In this example, this is geom.

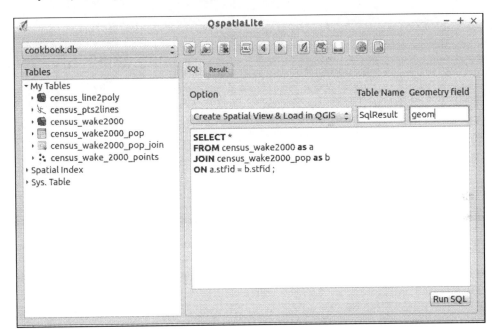

 You can explore your data table fields in the left-hand side to check the name of the fields that you need.

The SQL method is as described, as follows:

1. In **Database | DB Manager**, open **SQL Window**.

2. Write a query. In this example, this is the Join query from the previous recipe.

3. Convert this query to a view by adding CREATE VIEW <name> as SELECT:

```
CREATE VIEW census_wake2000_pop_join AS
SELECT *
FROM census_wake2000 as a
JOIN census_wake2000_pop as b
ON a.stfid = b.stfid;
```

4. Register the view with the SpatiaLite metadata backend with a follow up query. This function is case sensitive:

```
CREATE VIEW census_wake2000_pop_join AS
INSERT INTO views_geometry_columns
(view_name, view_geometry, view_rowid, f_table_name,
f_geometry_column, read_only)
VALUES ('census_wake2000_pop_join', 'geom', 'rowid',
'census_wake2000', 'geom',1);
```

 This only works when the view geometry is based on the geometry of a single table. If you need to generate new geometries, you probably need a table.

5. The pattern is ('name of view','name of view geometry field','A Unique ID','name of table the view gets its geometry from','name of geometry field in the original table',read-only (1) or writable(0)).

6. After running the second query, you should be able to load the view in QGIS and see the same fields as the join query.

How it works...

A view is actually stored in the database and is triggered when you load it. In this way, if you change the original data tables, the view will always be up to date. By comparison, creating new tables makes copies of the existing data, which is stored in a new place, or creates a snapshot or freeze of the values at that time. It also increases the database's size by replicating data. Whereas, a view is just the SQL text itself and doesn't store any additional data.

QGIS reads the metadata tables of SpatiaLite in order to figure out what layers contain spatial data, what kind of spatial data they contain, and which column contains the geometry definition. Without creating entries in the metadata, the tables appear as normal SQLite tables, and you can only load attribute data without spatial representation.

As it's a view, it's really reading the geometries from the original tables. Therefore, any edits to the original table will show up. New in SpatiaLite 4.x series, this makes it easier to create writable views. If you use the spatialite-gui standalone application, it registers all the database triggers needed to make it work, and the changes made will affect the original tables.

There's more...

You don't have to use ROWID as unique id, but this is a convenient handle that always exists in SQLite, and unlike an ID from the original table, there's no chance of duplication in an aggregating query.

See also

▶ Read more about writable-view at https://www.gaia-gis.it/fossil/libspatialite/wiki?name=writable-view. This recipe is extremely similar to the next one on PostGIS and demonstrates how interchangeable the two can be if you are aware of the slight differences.

Creating views in PostGIS

In a database, a view is a stored query. Every time that you open it, the query is run and fresh results are generated. To use views as layers in QGIS takes a couple of steps.

Getting ready

For this recipe, you'll need a query that returns results containing a geometry. The example that we'll use here is the query from the *Joining tables in databases* recipe where attributes were joined 1:1 between the census polygons and the population CSV.

How to do it...

The SQL method is described as follows:

1. In **Database | DB Manager**, open **SQL Window**.

2. Write a query; in this example, this is the join query that was written in the previous exercise. If you want to see it right away but not necessarily retain it, check the **Load as new layer** checkbox near the bottom:

```
SELECT *
FROM census_wake2000 as a
JOIN census_wake2000_pop as b
ON a.stfid = b."STFID";
```

3. Now, execute the query by clicking on the **Execute (F5)** button:

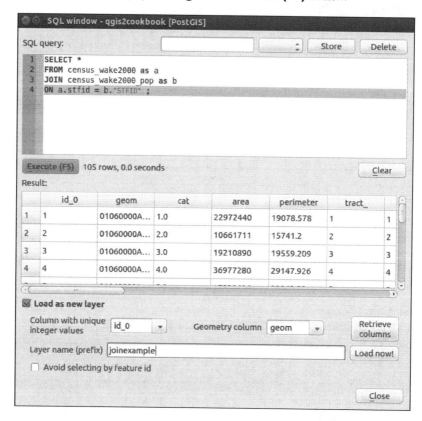

4. After executing the query, to load it to the map check the **Load as new layer** box, which will expand some additional options. Pick your unique integer (id_0) for **Column with unique integer values** and geom for **Geometry column**. Name your result in the **Layer name (prefix)** textbox and click on **Load now!**.

> If you only needed to see this data in this particular QGIS project, you can stop here. In order to make the database store this query for other projects and users, continue this recipe.

5. Convert this query to a view by adding CREATE VIEW <name> AS SELECT:

```
CREATE VIEW census_wake2000_pop_join AS SELECT *
FROM census_wake2000 as a
JOIN census_wake2000_pop as b
ON a.stfid = b."STFID";
```

6. Go back to **DB Manager** and hit the **Refresh** button (on the left). You should now see your new view listed and be able to add it to the map.

How it works...

QGIS reads the metadata tables or views of PostGIS in order to figure out what layers contain spatial data, what kind of spatial data they contain, and which column contains the geometry definition. Without creating entries in the metadata, the tables appear as normal PostgreSQL tables, and you can only load attribute data without spatial representation.

As this is a view, it's really reading the geometries from the original tables. Therefore, any edits to the original table will also show up.

There's more...

QGIS is really picky about having a unique ID for PostGIS tables and views. There are a few tips to make this always work. Always include a numeric unique ID (as the first column is recommended but not required, IDs must be integer columns (usually int4, but int8 should work now too). Autoincrementing IDs are good idea. When you don't have such an ID field to use from one of the underlying tables, you can add an ID on the fly with the following:

```
SELECT row_number() OVER() AS id_qgis, <add the other fields you
want here> FROM table;
```

The downside of this is that you now have to list out all the fields that you want to use in the view rather than using *. When creating tables, you'll want to turn this id_qgis field into an auto-incrementing field if you plan to add records.

The other big catch is that if you make a new geometry by manipulating existing geometries, QGIS isn't always aware of the results. In the previous example, the geometry is just passed from the original table to the view unchanged, so it is properly registered in the geometry_columns metadata of PostGIS. However, a new geometry doesn't exist in the original table, so the trick is to cast the geometry result, as follows:

```
CREATE VIEW census_wake2000_4326 AS
SELECT id_0,
stfid,tractid,ST_Transform(geom,4326)::geometry(GeometryZ, 4326)
As geom
FROM census_wake2000;
```

QGIS doesn't always think that this is a valid spatial layer but adding to the Canvas should work.

 The more specific you can be, the better. If you're not sure what geometry type it is or if you have 3D (aka Z), check the entries in the geometry_columns view.

Also, keep your eyes on Postgres's relatively new feature called Materialized Views. This is a method of caching view results that don't update automatically, but they also don't require whole new tables.

See also

▸ Finer details from the PostGIS manual can be read at `http://postgis.refractions.net/docs/using_postgis_dbmanagement.html#Manual_Register_Spatial_Column`. This recipe is extremely similar to the previous one and demonstrates how interchangeable these two can be if you are aware of the slight differences.

▸ Read more about *Materialized Views* at `http://www.postgresql.org/docs/9.3/static/rules-materializedviews.html`

Creating spatial indexes

Spatial indexes are methods to speed up queries of geometries. This includes speeding up the display of database layers in QGIS when you zoom in close (it has no effect on viewing entire layers).

This recipe applies to SpatiaLite and PostGIS databases. In the event that you've made a new table or you have imported some data and didn't create a spatial index, it's usually a good idea to add this.

 You can also create a spatial index for shapefile layers. Take a look at **Layer Properties | General** for the **Create Spatial Index** button. This will create a `.qix` file that works with QGIS, Mapserver, GDAL/OGR, and other open source applications. Refer to `https://en.wikipedia.org/wiki/Shapefile`.

Getting ready

You'll need a SpatiaLite and a Postgis database. For ease, import a vector layer from the provided sample data and do not select the **Create spatial index** option when importing. (Not sure how to import data? Refer to *Chapter 1, Data Input and Output*, for how to do this.)

How to do it...

Using the **DB Manager** plugin (in the **Database** menu), perform the following steps:

1. Check whether the index does not exist. In **DB Manager**, open the database and then open the table that you want to check. Looking at the properties on the right, you should see a message just above **Fields** that looks like this:

2. However, what if no index was listed for the geom column? Then, we can make one just by clicking the **create it** link. Or you can do this in a SQL window, as follows:

   ❑ For SpatiaLite, use the following:

   ```
   SELECT CreateSpatialIndex('schools_wake', 'geom');
   ```

   ❑ For PostGIS, use the following:

   ```
   CREATE INDEX sidx_census_wake2000_geom
       ON public.census_wake2000 USING gist(geom);
   ```

3. Verify that the index exists, as follows:

   ❑ For PostGIS (the left-hand side of the following screenshot), on the right-hand side, scroll to the bottom looking for the **Indexes** section

   ❑ For SpatiaLite (the right-hand side of the following screenshot), you can see the `idx_nameoftable_geomcolumn` listed as a table:

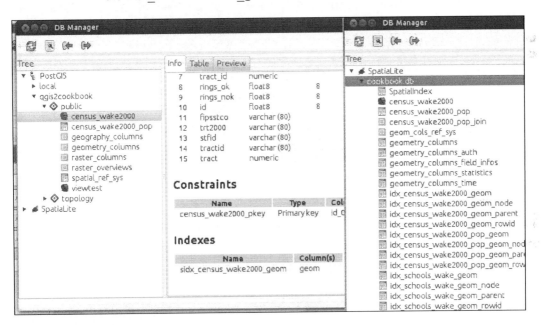

How it works...

When you create a spatial index, the database stores a bounding box rectangle for every spatial object in the geometry column. These boxes are also sorted so that boxes near each other in coordinate space are also near each other in the index.

When queries are run involving a location, a comparison is made against the boxes, which is a simple math comparison. Rows with boxes that match the area in question are then selected to be tested in depth for a precise match, based on their real geometries. This method of searching for intersection is faster than testing complex geometries one by one because it quickly eliminates items that are clearly not near the area of interest.

There's more...

Spatial indexes are really important to speed up the loading time of database spatial layers in QGIS. They also play a critical role in the speed of spatial queries (such as intersects). Note that PostGIS will automatically use a spatial index if one is present. SpatiaLite requires that you write queries that intentionally call a particular spatial index (Refer to Haute Cuisine examples from the *SpatiaLite Cookbook*)

Also, keep in mind that only one spatial index per table can be used in a single query. This really comes into play if you happen to have more than one spatial column or create a spatial index in a different projection than the geometry (check out the *PostGIS Cookbook* by Packt Publishing for more information).

 If you plan to insert many records into a table with an existing spatial index, you may want to disable or drop the index and recreate it after the import is done. Otherwise, the index will be recalculated after each row is inserted. This applies to nonspatial indexes too.

Do you want to check lots of tables at once? You can list all GIST indexes in PostGIS at once:

```
SELECT i.relname as indexname, idx.indrelid::regclass as
  tablename,
  am.amname as typename,
ARRAY(SELECT pg_get_indexdef(idx.indexrelid, k + 1, true)
  FROM generate_subscripts(idx.indkey, 1) as k
  ORDER BY k
  ) as indkey_names
FROM pg_index as idx
JOIN pg_class as i  ON  i.oid = idx.indexrelid
JOIN pg_am as am  ON  i.relam = am.oid
JOIN pg_namespace as ns  ON  ns.oid = i.relnamespace
AND ns.nspname = ANY(current_schemas(false))
Where am.amname Like 'gist';
```

To do something similar in SpatiaLite, use the following:

```
SELECT * FROM geometry_columns WHERE spatial_index_enabled = 1;
```

See also

- ▸ Information on SpatiaLite spatial index implementation can be found at `https://www.gaia-gis.it/fossil/libspatialite/wiki?name=SpatialIndex`

- ▸ More details on using spatial indexes can be found at `https://www.gaia-gis.it/fossil/libspatialite/wiki?name=SpatialIndex`

- ▸ Information about PostGIS implementation is at `http://postgis.net/docs/manual-2.0/using_postgis_dbmanagement.html#gist_indexes`

- ▸ You can also check out *Chapter 10, Maintenance, Optimization, and Performance Tuning,* of *PostGIS Cookbook* by Packt Publishing,

Georeferencing rasters

Sometimes, you have a paper map, an image of a map from the Internet, or even a raster file with projection data included. When working with these types of data, the first thing you'll need to do is reference them to existing spatial data so that they will work with your other data and GIS tools. This recipe will walk you through the process to reference your raster (image) data, called georeferencing.

Getting ready

You'll need a raster that lacks spatial reference information; that is, unknown projection according to QGIS. You'll also need a second layer (reference map) that is known and you can use for reference points. The exception to this is, if you have a paper map that has coordinates marked on it or a spatial dataset that just didn't come with a reference file but you happen to know its CRS/SRS definition. Load your reference map in QGIS.

This book's data includes a scanned USGS topographic map that's missing its `o38121e7.tif` projection information. This map is from Davis, CA, so the example data has plenty of other possible reference layers you could use, for example, the streets would be a good choice.

 Actually, the world file was just renamed to `o38121e7.tfw.orig` so that QGIS wouldn't detect it. You can use this later to compare your georeference quality.

How to do it...

On the **Raster** menu, open the **Georeferencing** tool and perform the following steps:

1. Use the file dialog to open your unknown map in the **Georeferencing** tool.

2. Create a **Ground Control Point** (**GCP**) of matches between your start coordinates and end coordinates.

 Building corners, street intersections, and things where line features intersect or significant edge features can be found.

3. Add a point in your unknown map with **GCP Add +**. You can now enter the coordinates (that is, if it's a paper map with known coordinates marked on it), or you can select a match from the main QGIS window reference layer.

4. Repeat this process to find at least four matches. If you want to get a really good fit do between 10-20 matches.

5. (Optional) Save your GCPs as a text file for future reference and troubleshooting:

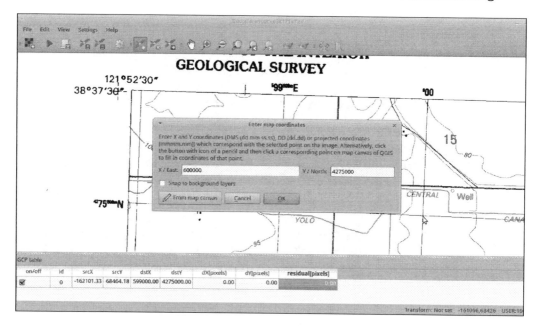

 Try to spread out your control points so that you have good coverage of the whole map. It's all about averaging the differences.

6. Now, choose **Transformation Settings**, as follows:

7. You have a choice here. Generally, you'll want to use Polynomial. If you set 4+ points for the first order, 6+ points for the second order and 10+ points for the third order, The second order is the currently recommend one. This will be discussed in the *There's more...* section of this recipe.

8. Set **Target SRS** to the same projection as the reference layer. (In this case, this is **EPSG:26910 UTM Zone 10n**)

9. **Output Raster** should be a different name from the original so that you can easily identify it.

> Save your GCP list to the file. If you don't like the results, come back and try a different algorithm or change the number of GCPs used. If you want a reference for comparison, look at the text `o38121e6.tif.points` file in this book's data folder.

10. When you're happy with your list of GCPs click on **Start Georeferencing** in **File** or on the green triangular button.

How it works...

A mathematical function is created based on the differences between your two sets of points. This function is then applied to the whole image, stretching it in an attempt to fit. This is basically a translation or projection from one coordinate system to another.

There's more...

Picking transformation types can be a little tricky, the list in QGIS is currently in alphabetical order and not the recommended order. Polynomial 2 and Thin-plate-spline (TPS) are probably the two most common choices. Polynomial 1 is great when you just have minor shift, zooming (scale), and rotation. When you have old well-made maps in consistent projections, this will apply the least amount of change. Polynomial 2 picks up from here and handles consistent distortion. Both of these provide you with an error estimate as the Residual or **RMSE** (**Root Mean Square Error**). TPS handles variable distortion, varying it's correction around each control point. This will almost always result in the best fit, at least through the GCPs that you provide. However, because it varies at every GCP location, you can't calculate an error estimate and it may actually overfit (create new distortion). TPS is best for hand-drawn maps, nonflat scans of maps, or other variable distorted sources. Polynomial methods are good for sources that had high accuracy and reference marks to begin with.

If you really want a good match, once you have all your points, check the RMSE values in the table at the bottom. Generally, you want this near or less than 1. If you have a point with a huge value, consider deleting it or redoing it. You can move existing points, and a line will be drawn in the direction of the estimated error. So, go back over the high values, zoom in extra close, and use the GCP move option.

Sometimes, just changing your transformation type will help, as shown in the following screenshot that compares Polynomial 1 versus Polynomial 2 for the same set of GCP:

GCP table

on/off	id	srcX	srcY	dstX	dstY	dX[pixels]	dY[pixels]	residual[pixels]
☑	0	-162100.01	68464.42	599000.00	4275000.00	-1.27	1.65	2.08
☑	1	-161099.60	68430.25	600000.00	4275000.00	-2.41	0.22	2.42
☑	2	-154113.88	68203.95	607000.00	4275000.00	0.76	-1.33	1.53
☑	3	-161493.07	56413.39	600000.00	4263000.00	1.82	-1.25	2.20
☑	4	-153496.71	56161.93	608000.00	4263000.00	-2.87	1.67	3.32
☑	5	-159301.27	62357.43	602000.00	4269000.00	1.16	-0.79	1.40
☑	6	-156178.82	66267.28	605000.00	4273000.00	2.81	-0.16	2.81

Polynomial 1

Note the residual values difference when changing to Polynomial 2 (assuming that you have the minimum number of points to use Polynomial 2):

GCP table

on/off	id	srcX	srcY	dstX	dstY	dX[pixels]	dY[pixels]	residual[pixels]
☑	0	-162100.01	68464.42	599000.00	4275000.00	0.79	0.36	0.87
☑	1	-161099.60	68430.25	600000.00	4275000.00	-0.96	-0.43	1.05
☑	2	-154113.88	68203.95	607000.00	4275000.00	-0.58	-0.26	0.63
☑	3	-161493.07	56413.39	600000.00	4263000.00	0.19	0.09	0.21
☑	4	-153496.71	56161.93	608000.00	4263000.00	-0.05	-0.02	0.05
☑	5	-159301.27	62357.43	602000.00	4269000.00	-0.74	-0.33	0.81
☑	6	-156178.82	66267.28	605000.00	4273000.00	1.34	0.60	1.46

Polynomial 2

Resampling methods can also have a big impact on how the output looks. Some of the methods are more aggressive about trying to smooth out distortions. If you're not sure, stick with the default nearest neighbor. This will copy the value of the nearest pixel from the original to a new square pixel in the output.

See also

▸ When performing georeferencing in a setting where you need it to be very accurate (science and surveying), you should read up on the different transformations and what RMSE values are good for your type of data. Refer to the general GIS or Remote Sensing textbooks for more information.

▸ For full details of all the features of the QGIS georeferencer, refer to the online manual at `https://www.qgis.org/en/docs/user_manual/plugins/plugins_georeferencer.html`.

▸ The QGIS documentation has some basic information about how to pick transformation type at `http://docs.qgis.org/2.8/en/docs/user_manual/plugins/plugins_georeferencer.html#available-transformation-algorithms`.

Georeferencing vector layers

For various reasons, sometimes you have a vector layer that lacks projection information. This is often the case with CAD layers that were created only in local coordinates. When it is possible, try to track down the original projection information. As a last resort, you can attempt to warp the vector layer to match a known reference layer with the recipe described here.

Getting ready

You can open two instances of QGIS (or use one as you'll just be zooming back and forth a lot). In one instance, load a reference layer, something in the projection that you want your data to be in. Activate **Coordinate Capture Plugin** from the **Manage Plugins** menu.

 In Windows, you need the osgeo4w shell for this recipe. If you don't have a start menu item, look for the `OSGeo4W.bat` launcher in your QGIS or OSGeo4w installation folder.

This example uses `cad-lines-only.shp`, which is the line layer extracted from the `CSS-SITE-CIV.dxf` file. This file is a CAD rendering of design plans for Academy St. in the town of Cary, Wake County, North Carolina.

How to do it...

1. Create a list of GCP matches between your unknown layer (`cad-lines-only.shp`) and your reference layer (`CarystreetsND83NC.shp`).

2. Here are some specific adjustments to help with `cad-lines-only.shp` referenced to `CarystreetsND83NC.shp`. These will make it easier to find matches between the two layers:

    1. Load `cad-lines-only.shp`, and adjust its style properties using a rule-based style. Use the "Layer" = 'C-ROAD-CNTR' rule, which will only show you street centerlines.

    2. In your other QGIS session, load `CarystreetsND83NC.shp` in order to find the matching area, open the attribute table, and apply the following select expression: `"Street" LIKE '%N ACADEMY%' OR "Street" LIKE '%S ACADEMY%' OR "Street" LIKE '%CHATHAM%'`. The filter here highlights the three main streets of the original project, which is at the intersection of Chatham and N/S Academy streets in the center of the town. This may also be useful to change the color of the selected features to make it easier to find. The traffic circles at either end of the project are good landmarks:

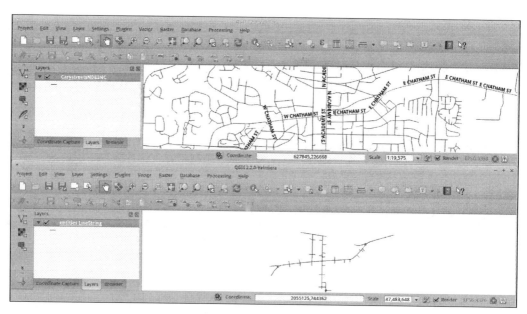

    3. Find an easy-to-identify feature that matches in both layers (street intersections).

4. Use the coordinate capture plugin to copy the x,y value for the point in both layers.

5. Save the coordinates in a text editor while you work.

6. Repeat this procedure until you have at least four pairs of points. Try to pick points spread out across the whole layer:

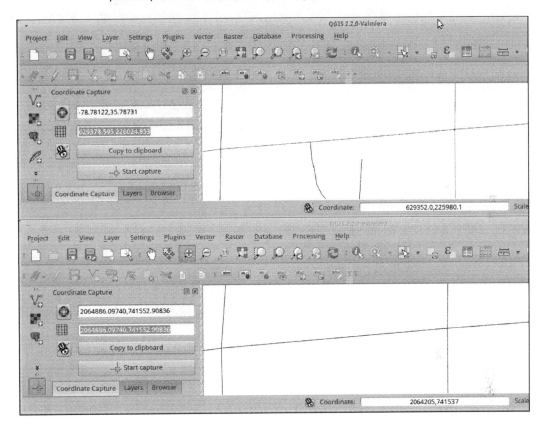

 There is currently no graphical interface in QGIS for the next step, which uses the OGR library that comes with QGIS. Take the list of points and using the ogr2ogr command-line, you're going to apply the GCP to the unknown layer.

3. Each set of coordinate pairs will look as follows:

```
-gcp sourceX sourceY destinationX destinationY
```

4. Open a terminal (Mac or Linux) or an OSGeo4w shell (Windows).

5. Change to the directory where you have the data (Hint: `cd /home/user/Qgis2Cookbook/`):

```
ogr2ogr -a_srs EPSG:3358 -gcp 2064886.09740 741552.90836
629378.595 226024.853 -gcp 2066610.97021 741674.39817
629903.420 226064.049 -gcp 2064904.46214 743055.63847
629384.784 226485.725 -gcp 2062863.85707 741337.65243
628762.587 225960.900 cad_lines_nd83nc.shp cad-lines-only.shp
```

`-a_srs` is the proj code for your reference layer.

The command pattern is `ogr2ogr <options> <destination> <source>`.

 Other useful advanced options include `-order <n>` to indicate polynomial level (default is based on the number of GCPs) or `-tps` to use Thin-plate-spline instead of polynomial. For more options refer to `http://www.gdal.org/ogr2ogr.html`.

6. Now, load your new `cad_lines_nd83nc.shp` file in the same project, as `CarystreetsND83NC.shp`. They should line up without the need to enable projection-on-the-fly:

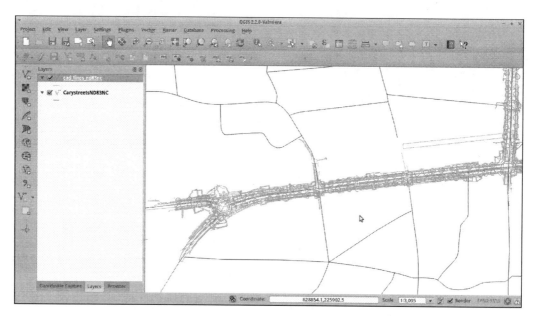

How it works...

Given the list of input coordinates and matching output coordinates, a math formula is derived to translate between the two sets. This formula is then applied to all the points in the original data. The result of this is a reprojected dataset from an unknown projection to a known projection.

 The original data is actually EPSG:102719, but we're pretending that we didn't have this piece of information to demonstrate this example.

There's more...

When picking a reference layer, try to pick something in the projection that you want to use for your maps and analysis. That way you only have to reproject once, as each additional transformation can add an error. There's also more than one way to go about accomplishing this task, including moving the data by hand.

In this particular, example the transformation is autoselected based on the number of GCP point pairs. 4-5 is the first order polynomial, 6-9 is the second order polynomial, and 10+ is the third order polynomial. Refer to the previous recipe in this chapter for more information.

A related topic is *Affine transformations* when you simply want to shift or rotate a vector layer by a known amount. The QgsAffine plugin is great if you already know the parameters, or roughly know how far you want to rotate and shift the vector layer, as it then just needs some math to get the parameters.

 Maybe by the time you read this, all of the difficult things here will be worked in a plugin. Keep an eye open, and try the experimental plugins Vector Bender, vectorgeoref, and Affine Transformations.

See also

- This method is very similar to the *Georeferencing Rasters* recipe and many of the same tips apply to both
- If you want to see how we got the CAD file into an SHP to begin with, look at Importing *DXF/DWG files* in the *Chapter 1, Data Input and Output*
- See the *Using Rule Based Rendering* recipe in *Chapter 10, Cartography Tips*, for tips on how to visualize the resulting CAD import better by applying attribute based rule filtering

- ▸ Refer to the original files at `ftp://199.72.17.76/Engineering/Academy%20Street%20Improvements%202013/DWGs/CSS-WATER%20&%20SEWER/CSS-SITE-CIV.dwg`

- ▸ Too lazy to do the math? You can also just use GvSig to do the math and make a world file; refer to `http://foss4gis.blogspot.com/2011/05/computing-and-applying-affine.html`

- ▸ If you want to do the math yourself see `http://press.underdiverwaterman.com/rotating-a-point-grid-in-qgis/`

Creating raster overviews (pyramids)

Overviews, or pyramids, and resampling are all about making raster layers load faster when zooming and panning in your map canvas, by reducing the amount of data loaded when not zoomed in all the way.

Getting ready

You will need a large raster image.

Generally, you want to make a copy of the data as this method will likely alter the original file if you choose to make 'internal' pyramids (easy to do on accident).

How to do it...

1. Load your raster in QGIS. `elev_lid792_1m.tif` will work fine for this example.

2. Right-click on the layer name and open **Properties**.

3. Go to the **Pyramids** item on the left:

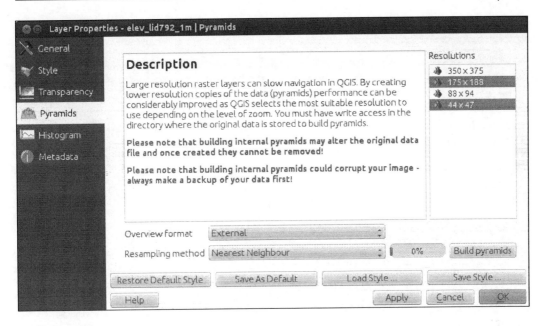

4. Select the image sizes that you want to create pyramids for:

   ❏ Optionally, choose whether to store externally (safer) or internally (less files to keep track of).

   ❏ Optionally, choose a resampling algorithm; **Nearest Neighbor** is the simplest, but other methods may look smoother at the cost of more data manipulation and compute time

5. Click on **Build pyramids**.

6. When this is completed, you'll notice the red X on the sizes that you picked will now show a pyramid.

How it works...

Generating pyramids essentially makes copies of your original data resized for different zoom levels. As you zoom out, the original data is resampled to fit the size of the screen. The pyramids do the same thing, but they let you decide what resampling method to use and generate this overview ahead of time. By generating them ahead of time, QGIS can load the image faster when you change zoom levels.

There's more...

Resampling is a fancy way of saying that at each zoom level that is now 1 pixel is more than 1 pixel from the original data, so they need to be averaged in some way and the result assigned to the 1 pixel that is now available. Each of the different methods uses a different math formula to decide the new value and how much to smooth that value with neighboring pixels (so that it looks aesthetically pleasing). This is the same concept as when you shrink pictures so that you can e-mail them to your friends.

If you chose to save them externally, your overviews are stored in `elev_lid792_1m.tif.ovr`. Some other programs store the same thing in the `.aux` files; however, pyramid formats are not universally compatible between GIS applications.

See also

▶ This is the same effect as using the GDAL `gdaladdo` command; refer to `http://gdal.org/gdaladdo.html`

▶ More details from the QGIS documentation can be found at `https://www.qgis.org/en/docs/user_manual/working_with_raster/raster_properties.html`

Building virtual rasters (catalogs)

When you have a lot of rasters (instead of one big raster) that are all part of the same dataset (typically adjacent to each other), you don't want to load each file individually and then style it. It's much easier to load one file and treat it as one layer. This recipe lets you do this without actually creating a single monstrous raster, which can be difficult to work with.

Getting ready

You will need two or more raster files that have adjacent extents or only overlap partially around the edges and are in the same projection. Ideally, the files should be of the same type, such as all elevations, all air photos, and so on. For this recipe, the elevation rasters from the OSGeo EDU (North Carolina) dataset will work.

How to do it...

1. (Optional) Load the elevation rasters to your current map.
2. Go to **Raster Menu | Miscellanous | Build Virtual Raster (Catalog)**.
3. Check the **Use visible raster layers** checkbox or choose **SELECT**, browse to the example data, and select all four.

4. **SELECT** and name an output file using the `.vrt` extension.

5. (Optional) Check the **Load into canvas when finished** checkbox if you want to see the results immediately:

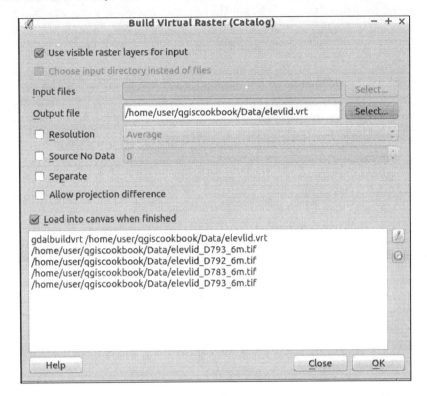

 GDAL command line equivalent: `<command>` `<output.vrt>` `<list of inputs... space between each...>`

For example, `gdalbuildvrt elevlid.vrt elevlid_D782_6.tif elevlid_D783_6m.tif elevlid_D792_6m.tif elevlid_D793_6m.tif`.

How it works...

GDAL VRT format is an XML file that defines the location of each raster file relative to an anchor file. It uses the existing spatial extent information of the rasters to figure out their positions relative to each other and then anchors the set in the given coordinate system.

There's more...

Using a VRT is all about saving time. When you have hundreds of raster files for one particular dataset, you can combine them into a single file. However, this file could be gigantic in size and somewhat impossible to work with. This is a quick way to be able use the files as a seamless background layer. If you need to perform analysis, you'll likely need to either combine the layers or loop over them individually.

You could also generate **Tile Index** (also in the **Miscellaneous** menu), which makes a shapefile of the outlines of the rasters and puts the ID and path of the raster in the attribute table. This would allow you to figure out which image you want to load for a given map without having to load them all.

Finally, if you really want to make all of the files a single large file, use the context menu (right-click on the loaded VRT layer and choose **Save As**). If you have overlaps, more complicated situations, or want to merge without loading the files, first use the **Merge** tool (also in the **Miscellaneous** menu). This can be tricky if your files overlap, you'll need to decide how to handle the double data.

See also

> ▸ For another example, please refer to http://manual.linfiniti.com/en/rasters/data_manipulation.html#basic-fa-create-a-virtual-raster

> ▸ GDAL's gdalbuildvrt is the underlying tool; it's documentation can be found at http://gdal.org/gdalbuildvrt.html

3

Common Data Preprocessing Steps

In this chapter, we will cover the following recipes:

- ▶ Converting points to lines to polygons and back – QGIS
- ▶ Converting points to lines to polygons and back – SpatiaLite
- ▶ Converting points to lines to polygons and back – PostGIS
- ▶ Cropping rasters
- ▶ Clipping vectors
- ▶ Extracting vectors
- ▶ Converting rasters to vectors
- ▶ Converting vectors to rasters
- ▶ Building DateTime strings
- ▶ Geotagging photos

Introduction

When working with other people's data, it is often not the exact format that you need for a particular use. This chapter is all about taking the data that you do have and converting it to what you actually need. It covers converting between different types of vectors (points, lines, and polygons), between vectors and polygons, and cutting out only the parts that you need. Taking data from how you get it and converting it to the format and layout that you need in order to work with is often called 'data preprocessing'.

Converting points to lines to polygons and back – QGIS

Sometimes your data is vector formatted (point, line, or polygon), but it is not the right kind of vector for a particular type of analysis. Or perhaps you need to split a vector in a particular way to facilitate some analysis or cartography. Thankfully, all vector formats are related, lines are two or more connected points, polygons are lines whose first and last point are the same, multipolygons are two or more polygons for the same record, and rings are nested polygons where the inner polygon outlines an area to be excluded. This recipe covers how to convert between the different vector types using built-in QGIS methods.

Getting ready

To convert points to lines or polygons, you will need a shapefile with an ID column that has a single value shared between the points of the same line or polygon. In the following example, we will use census_wake_2000_points.shp.

You will also need to install and activate the Points2One plugin. Refer to the following website for how install plugins, http://docs.qgis.org/2.8/en/docs/user_manual/plugins/plugins.html.

How to do it...

The following instructions show four different conversion methods, depending on the starting data and the end data type. All of the tools are in the **Vector** menu:

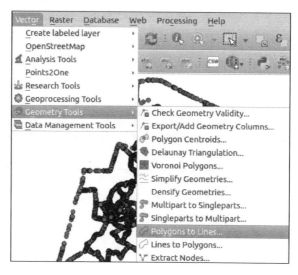

Start by loading the census_wake_2000_points.shp layer.

Converting points to lines (or polygons)

1. Go to **Vector | Points2One**.

2. Choose to create either lines or polygons.

3. Pick the group ID; in this case, this is STFID.

4. Create the output filename: `census_wake_2000_pt2lines.shp`:

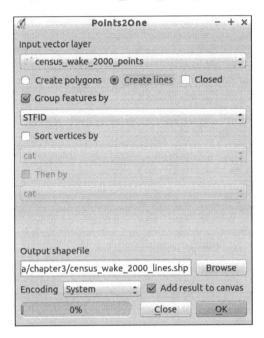

Converting lines to polygons

1. Go to **Vector | Geometry Tools | Lines to Polygons**.

2. Create the output filename: `census_wake_2000_lines2poly.shp`.

Converting polygons to lines

1. Go to **Vector | Geometry Tools | Polygons to Lines**.

2. Create the output filename: `census_wake_2000_poly2lines.shp`.

Converting polygons or lines to points

1. Go to **Vector | Geometry Tools | Extract Nodes**.

2. Create the output filename: `census_wake_2000_poly2pts.shp`.

How it works...

Converting to simpler types from more complex ones is fairly straightforward in simple cases. Lines are just multiple points connected together and polygons are lines that start and end with the same point. So, it's pretty easy to see how to deconstruct one geometry to simpler geometries.

It's building up from points, which is a little trickier. In a line with three or more points, you need to make sure that you have them in the correct order; otherwise, you'll end up with a squiggle. When going to polygons, this can create bigger issues by leaving you with invalid polygons that self-intersect. So, it's really important to order your points in your source table in the same order that they will be combined. Reordering your data can be somewhat tricky. The Points2One plugin now includes a sort order option; to use this, make sure that your attribute table has a numeric column with the order of the points specified per group (you can restart the numbering at 1 for each distinct grouping).

There's more...

You can also split or combine multipolygons with the **Singleparts to Multiparts** and **Multiparts to Singleparts** commands.

When things get really tricky, you may need to switch to editing the shapes by hand or custom scripts. A good example of this is when you want a polygon with a hole in the middle. If you do go the route of editing by hand, make sure to turn on snapping so that your lines are automatically snapped to existing points. The official documentation on snapping can be found at `http://docs.qgis.org/2.8/en/docs/user_manual/working_ with_vector/editing_geometry_attributes.html#setting-the-snapping- tolerance-and-search-radius`.

The **Editing** and **Advanced Editing** toolbars and additional editing related plugins offer the ability to manipulate particularly tricky geometries, one at a time, if you need to.

Converting points to lines to polygons and back – SpatiaLite

The goal of this recipe is identical to the previous recipe, but it covers how to perform the process with data in a SpatiaLite database. You will to turn points into lines and lines into polygons.

Not all methods are available; for those that are not available, you can use the previous recipe. It will also work on a database layer; it just doesn't save the results to the database. So, the results will need to be imported to the database after completion.

Getting ready

You need to load a vector layer of points with a numeric ID indicating order, and an identifier of unique lines or polygons that is shared between points of the same geometry. For example, you can use `census_wake_2000_points` loaded into SpatiaLite with the geometry field called `geom`.

How to do it...

Using **DB Manager Plugin** (comes with QGIS and is in the **Database** menu), the **QspatiaLite** plugin, or an alternate SpatiaLite SQL application (command line or GUI), the following SQL examples will perform the conversions between vector types.

Points to lines

1. Create a table with points grouped by common ID:

```
--Create table grouping points with shared stfid into lines
CREATE Table census_pts2lines AS
SELECT stfid,MakeLine(geom) as geom
FROM census_wake_2000_points
GROUP BY stfid;
```

The following screenshot shows what the screen will look like:

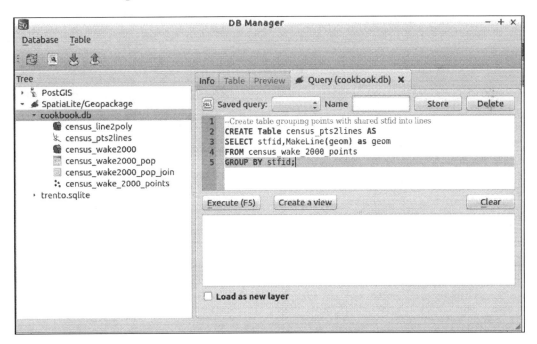

2. Register the new table as spatial:

```
--Register the new table's geometry so QGIS knows its a
spatial layer
SELECT
RecoverGeometryColumn('census_pts2lines','geom',3358,'LINES
TRING',2);
```

Some SQL interfaces can run multiple SQL statements in a row, separated by a semicolon. However, there are also many interfaces that can only perform one query at a time. Generally, run one query at a time unless you know your software supports multiple queries; otherwise, this may fail or silently only run the first query.

Lines to polygons

1. Create a table with lines grouped by common ID:

```
--Create table grouping lines with shared stfid into polygons
CREATE Table census_line2poly AS
SELECT stfid,ST_Polygonize(geom) as geom
FROM census_pts2lines
GROUP BY stfid;
```

2. Register the new table as spatial:

```
--Register the new table's geometry so QGIS knows its a
spatial layer
SELECT
RecoverGeometryColumn('census_line2poly','geom',3358,'POLYGON',2);
```

Double dashes (--) is the SQL character for a comment line. It is used to include descriptive text that is ignored in a query.

How it works...

Based on the common identifier specified in GROUP BY, the SQL statement aggregates multiple points into a new geometry of the type specified. After creating the new geometry and saving the results to a table, registration of the spatial metadata allows Spatialite and QGIS to know the table is a spatial layer.

There's more...

In the second example, lines were converted to polygons. You could also go directly from points to polygons with `ST_Polygonize(ST_MakeLine(geom))`.

Under the current versions of SpatiaLite, only aggregation to higher levels is fully supported. If you wish to disaggregate geometries, you can use the QGIS vector tools from the previous recipe.

See also

▸ SpatiaLite does have functions to dump specific points by first, last, or ID, one at a time. Refer to the index of functions online for details at `http://www.gaia-gis.it/gaia-sins/spatialite-sql-4.1.0.html`

▸ The *Converting points to lines to polygons and back – QGIS* recipe in this chapter for nondatabase methods

Converting points to lines to polygons and back – PostGIS

The goal of this recipe is identical to the previous two recipes, but it covers how to perform the process with data in a PostGIS database. You will use it to turn points into lines, and lines into polygons.

Not all methods are available; for those not available, you can use the previous recipe. It will also work on a database layer; it just doesn't save the results to the database. So, the results will need to be imported to the database after completion.

Getting ready

You need to load a vector layer of points with a numeric ID indicating order, and an identifier of unique lines or polygons that is shared between points of the same geometry. For example, you can use `census_wake_2000_points` loaded into PostGIS with the geometry field called `geom`. (Refer to *Chapter 1, Data Input and Output,* the *Loading Vector Data into PostGIS* recipe to see how to load data into PostGIS.)

 Import as single not multigeometries. Otherwise, you'll need to carry out some extra steps in the queries to split the multigeometries before they can be converted.

How to do it...

Using **DB Manager Plugin** (this comes with QGIS and is in the **Database** menu) or an alternate PostGIS SQL application (command line—pgsql or GUI—pgadmin III), the following SQL examples will perform the conversions between vector types.

Converting points to lines

1. Run the following query:

```
CREATE VIEW pts2line AS
SELECT ROW_NUMBER() over (order by census_wake_2000_points
.stfid) as id, stfid, ST_MakeLine(geom) as geom
FROM census_wake_2000_points
GROUP BY stfid;
```

The following screenshot shows what the screen will look like:

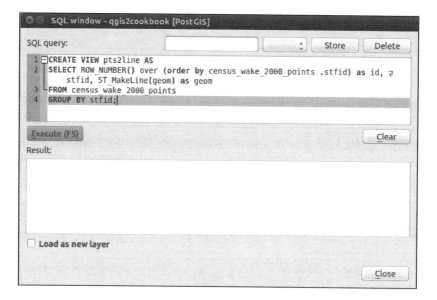

 To test the creation of new geometries, wrap the queries in CREATE VIEW, as demonstrated in *Chapter 2, Data Management*. If the data is large or you are happy with the results, you can swap in CREATE TABLE to make a new table for more permanent storage.

Converting lines to polygons

Run the following query:

```
CREATE VIEW line2poly AS
SELECT id,stfid,ST_MakePolygon(geom) as geom
FROM pts2line;
```

> Want to go straight from point to polygons? Try ST_
> MakePolygon(ST_MakeLine(geom)); the rest is
> as shown in the first example: points to lines query.

Converting lines or polygons to points

Run the following query:

```
CREATE VIEW pts AS
SELECT ROW_NUMBER() over (order by a.id_0) as id,id_0 as
grpid,(a.a_geom).path[2] as path,
ST_GeometryType((a.a_geom).geom), ((a.a_geom).geom) as geom
FROM (SELECT id_0,(ST_DumpPoints(geom)) as a_geom FROM
"census_wake2000") as a;
```

> What's ROW_NUMBER() about? This is a trick to ensure a
> unique integer for each row. Some tools complain if you don't
> have this; for example, DB Manager won't preview or load the
> layer, even though direct loading in QGIS works fine.

How it works...

Based on the common identifier specified in GROUP BY, the SQL statement aggregates multiple points into a new geometry of the specified type.

When dumping geometries to points, PostGIS actually dumps an array, including ID information. This is why the example query is actually a nested set of queries. The first is to dump the array of geometry information, and the second to extract the relevant parts of the results in the format that we want them in.

There's more...

PostGIS has a few dump functions with different purposes in mind. Splitting geometries is apparently a difficult concept for databases because aggregation is usually the only direction functions can logically go. Disaggregation is claimed by some to be counter to how SQL conceptually works and would require non-SQL logic.

See also

▸ For more details on the dump functions of PostGIS (ST_Dump, ST_DumpPoints, and ST_DumpRings), refer to the PostGIS manual at http://postgis.net/docs/manual-2.1/reference.html

▸ Refer to the *Converting points to lines to polygons and back – QGIS* recipe in this chapter for the non-database methods

Cropping rasters

Sometimes, the raster data you have for a theme is just much larger than the actual extent of your study area or map. Or, in the case of scanned maps, you have extra nonmap information around the outside edge. In these cases, you want to cut out a portion of your raster.

Getting ready

You'll need a raster file that you want to cut a portion of. In this example, we will use the North Carolina whole state elevation model (elev_state_500m.tif) and cut it with the outline of Wake County (county_wake.shp). Load both of these files in a fresh QGIS project.

How to do it...

The easiest way to do this is to use a polygon mask layer. The vector mask can be a rectangle, but it doesn't have to be. The outline of a single polygon works best, though.

 An alternate method would be to determine the bounding box (bbox) coordinates of the extent that you want with the Capture Coordinate tool or to draw the rectangle directly on the map.

1. Go to **Raster | Extraction | Clipper**.
2. Set **Input file (raster)** as elev_state_500m.tif.
3. Set **Output file** using the **Select** button to pick a directory, and name the output elev_wake_500m.tif.

4. Set **No data value** to **-9999**.

 Why -9999? Setting **No data value** to something impossible makes it more obvious later to other users. The value 0 is a really bad choice as data can legitimately have a value of zero. As some raster formats only support numbers and, in particular, integers, a large negative number is a common choice.

5. Now change **Clipping mode** to **Mask Layer** and select `county_wake.shp` as **Mask Layer**:

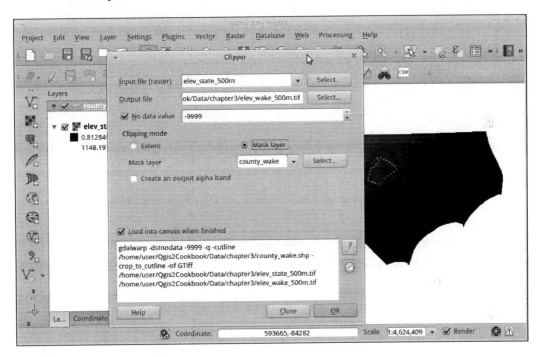

How it works...

The shape of your mask and the size of the raster cells in the source data will determine how pixelated the resulting raster will be. Zoom in to the results and compare the edge of the new raster to the vector outline of the county. You'll notice that because of the 500 m wide pixels, it's hard to exactly match the edge of the county exactly with whole pixels.

Note that this tool, as with all other tools in the GDAL **Tools** menu, is actually a graphical interface to GDAL command-line tools.

There's more...

You'll notice that with this particular example, an issue that arises with converting rasters to nonrectangular shapes; the edges are jagged as compared to the vector. If you need it to be really smooth, there are a few options. You can decrease the pixel size, splitting current pixels into multiple pixels using the `-tr` option. As with other Raster tools, you can use the pencil icon to override the GDAL command-line options to add features not included in the interface. In this case, the `-tr` option inline with the rest of the already formatted command:

```
gdalwarp -tr 100 100
```

This would make each pixel 100 units instead of the current 500 x 500.

> Some important options to remember when saving TIFF files with GDAL are number type (Integer versus Float) and compression. Both of these can greatly impact the final file size. Refer to the *Converting Vectors to Rasters* recipe later in this chapter for an example. Also, if you have a multicore CPU, add `-multi` to take advantage of your CPU cores for faster processing of most raster operations.

See also

 ▸ For a full list of the gdalwarp options refer to `http://gdal.org/gdalwarp.html`

Clipping vectors

Like rasters, occasionally you only need vector data to cover a certain area of study (area of interest). Also, like rasters, you can use a layer defining the extent that you want to select only for a portion of a vector layer to make a new layer. The tool that is used for this job is Clip; that is, 'Cookie Cutter' because of how the results look afterwards.

Getting ready

For the example in this recipe, we will use `geology.shp` and clip it to the extent of Wake County using `census_wake2000.shp`. Any vector layer with the aggregation of polygons covering all of the county will work.

How to do it...

1. Load the two, `geology.shp` and `census_wake2000.shp`, layers.

2. Open the clipping tool from **Vector | Geoprocessing Tools | Clip**:

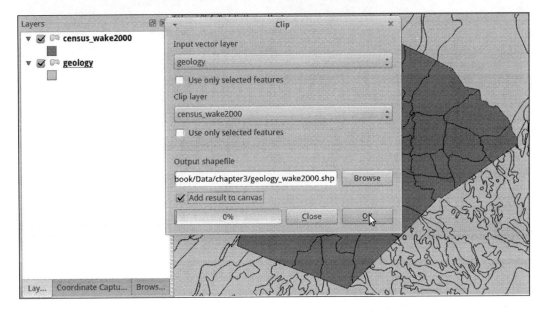

3. Input layer is the layer that has to be cut; this is `geology.shp`.

4. Clip layer defines the boundaries that have to be cut.

 There is no requirement that clip layer be contiguous. You can cut any combination of shapes that you want, circles, squares, triangles, and so on. They just need to be polygons.

5. (Optional) Check **Add result to canvas** so that you see the results immediately.

6.   Select **OK** to run the tool:

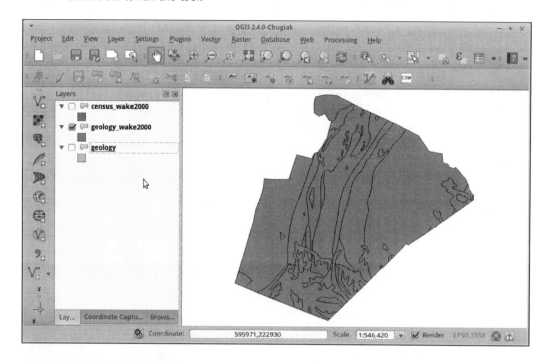

How it works...

All clipping is based on the principle of intersection features. For each feature in Input, the tool checks to see whether it intersects with the overall shape of clip layer. When it does intersect, the algorithm then checks whether any part falls outside the intersection. When a part lands outside, it is cut off.

There's more...

You have to be careful when using clip. If the original table contained columns that included measurements such as area and perimeter, these values are copied from the original. Therefore, they may not reflect the new size of and shapes that were cut.

Generally, all geometry operations and analysis should be done with layers in the same projection in order to ensure consistent results. Also, many tools are not projection aware and won't compensate for two source layers being in different projections.

Tools that create the intersection of objects (for example, in PostGIS's and SpatiaLite's ST_Intersection) can provide you with similar results. However, you may need to perform multiple steps: Intersect, then select by contains or intersection to eliminate unwanted data.

See also

Refer to the next recipe in the chapter if you want a way to limit features without altering the original spatial data

Extracting vectors

Clipping is great, except when you don't want to alter the original geometries, such as when you want to select overlapping features. Or, in other cases, you just want filter the geometries based on nonspatial attributes. To achieve both of these results, you can utilize the Selection tools in combination with **Save Layer As..** to extract just the features of interest. This recipe uses spatial selection methods to extract a subset of original polygons without altering them.

Getting ready

We'll use the same data as the previous recipe, `geology.shp` and `census_wake2000.shp`.

How to do it...

1. Select polygons from `geology.shp` that overlap with Wake County (`census_wake2000.shp`) by navigating to **Vector | Research Tools | Select by location**.

2. Select the feature in **geology**.

3. Intersect the features in `census_wake2000`.

4. Modify the current selection by **creating new selection**.

5. Click on **OK**:

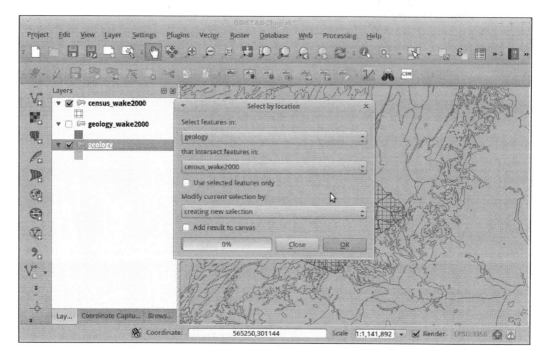

6. Now, you will see the matching features highlighted (by default in yellow):

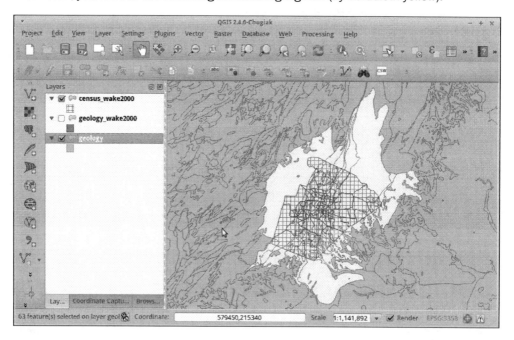

7. If the selection looks good, use the **Layer context** menu, right-click, and click on **Save As...** to create a file containing only the selection.

 When in the **Save As...** (as described in *Chapter 1, Data Input and Output*) dialog make sure to check the box next to **Save only selected features**.

How it works...

This really goes back to the same fundamental concept of Intersection that most vector analysis rely on. When you can test whether two features overlap, there are many different operations possible based on the answer. You can select, deselect, or, as in the previous recipe, select then cut to fit. In these cases, each polygon is tested for at least a partial intersection, and the matches are then highlighted as the results.

There's more...

While this recipe demonstrates how to select a subset of data based on location, you can also do the same thing based on attributes of the features with a query on the attribute table. Or, you can combine attribute based selection, spatial selection, and hand selection graphically on the map—any selection combination that you want can be saved as a new layer.

You may also notice in the **Select by location** tool that vectors can also be added or removed from existing selections in case you want to perform more complicated operations involving more than one type of criteria.

See also

▸ Refer to the documentation on PostGIS, SpatiaLite, or the *PostGIS Cookbook*, by Packt Publishing, for how to perform similar operations using SQL in PostGIS (SpatiaLite, queries are very similar)

Converting rasters to vectors

Sometimes, you need to convert data that is originally in raster format to a vector format in order to perform vector-based analysis methods. Generally speaking, as rasters are continuous datasets, converting them to polygons is more common than converting them to lines or points.

Getting ready

You need a raster layer, preferably one with groups of the same valued pixels next to each other. For this example, we'll use `geology_30m.tif`, as a 30 meter x 30 meter pixel should give decent results.

 The smaller the pixels, the smoother looking the resulting vector will appear when zoomed out.

How to do it...

1. Load `geology_30m.tif`.
2. Go to **Raster | Conversion | Polygonize**:

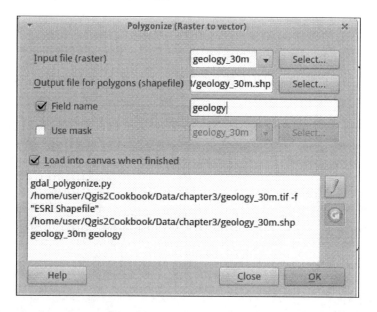

3. Name the output `geology_30m.shp`.
4. (Optional) Name the output column `geology`, `class` or `value`.
5. Press **OK** to run the process.

6. Compare the results (colors are in a similar but different scale):

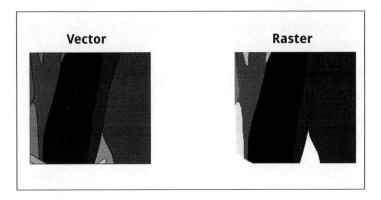

How it works...

For each pixel, the value is compared to its neighbors (there are different neighbor algorithms). When two pixels next to each other have the same value, they are lumped into a polygon. Additional neighbors of the same value get added to the polygon until pixels of differing values are encountered. As it's pixel-based, the edge of the result will usually follow the outline of the pixels, making for a jagged edge. This edge can be smoothed into straight lines with additional options or other tools, such as the QGIS smoothing tool.

There's more...

The minimum number of pixels required to make a polygon or the maximum allowed value difference to be counted as the same can be altered to drop out isolated pixels or to allow for a range of values to be counted together.

Note that if each pixel is unique as compared to its adjacent neighbors, then you'll just end up with a polygon for each pixel. Or if your raster is sufficiently large and varied, this process could take days. You may want to reconsider whether you really need to convert or whether your analysis can be done in raster. Another option would be to resample or reclassify the raster to larger polygons first to decrease the data density. Or, you need to investigate remote sensing type tools that perform classification to create related groupings of pixels based on similarity.

If you want to convert raster data to points, then you probably want to use the points sampling tool. If you want to convert some portion of a raster to lines then you may need more sophisticated feature extraction tools found; for example, in SAGA and GRASS, either through the Processing toolbox or as standalone software. Or, you may even need to result to a mix of pixel extraction and hand digitizing.

See also

> ▸ *Chapter 7, Raster Analysis I,* and *Chapter 8, Raster Analysis II,* on further raster methods

Converting vectors to rasters

Occasionally, you want to convert vectors to rasters to facilitate using raster analysis tools such as the raster calculator.

Getting ready

You'll need a vector layer; this can be a point, line or polygon layer. The best results generally come from polygon layers. We will use `geology_wake2000reclass.shp`. This file is the result of the earlier clipping vectors recipe with a new column added that codes the geology types as integers. For reference, you'll also use `elev_wake_500m.tif` as a matching raster for the area of interest.

How to do it...

In order to be useful in analysis, here's a checklist:

1. Is the vector data in the same projection as the rest of the raster analysis data? If not, reproject it first. Check the following URL for help, `https://docs.qgis.org/2.8/en/docs/training_manual/vector_analysis/reproject_transform.html`.

2. Clip the vector data to the analysis extent. You may need to convert a raster into a polygon mask to clip it (refer to the clipping vectors recipe earlier in this chapter).

     You can only pick numeric fields as raster formats only store a single number per cell. In order to keep the attribute that you want, you may need to use the field calculator to create a new field that reclassifies categories of text into a numeric scheme (for example, 1 = water, 2 = land, and so on) before performing the conversion. If you copy a unique ID as the attribute, there are some tools later that let you rejoin the original attribute table as a value attribute table (refer to the GRASS functions in **Processing Toolbox**).

3. Load `geology_wake2000reclass.shp` and `elev_wake_500m.tif`.

4. Open **Properties** of `elev_wake_500m.tif`:

    1. In the **Metadata** section, scroll down to **Dimensions**. You will want to match either the dimensions or resolution so that your new raster will match the existing elevation data pixels.

    2. Note that **Dimensions** are X: **134**, Y: **124** and Bands: **1**. The resolution is 499.637,-498.342 pixel size.

    3. Close the dialog.

5. Now, open the conversion dialog by navigating to **Raster | Conversion | Rasterize** and follow these steps:

    1. Input the file as `geology_wake2000reclass`.

    2. Name your output `geology_wake.tif` (you will get a warning to set the size or resolution).

    3. Set the raster size: **Width** to **134** and **Height** to **124**.

    4. Click on **OK** to run the process.

The following screenshot shows how the screen will look:

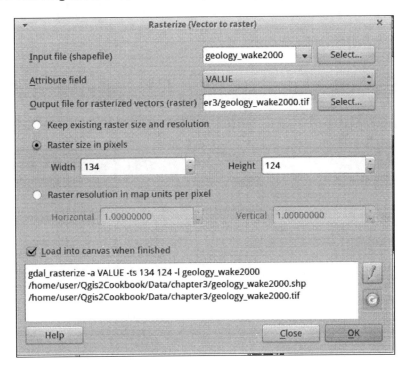

How it works...

A grid of pixels is created at the specified width, height, and extent. For each cell, an intersection is performed with the underlying vector layer. If more than 50% of the cell intersects with the vector, it's designated attribute is assigned to the cell.

There's more...

It's really important to match projection and extent before converting to raster. If you fail to do so, then your pixels in different raster layers won't line up perfectly with each other, and either tools won't work or they will introduce a resampling error. If this looks too pixelated (squares) for your liking, consider creating the raster at a higher pixel density.

If you compare the vector version to the new raster, you'll notice that the area in the middle all came out a similar color. This is due to the values used for classification, where the geology that started with the same major component was given the same starting value (for example, PZ all start with 40, and the last number changes based on the letters after PZ).

Looking at the new layer and want to get rid of the black surrounding the real data? This area is no-data, refer to *Chapter 8, Raster Analysis II*.

See also

> ▶ There are other methods to calculate the new value of a pixel to make smoother transitions or intermediate values when multiple polygons are with the same pixel. Refer to the GRASS and SAGA methods in Processing Toolbox for more sophisticated alternatives.

Building DateTime strings

Date and time data get stored in all sorts of ways. One of the more frustrating issues is that some common GIS formats (Shapefiles) can't store date and time in the same field without making it a string. This is fine for visual display but terrible for use with tools that use DateTime for their functionality, such as the TimeManager Plugin (refer to *Chapter 4, Data Exploration*).

Getting ready

Use `datetime-example.shp`, which contains a variety of date and time representations to play with.

How to do it...

1. Load `datetime-example.shp`.

2. Open the attribute table of `datetime-example`.

3. Create a new field. As this is a shapefile, we'll need to use a String of length 30 (or you can use the empty field called `calculated`).

4. Turn on layer editing (this is the pencil icon, which is the first icon to the left of the window toolbar).

5. From the drop-down list, select **Calculated**.

6. Now press the **Calculation** button.

 In older versions of QGIS, you'll need to open the Field calculator, which also works in newer versions but has slightly more steps.

7. In the calculator, we'll use the `substr` String operation (that is, Substring) in combination with the || concatenation to rearrange the values from existing fields into a valid `DateTime`:

   1. The simplest variant is just to combine `shpDate` with `Time` and put a space in between:

      ```
      "shpdate"  || ' '||  "Time"
      ```

   2. For a bit more of a challenge, use `Date`:

      ```
      substr("Date",7,4) ||'-'||substr("Date",1,2)||'-'||
          substr("Date",4,2) || ' '||  "Time"
      ```

 Note the use of single quotes (') to denote a string as opposed to double quotes ("), which indicate a field name.

8. Experiment with the formulas, checking the results with the calculator preview at the bottom. When satisfied, select **OK**, and then click on the **Update All** button:

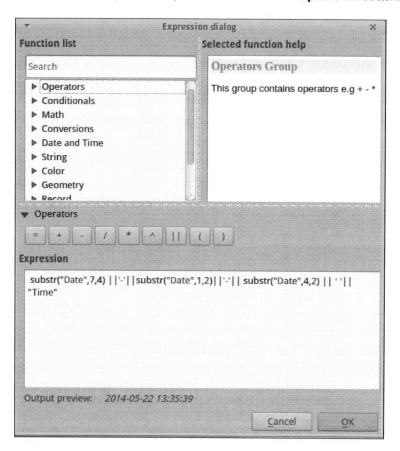

9. If you're happy with the results, save the edits; if not, toggle **editing off** and choose **Close without saving**.

How it works...

Substr takes three arguments: the field name, the starting position, and the number of characters after this to include. The position index starts at 1.

There's more...

Using string manipulation, we've combined multiple fields into an ISO standard format for DateTime, which other tools will recognize and be able to utilize.

The fields included in this example data are as follows:

Field	Type	Explanation
Time	String	This is time in a 24 hour format: hours:minutes:seconds.
datetime	String	This is a DateTime String from a typical GPS GPX file.
calculated	String	This is a String that is long enough to hold date and time with padding characters and a timezone UTC offset.
Date	String	This is a typical date format coming out of a spreadsheet.
shpdate	Date	This is a date format in the Date type within a shapefile, and it can not hold time.

See also

▶   If using database layers, this can all be performed with SQL in SpatiaLite or PostGIS. The ISO date time standard is 8601, and can be found at `http://en.wikipedia.org/wiki/ISO_8601`.

Geotagging photos

Newer cameras and phones with built-in GPS can be wonderful tools for data collection, as they help keep track of exactly where and when a picture was taken. However, not all cameras have a built-in GPS. You can add geotags afterwards, either with a GPS log from a separate GPS unit or just using a reference map and your memory or notes.

Getting ready

For this recipe, you'll need a some photos and either a GPS log (`*.gpx`), reference vector, reference raster, or coordinates. We've provided `centerofcalifornia.jpg` in the geotag folder, and the coordinates are in the image itself but also included as a point in `centerofcalifornia.shp`.

You will also need the Geotag photos plugin, which requires the exiftool program to be installed on your system. If exiftool didn't come with your install, you can easily get it from the Web at `http://www.sno.phy.queensu.ca/~phil/exiftool/` or at package repositories (Linux).

How to do it...

This particular plugin assigns location per folder, so all photos in a folder will get the same coordinates. This works well for batch assigning of general coordinates:

1. Start by loading your GPS log, or creating a new vector layer and digitizing the points that you want to assign to photos. In this case, load `centerofcalifornia.shp`.

 Don't have a lot of locations or just have coordinates written down by hand? You can manually enter the information into the plugin interface without an existing layer.

2. (Optional) Load a background reference layer.

3. Now that you have the layer that you want to associate with photos open the plugin in **Vector | Geotag and import photos | Geotag photos**.

4. Select the layer and then the field (location) that you want to use as the label.

5. Now, click on **Populate Table**. One row should have been added to the interface.

6. Now, pick the photos by clicking under **Path to Folder** in the empty box for the row that you want to assign:

    1. You can type in the path or browse by clicking on **....**

    2. Pick the `geotag` folder.

    3. Make sure to press **Enter** or click outside the box once you are back in the main screen:

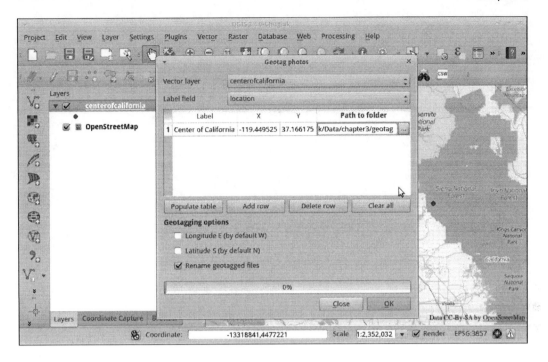

7. (Optional) Check the box to rename geotagged files if you want the geotagged version to be a new copy of the file instead of altering the original files (always keep an original backup).

8. Click on **OK**.

How it works...

Exiftools writes to the built-in metadata of an image file to a section called EXIF. It's a standard in photography to store extra data about photos that many software management tools can easily read from. Latitude and Longitude in WGS 84 coordinates are the standard method of encoding GPS data within the EXIF section.

There's more...

Now that you have a geotagged photo, you can upload it to sites such as Flickr, which will display it on a map, or skip to the recipe *Viewing Geotagged Photos* in *Chapter 4, Data Exploration,* for how to make a map in QGIS.

This plugin is very manual and assigns location per folder as it was created to work specifically with camera traps. Instead, if you were travelling between each photo location and have a GPS log, there are other non-QGIS tools to help you match GPS points with your photos. Digikam (a photography management tool) has a function to geotag based on timestamp matches.

See also

▸ The OpenStreetMap wiki lists other free and paid options out there at
`http://wiki.openstreetmap.org/wiki/Geotagging_Source_Photos`

4
Data Exploration

In this chapter, we will cover the following recipes:

- ▸ Listing unique values in a column
- ▸ Exploring numeric value distribution in a column
- ▸ Exploring spatiotemporal data using Time Manager
- ▸ Creating animations using Time Manager
- ▸ Designing time-dependent styles
- ▸ Loading BaseMaps with the QuickMapServices plugin
- ▸ Loading BaseMaps with the OpenLayers plugin
- ▸ Viewing geotagged photos

Introduction

This chapter focuses on recipes that will help you visually inspect and better comprehend your data. The recipes in this chapter include methods of summarizing, inspecting, filtering, and styling data, based on spatial and temporal attributes so that you can get a better feeling for your data before you perform analysis. The primary goal is to create some visuals or summaries of data that allow you, the human, to utilize your brain's ability to identify patterns of interest. The better you understand your data, the easier it is to pick appropriate analysis methods later.

Listing unique values in a column

When investigating a new dataset, it is very helpful to have a way to quickly check which values a column contains. In this recipe, we will use different approaches using both the GUI and the Python console to list the unique values of POI classes in our sample POI dataset.

Getting ready

To follow this recipe, please load `poi_names_wake.shp`.

How to do it...

If you are simply looking for a solution based on the GUI, the **List unique values** tool is available both in **Vector | Analysis Tools** as well as in the **Processing Toolbox** menu. You can use either one of these to get a list of the unique values in a column. Having this tool available in the **Processing Toolbox** menu makes it possible to include it in processing models and, thus, automate the process. The following steps to list unique values use the **Processing Toolbox** menu:

1. Start **List unique values** from the **Processing Toolbox** menu.
2. Select the `poi_names_wake` layer as **Input layer** and the `class` attribute as **Target field**.
3. Click on **Run** and wait for the tool to finish. The results will be displayed in the **Results** view, which will open automatically.

If you want to further customize this task, for example, by counting how often the values appear in this dataset, it's time to fire up Python console:

1. Start **Python Console**, which you will find in the **Plugins** menu, and click on the **Show editor** button (in the toolbar to the left of Python console) to open the editor window.
2. Paste the following short script into the editor, save it, and then click on the **Run script** button. (Make sure that the POI layer is selected in the layer list.) It loops through all features in the active layer and creates a dictionary object, which contains all unique values and the corresponding counts:

```
import processing
layer = iface.activeLayer()
classes = {}
features = processing.features(layer)
for f in features:
  attrs = f.attributes()
  class_value = f['class']
  if class_value in classes:
```

```
        classes[class_value] += 1
    else:
        classes[class_value] = 1
print classes
```

The following screenshot shows what the screen looks like:

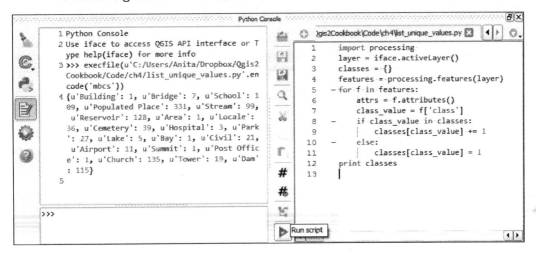

How it works...

In the first line, we use `import processing` because it offers a very handy and convenient function, `processing.features()`, to access layer features, which we use in line 7. It is worth noting that, if there is a selection, `processing.features()` will only return an iterator of the selected features.

In line 3, we get the currently active layer object. Line 5 creates the empty dictionary object, which we will fill with the unique values and corresponding counts.

The `for` loop, starting on line 5, loops through all features of the layer. For each feature, we get the value in the classification field (line 7). You can change the column name to analyze other columns. Then, we only need to check whether this value is already present in the `classes` dictionary (line 8) or whether we have to add it (line 11).

There's more...

If you are using an SQL database, such as Spatialite or PostGIS, you can achieve similar results with a query using the COUNT and GROUP BY functions to count the number of features or records per class:

```
SELECT class, COUNT(*)
FROM poi_name_wake
GROUP BY class
```

Exploring numeric value distribution in a column

In this recipe, we will look at how to explore the properties of a column of numeric values. We will look at the tools that QGIS offers and apply them to analyze the elevation values in our sample POI dataset.

Getting ready

To follow this recipe, please load `poi_names_wake.shp`. If you followed the previous recipe, *Listing unique values in a column*, you can continue directly from there.

How to do it...

A good way to get a first impression of the properties of a numeric column is using the **Basic Statistics** tool from **Vector**. This allows you to calculate statistical values, such as the minimum and maximum values, mean and median, standard deviation, and sum.

If you want to examine the distribution of elevation values, there is the handy Statist plugin. Statist generates an interactive histogram representation of the value distribution:

1. Install **Statist** using **Plugin Manager**.

2. Start **Statist** from the **Vector** menu.

3. Specify **Input vector layer** and the attribute that you want to analyze (**Target field**), then click on **OK** to compute the statistics.

4. Using the buttons below the diagram, you can zoom and pan the diagram, as well as save the diagram image.

5. You can even customize the diagram by changing the title and axis labels and ranges. Just use the right-most button with the green tick mark on it to open the customization dialog:

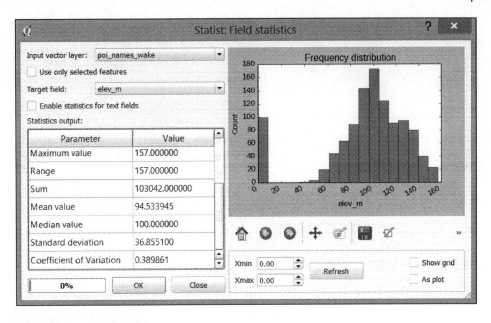

How it works...

Thanks to **Python Console** and the editor, we are not limited to the existing tools and plugins. Instead, we can create or own specialized scripts such as the following one. This script creates a short layer statistics report using HTML and the Google Charts Javascript API (for more information and API docs refer to `https://developers.google.com/chart/`), which it then displays in a `QWebView` window. Of course, you can use any other JavaScript charting API as well. (Note that you need to be connected to the Internet for this script to work because it has to download the Javascript.) We recommend using the editor that was introduced in the previous recipe. Don't forget to select the layer in the legend:

```
import processing
from PyQt4.QtWebKit import QWebView
layer = iface.activeLayer()
values = []
features = processing.features(layer)
for f in features:
  values.append( f['elev_m'])
myWV = wQWebView(None)
html='<html><head><script type="text/javascript"'
html+='src="https://www.google.com/jsapi"></script>'
html+='<script type="text/javascript">'
html+='google.load("visualization","1",{packages:["corechart"]});'
html+='google.setOnLoadCallback(drawChart);'
```

```
html+='function drawChart() { '
  html+='var data = google.visualization.arrayToDataTable(['
    html+='["%s"],' % (field_name)
    for value in values:
      html+='[%f],' % (value)
  html+=']);'
  html+='var chart = new google.visualization.Histogram('
    html+='document.getElementById("chart_div"));'
  html+='chart.draw(data, {title: "Histogram"});}</script></head>'
html+='<body><h1>Layer: %s</h1>' % (layer.name())
html+='<p>Values for %s range from: ' % (field_name)
html+='%d to %d</p>' % (min(values),max(values))
html+='<div id="chart_div"style="width:900px; height:500px;">'
html+='</div></body></html>'
myWV.setHtml(html)
myWV.show()
```

Of course, custom reports such as this one lend themselves to adding more details. For example, we can create separate histograms for each POI class or add other types of charts, such as scatter charts:

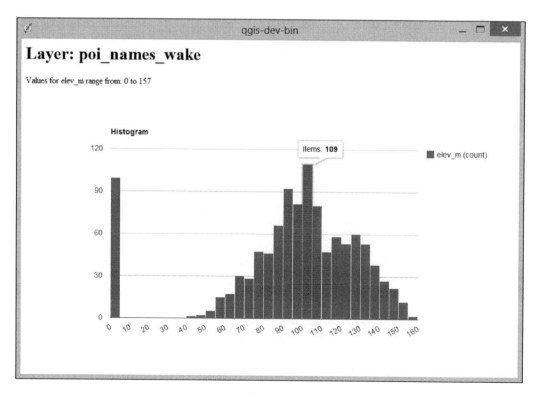

The first part (lines 1 to 12) is very similar to the script explained in the previous recipe, *Listing unique values in a column:* We get the active layer and collect all elevation values in the `values` list.

The `QWebView` created on line 14 enables us to display the HTML content, which we then generate in the following section (lines 16 to 34). First, we load the Google Charts Javascript. The actual magic happens in the `drawChart()` function starting on line 21. Lines 22 to 26 create the `data` object, which is filled with the elevation values from our `values` list. The last three lines of the function (lines 27 to 29) finally create and draw the histogram chart. Finally, lines 30 to 34 contain the HTML body definition with the header stating the layer name and a short introduction text that states the min and max elevation values.

See also

▸ For those who want to perform more advanced graphing and numerical analysis, consider using the matplotlib python library or reading your data sources into R. Aggregate functions in SatialLitetgis PostGIS can also provide you with min, max, average, sum, and other summarization functions. For PostGIS, refer to `http://www.postgresql.org/docs/9.1/static/functions-aggregate.html`.

Exploring spatiotemporal vector data using Time Manager

In this recipe, we will look at exploring spatiotemporal vector data using the Time Manager plugin. We'll use event data from the **ACLED (Armed Conflict Location and Event Data Project)** at `http://www.acleddata.com/about-acled/`.

Getting ready

To follow this recipe, please load `ACLED_africa_fatalities_dec2013.shp`. The layer style that you will see in the following screenshots consists of a simple circle marker at 50% transparency with the data-defined size set to the number of fatalities of the incident. (You can read more about styling in *Chapter 10, Cartography Tips*, and *Learning QGIS* book by Packt Publishing.) If you want some additional geographic context, you can also load `NE_africa.shp`, which contains the outline of Africa.

How to do it...

Once the data is loaded, all event positions will be displayed. The default way to filter the events, for example, to only see the events from December 1, is to use Layer | Query and enter a filter expression or query, such as the following:

```
"EVENT_DATE" >= '2013-12-01' AND "EVENT_DATE" < '2013-12-02'
```

1. It's easy to see that updating this query manually for each day will not be a very convenient way to explore spatiotemporal data. Therefore, we will use the Time Manager plugin (installed using Plugin Manager).

2. The Time Manager panel will be added to the bottom of the QGIS window once the plugin is installed. Click on the **Settings** button to open the **Time manager settings** dialog. We can configure Time Manager here.

3. Click on **Add Layer** to open the **Select layer and column(s)** dialog.

4. Select the **ACLED_africa_fatalities_dec2013** layer and **EVENT_DATE** as starting time and then click on **OK** to add the event point layer to the list of managed layers, as shown in the following screenshot:

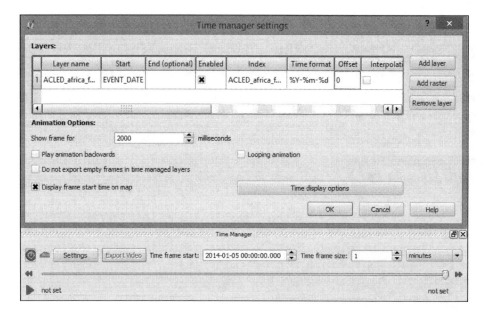

 Optionally, you can enable **display frame start time on map** to add a small label with the corresponding timestamp to the rendered map.

5. Click on **OK** when you are done. At this point, Time Manager applies the temporal filter to the dataset, so this can take some time depending on the size of the dataset used.

6. By default, after the first layer has been added, Time Manager will display all the events that occurred during the first day of the dataset. It is easy to adjust the filter by changing the **Time frame size** settings. You can increase the number of days that should be displayed or change to one of the other time units, including seconds, minutes, hours, weeks, and months, as shown in the following screenshot:

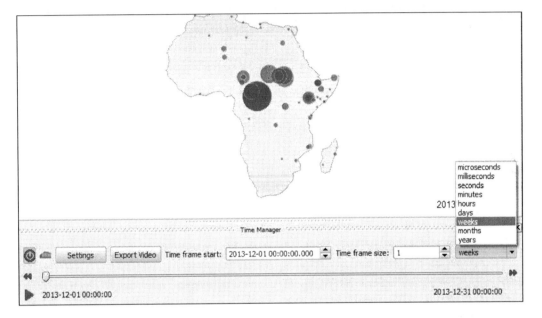

7. Once you are happy with the settings, you have multiple options to navigate through time:

   ❑ Click on the play button in the bottom-left corner of the Time Manager panel to start an automatic animation

   ❑ Move the time slider to the center of the panel like you would do to navigate within a video or music player application

   ❑ Click on the forward or backward button on either side of the slider to advance or go back by one time frame

   ❑ Of course, you can also edit the **Time frame start** setting directly

How it works...

For performance reasons, Time Manager relies on the layer query/filter expression capability of QGIS. This comes with the following limitations:

- ▶ Time Manager can only be used with data sources that support layer queries or filter expressions. Most notably, this means that it cannot be used with delimited text layers.

- ▶ As the layer queries or filter expressions have to work with strings, it has to be possible to order the date-time values correctly using text sort. Therefore, the values have to be stored in one of the following formats:

```
%Y-%m-%d %H:%M:%S.%f
%Y-%m-%d %H:%M:%S
%Y-%m-%d %H:%M
%Y-%m-%dT%H:%M:%S
%Y-%m-%dT%H:%M:%SZ
%Y-%m-%dT%H:%M
%Y-%m-%dT%H:%MZ
%Y-%m-%d
%Y/%m/%d %H:%M:%S.%f
%Y/%m/%d %H:%M:%S
%Y/%m/%d %H:%M
%Y/%m/%d
%H:%M:%S
%H:%M:%S.%f
%Y.%m.%d %H:%M:%S.%f
%Y.%m.%d %H:%M:%S
%Y.%m.%d %H:%M
%Y.%m.%d
%Y%m%d%H%M%S
```

 If your data uses a different format, which is ordered correctly as well, you can add it to `timevectorlayer.py` or change the format using Field Calculator.

See also

- ▶ The following recipes will show you how to create videos and more sophisticated time-dependent styles using Time Manager.

Creating animations using Time Manager

In this recipe, we will use the Time Manager plugin to create an image series out of our spatiotemporal QGIS project and turn it into a video, which is ready to be uploaded on Youtube or added into a presentation using easily available and free tools.

Getting ready

To follow this recipe, it's advisable that you complete the previous recipe, *Exploring spatiotemporal vector data using Time Manager,* to set up this project.

To turn the image series exported by Time Manager into a video, we can use external programs, such as the command-line tool Mencoder, or the free Windows Movie Maker.

Mencoder is a very useful command-line tool to encode videos, which is available from repositories for many Linux distributions and for Mac. Windows users can download it from Gianluigi Tiesi's site at `http://oss.netfarm.it/mplayer-win32.php`.

If you're using Windows, you can also create the video using the free Windows Movie Maker application, which can be downloaded from `http://windows.microsoft.com/en-us/windows/get-movie-maker-download`.

How to do it...

Before starting the export, it is a good idea to check all the settings, as follows:

1. The time slider should be moved to the beginning of the time line, and an appropriate **Time frame size** should be set.

2. Additionally, it can be useful to enable **display frame start time on map** (refer to the screenshots in the previous recipe) if you haven't done so already in the previous recipe because, otherwise, the exported animation frames won't contain any information about the time of the displayed events.

3. When you have found the best settings for your dataset, click on the **Export Video** button. A dialog will open, which will allow you to select the folder that you want to export your video to. After you click on the **Select Folder** button, Time Manager will automatically start to export the video frames. As displayed in the **Export video** information popup, you should now wait for the export to finish. There will be another popup once this process is finished, which looks like the following screenshot:

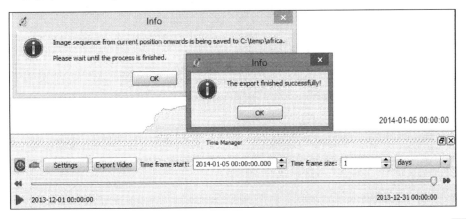

4. If you open the `export` folder, you will see the animation frames that Time Manager just created.

5. This is how you can use Mencoder to create an `.avi` video from all `.png` images in the current working directory. Make sure that you are in the folder containing the images before running the following command:

```
mencoder "mf://*.png" -mf fps=10 -o output.avi -ovc lavc
-lavcopts vcodec=mpeg4
```

6. You can control the speed of the animation using the frames per second (`fps`) parameter. Higher values create a faster animation.

If you're using Windows Movie Maker, perform the following steps:

1. Load the animation frame images.

2. To adjust the speed of the animation, go to **Video Tools | Edit**, and reduce the **Duration** value. Note that you should have all images selected if you want to apply the same duration to all images at once.

3. To save the animation, just go to **File | Save Movie** and select your preferred resolution and quality.

How it works...

Time Manager's Export Video feature uses the `QgsMapCanvas.saveAsImage()` function to export the image series. This means that the images will be of the same size as the map canvas in your QGIS window at the time of clicking on the **Export Video** button.

Designing time-dependent styles

In this recipe, we will use the `animation_datetime()` function, which is exposed by Time Manager to create a time-dependent style for our animation. The style will represent the age of the event feature: the event marker's fill color will fade towards gray the older the event gets.

Getting ready

To follow this recipe, please load `ACLED_africa_fatalities_dec2013.shp` and configure Time Manager, as shown in the *Exploring spatiotemporal vector data using Time Manager* recipe, with the following exception: when adding the layer to Time Manager, set the **End time** value to the `FOREVER` attribute.

How to do it...

To create a time-dependent style, we use the **Data defined properties** option of the Simple marker:

1. In the _Exploring spatiotemporal vector data using Time Manager_ recipe, we mentioned that we already used the **FATALITIES** attribute to scale the marker size. For the time-dependent style, we will add a new definition to the **Fill color** property, as shown in the following screenshot:

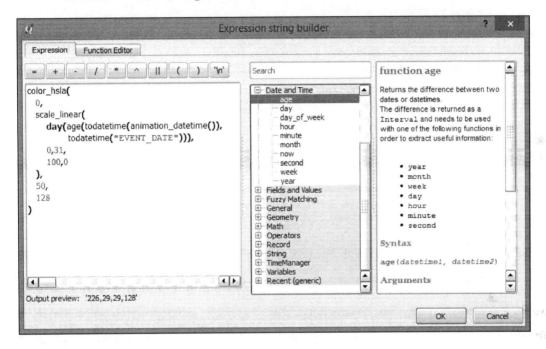

2. Confirm the changes and start the animation to watch the effect.

How it works...

Here is our color expression in more detail:

```
color_hsla(
  0,
  scale_linear(
    day(age(todatetime(animation_datetime()),
    todatetime("EVENT_DATE"))),
    0,31,
```

```
    100,0
  ),
  50,
  128
)
```

The expression consists of multiple parts, as follows:

- `day(age(todatetime(animation_datetime()),todatetime("EVENT_DATE")))`: This calculates the number of days between the current animation time given by `animation_datetime()` and calculates `EVENT_DATE`

- `scale_linear`: This transforms the age value (in days between 0 to 31 days) into a value between 100 and 0 which is suitable for the saturation parameter of the following color function

- `color_hsla`: This is one of many functions that are available in QGIS to create colors. It returns a string representation of a color, based on its attributes for hue (0 equals red), saturation (between 0 and 100 depending on our age function), lightness (50 equals medium lightness) and alpha (128 equals 50% transparency)

You can speed up the fading effect by reducing the `scale_linear` parameter, `domain_max`, from 31 days to a smaller value, such as 7, for a complete fade to gray within one week.

See also

- If you are interested in learning more about color models, such as the HSL color model used in this recipe, we recommend the Wikibook on color models at `http://en.wikibooks.org/wiki/Color_Models:_RGB,_HSV,_HSL`

Loading BaseMaps with the QuickMapServices plugin

Often, when exploring your data, you may feel somewhat lost. Without the context of the known world, a layer can seem like a blob of information floating in space. By adding an atlas-style map, air photos, or another BaseMap, you can begin to see how your data fits in the on-the-ground reality. However, adding such layers often takes considerable preprocessing work; sometimes, you just don't want to go through this until you know you need it. What's the solution? Use a premade layer, preferably fast-loading tiles, from a web service.

Getting ready

The QuickMapServices plugin works best when you have another dataset that you want to provide extra context for. Start by first loading such a layer and then zooming in to its extent.

You will need the following:

▸ A layer of interest to overlay (you can use `Davis_DBO_Centerline-wgs84.shp`)

▸ An active Internet connection (this may not work behind corporate proxies)

▸ You will need to install and activate the QuickMapServices plugin

How to do it...

Starting with a new QGIS project, follow these instructions to load BaseMap from the web with the QuickMapServices plugin:

1. Start by first loading your local map layers:

2. Verify that the projection definition is correctly identified by QGIS.

 The plugin will not turn on projection-on-the-fly for you unless you change its settings. However, in order for most tile services to work in QGIS, projection-on-the-fly must be enabled and set to EPSG:3857 Psuedo/Web/Popular Mercator. Other data will fail to line up if their projection is not defined or read properly by QGIS.

3. Go to **Web | QuickMapServices** and select a layer to load from the Web. Wait a few seconds for the tiles to be loaded:

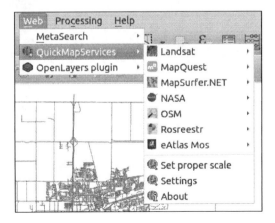

The default list of services is open and free. If you want to use other services that have more limited licensing restrictions, such as Google and Bing, you need to change some of the plugin's settings. Refer to the *There's more...* section of this recipe.

4. (Optional) Temporarily disable **Rendering** (the checkbox in the bottom panel) to avoid constant redrawing while rearranging the layer order.

5. Rearrange your layers to move the new **QuickMapService** added layer to the bottom of your layer list.

6. Zoom to your original layer's extent.

7. (Optional) If you turned **Rendering** off, reactivate **Rendering** now.

Are things not lining up? Try zooming in a little more or panning slightly. Most of all, be patient! Depending on your Internet connection, it can take a while to retrieve the tiles.

The following screenshot shows how the screen will look:

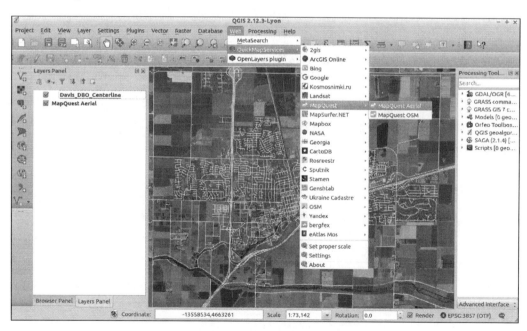

How it works...

The QuickMapServices plugin is a web-based tool. All of the BaseMaps come from the Internet as you pan and zoom; none of the data comes from your computer or QGIS itself.

There are a few things to be cautious of when using the QuickMapServices plugin. It doesn't always line up quite right, especially when zoomed out to big areas. First, check whether your other layers' projections are defined correctly and then try to reset the map by slightly panning to the side. The key idea to remember is that tiled services generally only exist for EPSG:3857 and at a very specific set of scales. QGIS will attempt to pick the closest matching scale and resample the scale to make it fit. This also explains why loading such layers can sometimes be slow.

There's more...

To add more restricted services, such as Google. Bing, and so on, perform the following steps:

1. Go to **Web | QuickMapServices | Settings | Contributed Services**.

2. Click on the **Get contributed pack** button:

While it may be legal to view the maps (most of the time), depending on layers that are selected, it may not be legal to digitize maps based on them, print them, or, otherwise, save them for offline use. The license varies by data source. So, make sure to check this for the sources you want to use by going online and reading the Terms of Service on their websites. If your use case is outside of generally viewing for quick reference, you will probably need to spend some time obtaining a license or permission for your use.

OpenStreetMap-based sources are often good choices as the licenses typically just require attribution with no restrictions on use. The main layers that originally come with the plugin are there because they have less restrictive licenses.

Finally, you may be wondering how QuickMapServices differs from the OpenLayers plugin mentioned in the next recipe. For starters, this plugin is newer and currently supported. It also solves some long-standing issues, especially in regards to printing. There is also the contributed layers GitHub repository, which should make it easier for people to contribute new layer definitions.

See also

> ▸ Additional tile services can be added by hacking the plugin code or using a GDAL TMS layer (Refer to *Chapter 9, QGIS and the Web*). You can also substitute in WMS services to serve a similar role without some of the same limitations of tiles. Refer to *Chapter 9, QGIS and the Web*, for information about creating your own web services.

Loading BaseMaps with the OpenLayers plugin

Often, when exploring your data, you may feel somewhat lost. Without the context of the known world, a layer can seem like a blob of information floating in space. By adding an atlas-style map, air photos, or another BaseMap, you can begin to see how your data fits in the on-the-ground reality. However, adding such layers often takes considerable preprocessing work; sometimes, you just don't want to go through this until you know you need it. What's the solution? Use a premade layer from a web service.

 This recipe is almost identical to the previous recipe. QuickMapServices is a replacement for the OpenLayers plugin, which is being discontinued (deprecated). We kept this recipe because it's still a commonly-mentioned plugin and works slightly differently. However, please consider using QuickMapServices.

Getting ready

The Openlayers plugin works best when you have another dataset that you want to provide extra context for. Start by first loading such a layer and then zooming in to its extent.

You will need the following:

- ▸ A layer of interest to overlay (you can use `Davis_DBO_Centerline-wgs84.shp`)
- ▸ An active Internet connection (this may not work behind corporate proxies)
- ▸ You will need to install and activate the OpenLayers plugin

How to do it...

Starting with a new QGIS project, follow these instructions to load BaseMap from the Web with the Openlayers plugin:

1. Start by first loading your local map layers.

2. Verify that the projection definition is correctly identified by QGIS.

 The plugin will set and turn on projection-on-the-fly for you. In order for most tile services to work in QGIS, projection-on-the-fly must be enabled and set to EPSG:3857 Psuedo/Web/Popular Mercator. Other data will fail to line up if their projection is not defined or read properly by QGIS.

3. Go to **Vector | OpenLayers Plugin** and select a layer to load from the Web. Wait a few seconds for the tiles to be loaded.

4. (Optional) Temporarily disable **Rendering** (the checkbox in the bottom panel) to avoid constant redrawing while rearranging layer order.

5. Rearrange your layers to move the new OpenLayers added layer to the bottom of your layer list.

6. Zoom to your original layer's extent.

7. (Optional) If you turned **Rendering** off, reactivate **Rendering** now.

 Are things not lining up? Try zooming in a little more or panning slightly. Most of all, be patient! Depending on your Internet connection, it can take a while to retrieve the tiles.

The following screenshot shows how the screen will look:

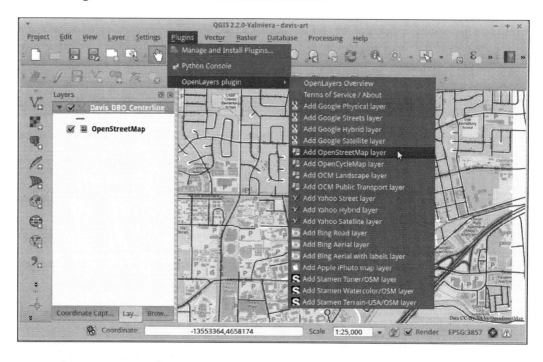

How it works...

The OpenLayers plugin is a web-based tool, based on the similarly named OpenLayers library to create web-based maps in an Internet browser. However, instead of displaying the maps in the browser, this plugin renders them into an active QGIS canvas (that is, a map).

There are a few things to be cautious of when using the OpenLayers plugin. It doesn't always line up quite right, especially when zoomed out to big areas. First, check whether your other layers' projections are defined correctly and then try to reset the map by panning slightly to the side. The key idea to remember is that tiled services generally only exist for EPSG:3857 and at a very specific set of scales. QGIS will attempt to pick the closest matching scale and resample the scale to make it fit. This also explains why loading such layers can sometimes be slow.

There's more...

While it may be legal to view the maps, depending on layers selected, it may not be legal to digitize maps based on them, print them, or, otherwise, save them for offline use. The license varies by data source. So, make sure to check for the sources you want to use by going online and reading the Terms of Service on their websites. If your use case is outside of generally viewing for quick reference, you will probably need to spend some time obtaining a license or permission for your use. OpenStreetMap-based sources are often good choices as the licenses typically just require attribution.

See also

▶ Additional tile services can be added by hacking the plugin code or using a GDAL TMS layer (Refer to *Chapter 9, QGIS and the Web*). You can also substitute in WMS services to serve a similar role without some of the same limitations of tiles. Refer to *Chapter 9, QGIS and the Web*, for information about creating your own web services.

Viewing geotagged photos

Keeping track of photographs by location can be an extremely useful tool, enabling you to easily pull up relevant photos of a place and time. They provide local context about other data collected in the same place, and they can provide office staff with a view of what people in the field saw. You can think of this as your own personal Street View, which is just more focused than Google's version.

Getting ready

For this recipe, you'll need a set of geotagged photos. We've included a set a photos in this book's data for you to learn with. This is a collection of photos from downtown Davis that highlights the density and variety of public art along several blocks.

This recipe also takes advantage of several plugins, as follows:

▶ Install and activate **Photo2Shape**

▶ Activate the core plugin, **eVis** (Event Visualization)

▶ (Optional) Install and activate OpenLayers Plugin

How to do it...

Follow these steps to view geotagged photo locations in QGIS:

1. In a QGIS project, enable the plugins listed in the *Getting ready* section.

2. (Optional) Load a reference layer to help you see the local context (`Davis_DBO_Centerline.shp` and/or `OpenStreetMap/Google Streets` via OpenLayers Plugin).

>
> Keep in mind that GPS locations and geotagged photos are almost always in Latitude and Longitude WGS84 coordinates (that is, EPSG:4326). So, you'll need to turn on projection-on-the-fly to make them line up with your reference layers.

3. Go to the **Vector** menu or locate the icon on the toolbar for **Photo2Shape**:

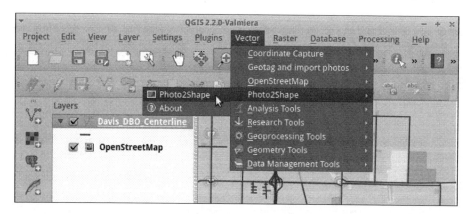

4. This will ask to you select the directory in which you have the geotagged photos and set an output shapefile. (Use the `davis-art` folder as the input directory.)

5. You should now get a new shapefile of the point locations of your photos loaded in the map. Use **Zoom to Layer Extent** to zoom in on the locations. You should see a camera icon at the location of each photo.

6. Looking at the attribute table, you can see all the information about the photos pulled into the table, including the path to the photos on your computer:

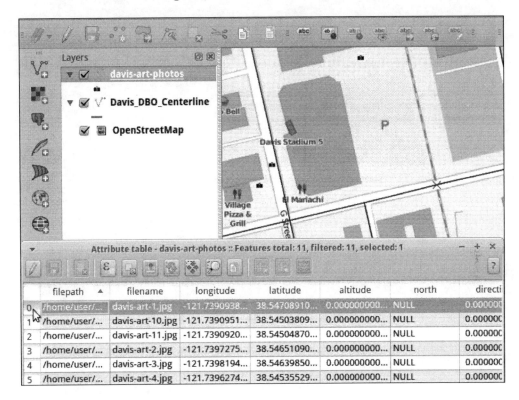

Going a little further

If you want to be able to see the actual photos in QGIS and not just the locations, continue with the next section of steps:

1. Enable the **eVis** plugin.

2. Once activated go to **Database | eVis | eVis Event Browser**.

3. In the new window that pops up, you can see the attributes in the bottom box the photo:

    1. If this is blank, go to the **Options** tab and check whether the correct field is selected for the path to the photo, in this case, this is **filepath**.

2. To make the tool remember this change, check the **Remember This** box and click on the **Save** button at the bottom:

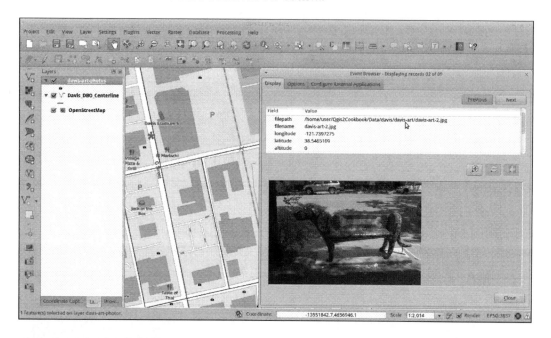

How it works...

In photography, there is a standard metadata format written by most cameras called Exif, which is stored as part of the image file format. Normally, all images store the timestamp, camera model, camera settings, and other general information about an image. When you take a picture with a GPS enabled camera, it should write the latitude and longitude to the photo's metadata. Other programs that are metadata-aware can then read this information at any time. If you happen to touch up these photos, make sure to tell your software to keep or copy the metadata from the original so that you retain the location information.

There's more...

Don't have a camera or phone with built-in geotagging? This is not a problem. There are many ways to add location information by yourself. One such method is with the **Geotag and import photos** plugin that lets you link photo data to known locations, and this can be found at `http://hub.qgis.org/projects/geotagphotos/wiki`.

If you need something more sophisticated, there are many other tools out there. Digikam, an open source photo management program, includes a geotagging tool that will attempt to automatch a GPX file from a GPS to your photos, based on timestamps.

Geotagged photos are also supported by many online photos services, so you can easily browse a map of the photos that you've uploaded. Flickr is probably the most well-known for this, and it also includes a concept of geo-fences, where you can exclude certain locations from being publicly known.

On the flip-side, you now have an idea about how to remove geotags from photos in case you don't want their locations known if you share them online.

See also

- There are other methods of seeing photos in the map besides eVis, including HTML map tips. Refer to Nathan's blog at `http://nathanw.net/2012/08/05/html-map-tips-in-qgis/`.

- More information about geotagging with Digikam can be found at `http://docs.kde.org/development/en/extragear-graphics/kipi-plugins/geolocation.html`.

- You can also use Flickr to geotag and re-export your images, you can or create online map mash-ups with their API.

5
Classic Vector Analysis

In this chapter, we will cover the following recipes:

- Selecting optimum sites
- Dasymetric mapping
- Calculating regional statistics
- Estimating density using heatmaps
- Estimating values based on samples

Introduction

This chapter will provide you with an introduction to some of the most-common GIS analysis use cases. The recipes focus on step-by-step instructions, as well as a closer explanation of the tools that are used to achieve the desired analysis results. This chapter includes recipes on optimum site selection, using interpolation, and creating heat maps, as well as calculating regional statistics.

Selecting optimum sites

Optimum site selection is a pretty common problem, for example, when planning shop or warehouse locations or when looking for a new apartment. In this recipe, you will learn how to perform optimum site selection manually using tools from the **Processing Toolbox** option, but you will also see how to automate this workflow by creating a Processing model.

In the optimum site selection in this recipe, we will combine different vector analysis tools to find potential locations in Wake County that match the following criteria:

- ▸ Locations are near a big lake (up to 500 m)
- ▸ Locations are close to an elementary school (up to 500 m)
- ▸ Locations are within a reasonable distance (up to 2 km) from a high school
- ▸ Locations are at least 1 km from a main road

Getting ready

To follow this exercise, load the following datasets, `lakes.shp`, `schools_wake.shp`, and `roadsmajor.shp`.

As all datasets in our test data already use the same CRS, we can get right to the analysis. If you are using different data, you may have to get all your datasets into the same CRS first. In this case, please refer to *Chapter 1, Data Input and Output*.

How to do it...

The following steps show you how to perform optimum site selection using the **Processing Toolbox** option:

1. First, we have to filter the lakes layer for big lakes. To do this, we use the **Select by expression** tool from the **Processing** toolbox, select the lakes layer, and enter `"AREA" > 1000000 AND "FTYPE" = 'LAKE/POND'` in the Expression textbox, as shown in the following screenshot:

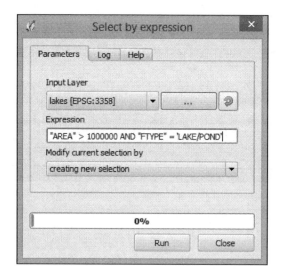

2. Next, we create the buffers that will represent the proximity areas around lakes, schools, and roads. Use **Fixed distance buffer** from the **Processing Toolbox** option to create the following buffers:

   1. For the lakes, select **Distance** of 500 meters and set **Dissolve result** by checking the box as shown in the following screenshot. By dissolving the result, we can make sure that the overlapping buffer areas will be combined into one polygon. Otherwise, each buffer will remain as a separate feature in the resulting layer:

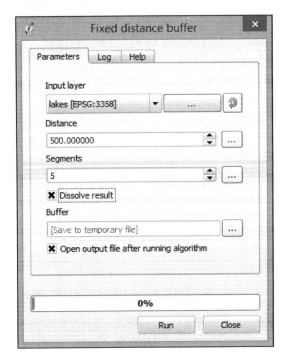

It's your choice whether you want to save the buffer results permanently by specifying an output file, or you just want to work with temporary files by leaving the Buffer output file field empty.

   2. To create the elementary school buffers, first select only the schools with "GLEVEL" = 'E' using the **Select by Expression** tool like we did for the lakes buffer. Then, use the buffer tool like we just did for the lakes buffer.

   3. Repeat the process for the high schools using "GLEVEL" = 'H' and a buffer distance of 2,000 meters.

   4. Finally, for the roads, create a buffer with a distance of 1,000 meters.

3. With all these buffers ready, we can now combine them to fulfill these rules:

    1. Use the **Intersection** tool from the **Processing Toolbox** option on the buffers around elementary and high schools to get the areas that are within the vicinity of both school types.

    2. Use the **Intersection** tool on the buffers around the lakes and the result of the previous step to limit the results to lakeside areas. Use the **Difference** tool to remove areas around major roads (that is, the buffered road layer) from the result of the previous (Intersection) steps.

4. Check the resulting layer to view the potential sites that fit all the criteria that we previously specified. You'll find that there is only one area close to **WAKEFIELD ELEMENTARY** and **WAKEFIELD HIGH** that fits the bill, as shown in the following screenshot:

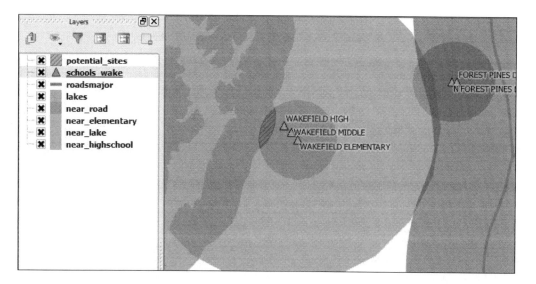

How it works...

In step 1, we used **Intersection** to model the requirement that our preferred site would be near both an elementary and a high school. Later, in step 3, the **Difference** tool enabled us to remove areas close to major roads. The following figure gives us an overview of the available vector analysis tools that can be useful for similar analyses. For example, **Union** could be used to model requirements, such as "close to at least an elementary or a high school". **Symmetrical Difference**, on the other hand, would result in "close to an elementary or a high school but not both", as illustrated in the following figure:

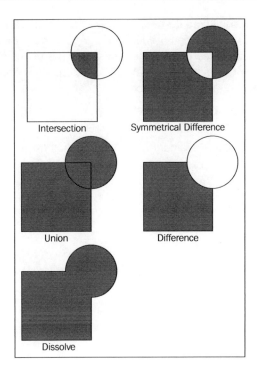

Intersection Symmetrical Difference

Union Difference

Dissolve

There's more...

We were lucky and found a potential site that matched all criteria. Of course, this is not always the case, and you will have to try and adjust your criteria to find a matching site. As you can imagine, it can be very tedious and time-consuming to repeat these steps again and again with different settings. Therefore, it's a good idea to create a Processing model to automate this task.

The model (as shown in the following screenshot) basically contains the same tools that we used in the manual process, as follows:

- Use two select by expression instances to select elementary and high schools. As you can see in the following screenshot, we used the descriptions **Select "GLEVEL" = 'E'** and **Select "GLEVEL" = 'H'** to name these model steps.

- For elementary schools, compute fixed distance buffers of 500 meters. This step is called **Buffer "GLEVEL" = 'E'**.

- For high schools, compute fixed distance buffers of 2,000 meters. This step is called **Buffer "GLEVEL" = 'H'**.

- Select the big lakes using `Select by` expression (refer to the **Select big lakes** step) and buffer them using fixed distance buffer of 500 meters (refer to the **Buffer lakes** step).

▸ Buffer the roads using **Fixed distance buffer** (refer to the **Buffer roads** step). The buffer size is controlled by the number model input called **road_buffer_size**. You can extend this approach of controlling the model parameters using additional inputs to all the other buffer steps in this model. (We chose to show only one example in order to keep the model screenshot readable.)

▸ Use **Intersection** to get areas near schools (refer to the **Intersection: near schools** step).

▸ Use **Intersection** to get areas near schools and lakes (refer to the **Intersection: schools and lakes** step).

▸ Use **Difference** to remove areas near roads (refer to the **Difference: avoid roads** step).

This is how the final model looks like:

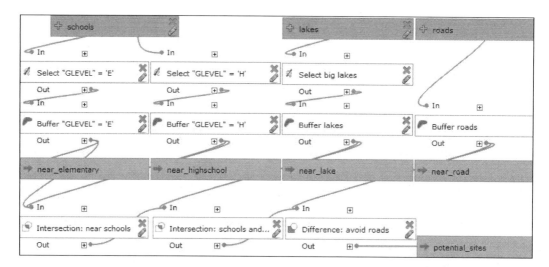

You can run this model from the **Processing Toolbox** option, or you can even use it as a building block in other models. It is worth noting that this model produces intermediate results in the form of buffer results (`near_elementary`, `near highschool`, and so on). While these intermediate results are useful while developing and debugging the model, you may eventually want to remove them. This can be done by editing the buffer steps and removing the **Buffer <OutputVector>** names.

Dasymetric mapping

Dasymetric mapping is a technique that is commonly used to improve population distribution maps. By default, population is displayed using census data, which is usually available for geographic units, such as census tracts whose boundaries don't necessarily reflect the actual distribution of the population. To be able to model population distribution better, Dasymetric mapping enables us to map population density relative to land use. For example, population counts that are organized by census tracts can be more accurately distributed by removing unpopulated areas, such as water bodies or vacant land, from the census tract areas.

In this recipe, we will use data about populated urban areas, as well as data about water bodies to refine our census tract population data.

Getting ready

To follow this exercise, please load the population data from `census_wake2000_pop.shp` (the file that we created in *Chapter 2, Data Management*), as well as the urban areas from `urbanarea.shp`, and the lakes from `lakes.shp`.

As all the datasets in our sample data already use the same CRS, we can get right into the analysis. If you are using different data, you may have to first get all datasets into the same CRS. In this case, please refer to *Chapter 1, Data Input and Output*, for details.

How to do it...

To create a new and improved population distribution map, we will first remove the unpopulated areas from the census tracts. Then, we will recalculate the population density values to reflect the changes to the area geometries by performing the following steps:

1. Use **Clip** from the **Processing Toolbox** option (or **Clip** by navigating to **Vector | Geoprocessing tools** if you prefer this option—the results will be identical) on the census tracts and urban area layers to create a new dataset, containing only those parts of the census tracts that are within urban areas.

2. Refine the results of the previous step further by removing the water bodies (the lakes layer) using the **Difference** tool. The following screenshot shows the results of this so far:

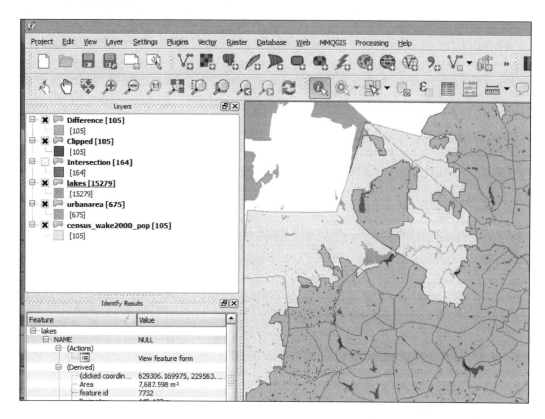

3. Now, we can calculate the population density of the resulting areas, as follows:

    1. Enable editing.

    2. Open **Field calculator**.

3. Calculate a new population density (inhabitants per square km) using the formula, **"_POP2000" / ($area / 1000000)**:

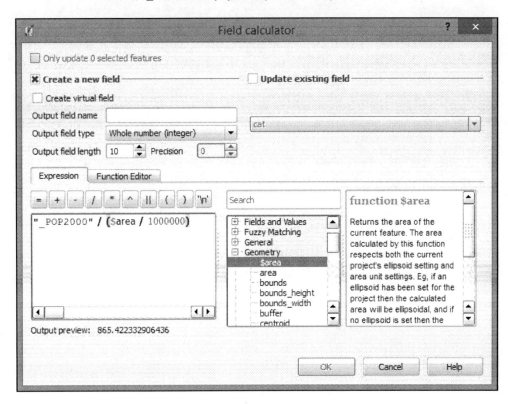

4. Deactivate editing and save the changes.

It is worth noting that you don't necessarily have to make a new column. If you only want to use the density values for styling purposes, you can also enter the expression directly in the style configuration. On the other hand, if you create a new column, you can inspect the density values in the attribute table, export them, or analyze them further.

We are done, and you can now visualize the results using a Graduated renderer with, for example, the Natural Breaks (Jenks) classification mode. The Jenks Natural Breaks classification is designed to arrange values into "natural" classes by maximizing the variance between different classes while reducing the variance within the generated classes. The following figure shows the population density based on the original census data (on the left) and the results after Dasymetric mapping (on the right):

How it works...

In the first step of this recipe, we used the **Clip** operation. As you most likely noticed, the results of a **Clip** operation look very similar to the results of the **Intersection** tool, which we used in the previous recipe of this chapter, *Selecting optimum sites*. Compare both the results, and you will see the following differences:

> ▸ The layer resulting from an **Intersection** operation contains attributes from both input layers, while the result of a **Clip** operation only contains attributes of the first input layer.

> ▸ This also means that the layer order is important when using **Clip**, but this does not change the output of **Intersection** (except for the attribute order in the attribute table).

> ▸ The **Intersection** result is also very likely to contain more features than the **Clip** result (164 instead of 105 if you use our sample data census tracts and urban areas). This is because the **Intersect** tool needs to create a new feature for every combination of intersecting census tracts and urban areas, while the **Clip** tool only removes the parts of the census tracts that are not within any urban area.

A popular way of thinking about the **Clip** operation is to imagine one layer as the cookie cutter and the other layer as the cookie dough.

Calculating regional statistics

Another classic spatial analysis task is calculating the areas of a certain type within regions, for example, the area within a county that is covered by certain land use types, or the share of different crops that is farmed in given municipalities.

In this recipe, we will calculate statistics of geological data for zip code areas. In particular, we will calculate the total area of each type of rock per zip code area.

Getting ready

To follow this recipe, load `zipcodes_wake.shp` and `geology.shp` from our sample data. Additionally, install and activate the **Group Stats** plugin using **Plugin Manager**.

How to do it...

Using the following steps, we can calculate the areas of certain rock types per zip code area:

1. Calculate the intersections between zip code areas and geological areas using the **Intersection** tool in the **Processing Toolbox** option or from the **Vector** menu.

2. Using the **Group Stats** plugin, you can now calculate the total area per rock type and zip code area, as follows:

    1. Select the **Intersection** result layer as the input **Layer**.

    2. Drag the **ZIPCODE** field to the **Rows** input area and the **GEO_NAME** field to the **Columns** input area.

    3. Drag the **sum** function and the **Area** value to the **Value** input area.

    4. Click on **Calculate** to start the calculations.

The following screenshot displays the complete configuration, as well as the results:

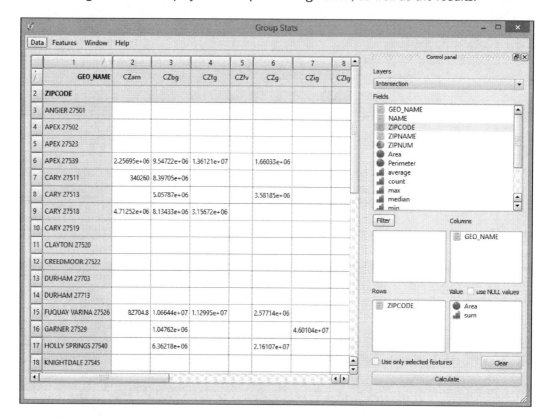

How it works...

The **Group Stats** plugin brings functionality, which is commonly known as pivot tables, to QGIS. A pivot table is a data summarization tool, which is commonly found in applications, such as spreadsheets or business intelligence software. As shown in this example, pivot tables can aggregate data from an input table. Additionally, the **Group Stats** plugin offers extended geometry functions, such as, **Area** and **Perimeter** for polygon input layers, or **Length** for line layers. This makes using the plugin more convenient because it is not necessary to first use **Field calculator** to add these geometric values to the attribute table.

It is worth noting that you always need to put the following two entries into the **Value** input area:

- An aggregation function, such as sum, average, or count
- A value field (from the input layer's attribute table) or geometry function, which should be aggregated

Estimating density heatmaps

Whether they are animal sightings, accident locations, or general points of interest, many point datasets can be interpreted more easily by visualizing the point density using a heatmap. In this recipe, we will estimate the density of POIs in Wake county to find areas with a high density.

Getting ready

Load the `poi_names_wake.shp` POI dataset from our sample data. Make sure that the **Heatmap** plugin, which comes with QGIS by default, is enabled in **Plugin Manager**.

How to do it...

Using the following steps, we can calculate the POI heatmap:

1. Start the **Heatmap** plugin from the **Raster** menu.
2. Make sure that **poi_names_wake** is selected as **Input point layer**.
3. Select a location and filename for **Output raster**. You don't need to specify the file extension because this will be added automatically, based on the selected **Output format**. GeoTIFF is usually the first choice.
4. Select a search **Radius** of `1000` **meters**.
5. The **Add generated file to map** option should be activated by default. Click on **OK** to create the default heatmap.

6. By default, the heatmap layer will be rendered using the **Singleband gray** render type. Change the render type to **Singleband pseudocolor** and apply a color ramp that you like to improve the visualization, as show in the following screenshot:

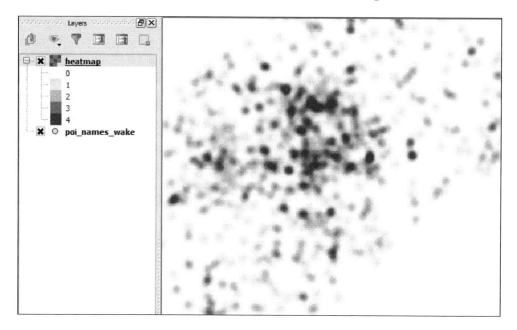

 If you want to control the size of the output raster, just enable the **Advanced** section and adjust the number of **Rows** and **Columns** or **Cell size X** and **Cell size Y**, accordingly. Note that changing rows and columns will automatically recalculate the size of the cell and vice versa.

How it works...

The search radius, which is also known as the kernel bandwidth, determines how smooth the heatmap will look because it sets the distance around each point at which the influence of the point will be felt. Therefore, smaller radius values result in heatmaps that display finer details, while larger values result in smoother heatmaps.

Besides the kernel bandwidth, there are also different kernel shapes to choose from. The kernel shape controls the rate at which the influence of a point decreases with increasing distance from the point. The kernel shapes that are available in the Heatmap plugin can be seen in the following figures. For example, a Triweight kernel (the first on the bottom row) creates smaller hotspots than the Epanechnikov kernel (the second on the bottom) because the Triweight shape gives features a higher influence for distances that are closer to the point:

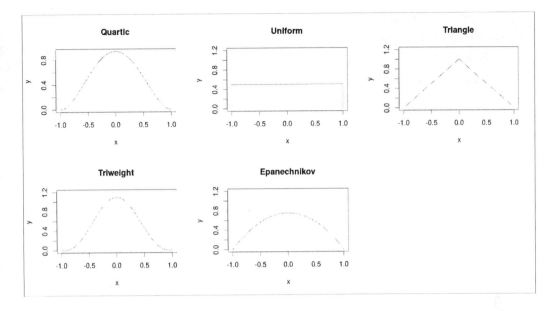

The triangular kernel shape can be further adjusted using the **Decay ratio** setting. In the preceding figure, you can see the shape for ratios of 0 (a solid red line), 0.5 (a dashed black line), and 1 (a dotted black line), which is equal to the uniform kernel shape. You can even specify values greater than 1. In this case, the influence of a feature will increase with the distance from the point.

Estimating values based on samples

Interpolation is the idea that, with a set of known values, you can estimate the values of additional points based on their proximity to these known values. This recipe shows you how to use known values at point locations to create a continuous surface (raster) of value estimates. Classic examples include weather data estimations that are based on weather station data (think temperature or rainfall maps), crop yield estimates that are based on sampling parts of a field, and like in this example in this recipe, elevation estimations that are based on the elevation of sampled points.

Getting ready

Activate **Interpolation Plugin** via **Plugin Manager**.

Load a point layer with numeric columns, representing the feature of interest. For this recipe, use the `poi_names_wake.shp`, and the `elev_m` column, which contains elevation in meters for each point.

How to do it...

1. Start by loading `poi_name_wake`.

2. Zoom to the layer extent.

3. Open the Interpolation tool by navigating to **Raster | Interpolation | Interpolation**.

 Yes, it's on the **Raster** menu; the source data must be a vector, but the results are a raster.

4. Select `poi_names_wake` for **Input**.

5. Select `elev_m` for **Interpolation attribute**.

6. Click on the **Add** button, your selection should appear in the box on the left-hand side.

7. Select **Inverse Distance Weighted (IDW)** for **Interpolation Method**.

8. Now, set the **Extent** and **Cell Size** properties. In **Cellsize X** and **Cellsize Y**, enter `100` and `100`. This forces the output cells to be 100x100 units of the current projection.

 Generally, if this was for analysis, you would attempt to match the region of interest or other raster layers. In this case, we just want to go for sensibly-sized cells. As the map is in UTM, we will want cells to be integers that represent metric units; 100 meters by 100 meters makes interpreting the results easier.

9. Click on the **Set to current extent** button in the middle.

10. Next to **Output file box**, click on the button labeled **...** to set the output path to save the results:

11. Pick the folder and type in a name with no file extension, such as `idw100m` (the result will be an ASCII raster `.asc` file), as shown in the following screenshot:

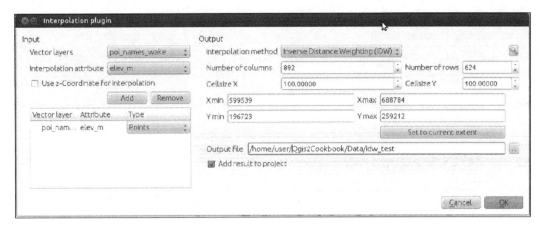

 The wrench tool in the upper-right corner will let you change the P value, which is the exponent in the denominator and directly sets how much a point influences a nearby location, as compared against more distanced points.

12. Check all your settings and then click on the **OK** button.

13. Now, wait patiently for your results, the smaller the size of the cell and the larger the number of columns and data points, the longer the calculation will take, as shown in the following screenshot:

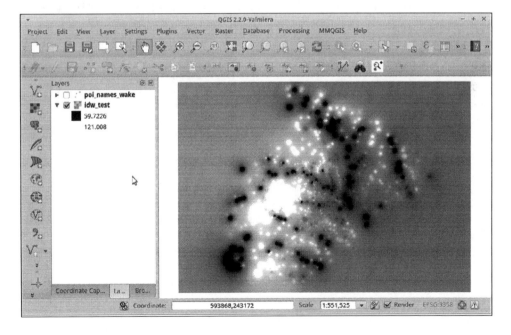

How it works...

The basic idea is that, at a given cell, you take the average of all the nearby points that are weighted by their distance to the cell in order to estimate the value at your current location. **Inverse Distance Weighted** (**IDW**) takes this one step further by giving more weight to values that are closer to the given cell and less weight to values that are further. This function uses an exponent factor P in order to greatly increase the role of closer points over distant points.

There's more...

Are the results not quite what you expected? There are a few parameters that can be adjusted; these are primarily the P value and the size of the cell. Is this still not coming out the way that you want? There are several other Interpolation tools that are accessible in Processing under the SAGA, GRASS, and GDAL toolboxes, which allow you to manipulate more of the formula parameters to refine the results.

Finally, depending on your data, IDW may not do a good job of interpolating. In the example here, you can actually see how there are distinct circles around isolated points. This is generally not a good result, and this needs a smoother transition to nearby points. If you have any control over field sampling to begin with, keep in mind that regularly-spaced grids will usually provide better results.

Do you not have control over the source data or you didn't get good results? Then, you may need to look into other more complicated formulas that compensate for skew, strong directionality, obstructions, and non-regular spacing of samples, such as Splines or Kriging, or **Triangulated Irregular Networks** (**TINs**). There is lot of science and statistics behind the methods and diagnostic tools to determine the best parameters. This is far too complicated a topic for this recipe, but it is well-covered in books on geostatistics.

See also

> ▶ http://docs.qgis.org/2.2/en/docs/user_manual/plugins/plugins_interpolation.html

> ▶ http://en.wikipedia.org/wiki/Inverse_distance_weightinging

6
Network Analysis

In this chapter, we will cover the following recipes:

- ▶ Creating a simple routing network
- ▶ Calculating the shortest paths using the Road graph plugin
- ▶ Routing with one-way streets in the Road graph plugin
- ▶ Calculating the shortest paths with the QGIS network analysis library
- ▶ Routing point sequences
- ▶ Automating multiple route computation using batch processing
- ▶ Matching points to the nearest line
- ▶ Creating a network for pgRouting
- ▶ Visualizing the pgRouting results in QGIS
- ▶ Using the pgRoutingLayer plugin for convenience
- ▶ Getting network data from the OSM

Introduction

This chapter focuses on the common use cases that are related to routing within networks. By far, the most common networks that are used to route are street networks. Other less common cases include networks for indoor routing, that is, through rooms inside buildings, or networks of shipping routes.

Networks and routing are in no way a GIS-only topic. You will find a lot of math literature related to this, called **Graph Theory**. In this chapter, we will use the following terms to talk about networks:

> ▸ A **network** (also known as **graph**) is a collection of connected objects

> ▸ These objects are called **nodes** (also known as vertices)

> ▸ The connections between nodes are called **links** (also known as **edges**)

The following figure explains these terms:

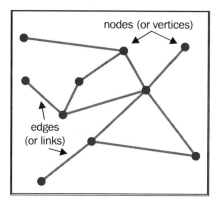

The two routing tools that are commonly used with QGIS are as follows:

> ▸ The Road graph plugin, which is one of the QGIS core plugins; that is, this plugin is available in every QGIS installation, but you may have to activate it in Plugin Manager

> ▸ The PostGIS extension pgRouting, which can be used directly through the QGIS DB Manager, or more comfortably through the pgRoutingLayer plugin, which can be installed from the QGIS plugin repository using Plugin Manager

Creating a simple routing network

In this recipe, we will create a routing network from scratch using the QGIS editing tools. Even though more and more open network data is available, there will still be numerous use cases where necessary network data does not exist or is not available for use. Therefore, it is good to know how to create a network and what to pay attention to in order to avoid common pitfalls.

For the task of network creation, the main difference between the Road graph plugin and pgRouting is that pgRouting needs a network node (that is, link start or end node) at each intersection while the Road graph plugin will also use intermediate link geometry nodes to infer intersections if two links share a node. In this recipe, we will create a network, which can be used in both tools.

Getting ready

To follow this recipe, you only need a new empty QGIS project. Additionally, make sure you have the **Digitizing** toolbar enabled (as shown in the following screenshot). We will create an imaginary network, but if you want you can load a background map and digitize this:

How to do it...

Before we can start to create the network, there are a few things that need to be set up first:

1. Create a new shapefile line layer for the network. You don't need to add any extra attributes besides the default ID attribute yet.

> You can read more about creating new shapefiles in the *Learning QGIS* book by Packt Publishing and the QGIS user guide at `http://docs.qgis.org/2.2/en/docs/user_manual/working_with_vector/editing_geometry_attributes.html#creating-a-new-shapefile-layer`.

2. To ensure that we can digitize the network with valid topology, we'll activate snapping next. Go to **Settings | Snapping Options** and activate snapping for your line layer by enabling the checkbox to the left of it. Additionally, set the mode to to vertex and choose a tolerance of at least **5.00000** pixels:

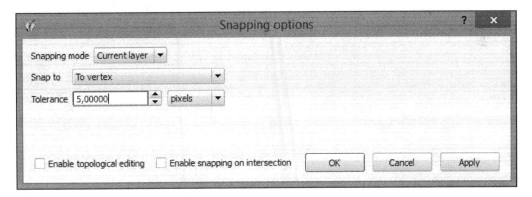

3. Now, we can enable editing for the line layer and then select the **Add Feature** tool from the **Digitizing** toolbar to start digitizing.

4. Create the first line feature now, and give it the ID number **1**. The line can have as many nodes as you wish. We'll create a line with four nodes, as shown in the following screenshot:

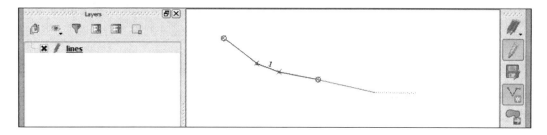

5. To draw the second line feature, start at the first or the last node of line 1. As we have activated snapping, you will see that the node is being highlighted if you hover over it with the mouse cursor. Draw a second line and give it the ID number **2**.

 The line in the preceding screenshot is drawn with a style that has circles on the starting and ending points. You can reproduce this style by adding the **Marker line** symbol levels to the line style or load `network_links.qml` from our sample data. For more details about styling features, please refer to *Chapter 10, Cartography Tips*.

6. Draw a few more lines (around 12 in total) forming a network. Make sure to pay attention to the snapping and assign link IDs:

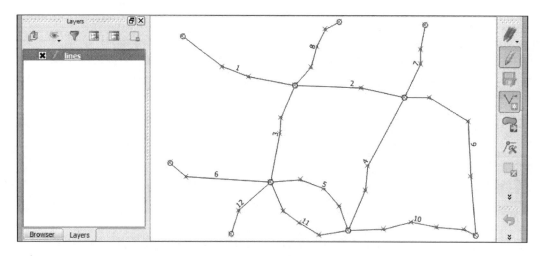

7. Disable editing, and confirm that you want to save the changes.

We will use this basic network as a starting point for the remaining recipes in this chapter.

How it works...

By setting the snapping mode to **to vertex**, we made it possible to digitize the line network in a way that ensures that lines, which should be connected, really contain a node at the exact same position.

There's more...

You can validate the network topology by running the Topology Checker plugin, which is installed with QGIS by default (you can read more about Topology Checker in *Chapter 12, Up and Coming*):

1. Start **Topology Checker** from the **Vector** menu.

2. Click **Configure** to set up a topology rule, as shown in the following screenshot, and click on **Add Rule** to add it to the list of rules to check. Then, close the settings by clicking on **OK**:

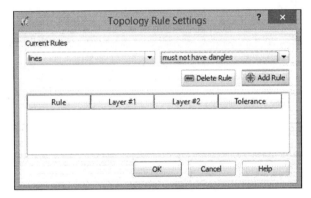

3. Once this tool is configured, click on **Validate All** (the button with the checkmark) to initiate the check. You will see the list of discovered errors displayed in the list above the buttons, as shown in the following screenshot. Additionally, the dangling ends are highlighted in red in the map:

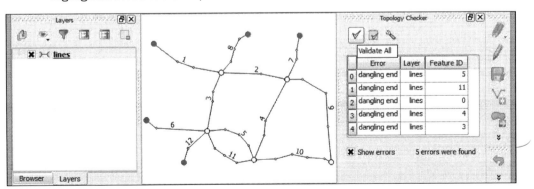

4. You can select the error entries in the list to jump to the line features that failed the check. In our network, only lines with dead-ends should be listed. If you see an error at an intersection, you should zoom closer and try to correct the node positions.

Calculating the shortest paths using the Road graph plugin

This recipe shows you how to use the built-in Road graph plugin to calculate the shortest paths in a network.

Getting ready

To follow this recipe, load `network_pgr.shp` from the sample data. Additionally, make sure that the Road graph plugin is enabled in Plugin Manager.

How to do it...

The Road graph plugin enables us to route between two points that are selected on the map. Before we can use this, we have to configure it first, as follows:

1. Enable the **Shortest path** panel by navigating to **View** | **Panels**. This should add the plugin panel to the user interface.

2. Go to **Vector** | **Road graph** | **Settings** to get to the configuration dialog. For now, the default settings, as shown in the following screenshot, should be fine. Note that the network layer is selected as **Transportation layer**. Click on **OK** to confirm the settings:

3. Once the settings are configured, we can calculate our first route. Select the **Start** and **Stop** locations using the buttons marked with crosshair icons. Activate the crosshair button and then click in the map to select a location. This location will be marked on the map, and the coordinates will be automatically inserted into the **Start** or **Stop** input field.

4. Click on **Calculate** to initiate route computation. Depending on the size of the network used, this step will either be very fast or it can take much more time. The route will be highlighted in the map, and the route length and travel time will be displayed, as shown in the following screenshot:

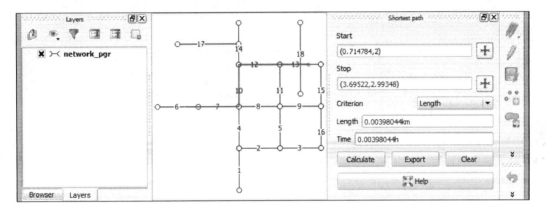

5. If you want to store the computed shortest path, click on **Export** and you will be able to choose whether you want to create a new layer for the path or add the route to an existing line layer.

6. To compute a new route, simply change the start and stop locations and click on **Calculate** again.

7. Click on **Clear** to remove the route highlights when you are done.

How it works...

The Road graph plugin uses the QGIS network analysis library, which implements Dijkstra's algorithm. For a given starting node, the algorithm finds the path with the lowest cost (that is, the shortest path if the cost criterion is length or the fastest path if the cost criterion is time) between this node and every other node in the network. This can also be used to find costs of the shortest paths from a start node to a destination node by stopping the algorithm once the shortest path to the destination node has been determined.

In contrast to many simple routing tools, the Road graph plugin builds the network topology automatically. As our network dataset is topologically sound (that is, there are no tiny gaps where network edges meet), we can set up Road graph plugin settings with **Topology tolerance** as **0**. If you are using a network from a different source, it may not have been created with the same attention to detail, and you may have to increase **Topology tolerance** to get routing to work.

See also

> ▸ If you are interested in learning more about this algorithm, you can start at `http://wiki.gis.com/wiki/index.php/Dijkstra's_algorithm`

Routing with one-way streets in the Road graph plugin

When it comes to vehicle routing, it is often necessary to go into more detail and consider driving restrictions, such as one-way streets. This recipe shows you how to use one-way street information to route with the Road graph plugin.

Getting ready

To follow this recipe, load `network_pgr.shp` from the sample data. Additionally, make sure that the Road graph plugin is enabled in Plugin Manager.

How to do it...

To demonstrate routing with one-way street information, we will first visualize the one-way values, and then we will configure the Road graph plugin to use the one-way information, as follows:

1. Before we start routing with one-way information, it is helpful to visualize the one-way streets. It is worth noting that the one-way direction will depend on the direction of the link geometry (that is, the direction the link was digitized in). The best way to visualize the link direction is by assigning arrow symbols, as shown in the following screenshot. You can load `network_pgr.qml` from our sample data to get the style:

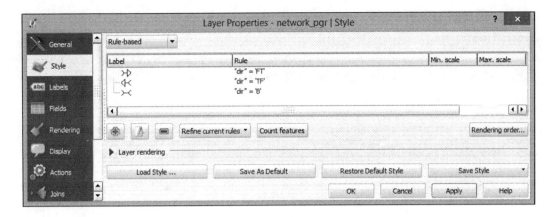

There are many different ways to encode one-way information. In our dataset, a forward direction is encoded as **FT** for "from-to", a backward direction as **TF** for "to-from", and both ways as **B** for "both".

2. Then, we can configure the Road graph plugin to use the one-way information. To do this, we have to choose the **dir** attribute as **Direction field** and enter the values for forward (in link geometry) direction and reverse (against link geometry) direction:

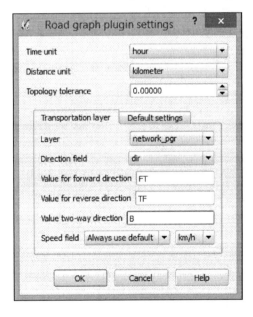

3. Once the plugin is configured, you can compute the shortest path as described in the previous recipe, *Calculating the shortest paths using the Road graph plugin*. You will see how the resulting routes differ from the normal (without one-way restrictions) paths, as shown in the following screenshot where the algorithm avoids the one-way links on the direct route and takes the longer route instead:

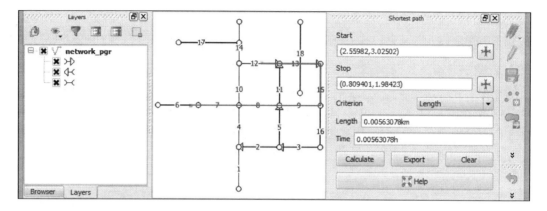

How it works...

When we use the default two-way setting, each network link is interpreted as a connection from the start to end node, as well as a connection from the end to start node. By adding one-way restrictions, this changes and the link is only interpreted as one connection now.

Besides **FT**, **TF**, and **B**, another common way to encode one-ways is **1** for in-link direction, **-1** for against-link direction, and **0** for both ways. In OpenStreetMap, you will find **yes** for the in-link direction, **no** for both ways and **-1** for the against-link direction (refer to `http://wiki.openstreetmap.org/wiki/Key:oneway` for more details).

Calculating the shortest paths with the QGIS network analysis library

As mentioned in the recipe, *Calculating the shortest paths using the Road graph plugin*, QGIS comes with a network analysis library, which can be used from the Python console, inside plugins, to process scripts, and basically anything else that you can think of. In this recipe, we will introduce the usage of the network analysis to compute the shortest paths in the Python console.

Getting ready

To follow this recipe, load `network_pgr.shp` from the sample data.

How to do it...

Instead of typing or copying the following script directly in the Python console, we recommend opening the Python console editor using the **Show editor** button on the left-hand side of the Python console:

1. Paste the following script into the editor:

```python
import processing
from processing.tools.vector import VectorWriter
from PyQt4.QtCore import *
from qgis.core import *
from qgis.networkanalysis import *

# create the graph
layer = processing.getObject('network_pgr')
director = QgsLineVectorLayerDirector(layer,-1,'','','',3)
director.addProperter(QgsDistanceArcProperter())
builder = QgsGraphBuilder(layer.crs())
from_point = QgsPoint(2.73343,3.00581)
to_point = QgsPoint(0.483584,2.01487)
tied_points =
   director.makeGraph(builder,[from_point,to_point])
graph = builder.graph()

# compute the route from from_id to to_id
from_id = graph.findVertex(tied_points[0])
to_id = graph.findVertex(tied_points[1])
(tree,cost) = QgsGraphAnalyzer.dijkstra(graph,from_id,0)

# assemble the route
route_points = []
curPos = to_id
while (curPos != from_id):
   in_vertex = graph.arc(tree[curPos]).inVertex()
   route_points.append(graph.vertex(in_vertex).point())
   curPos = graph.arc(tree[curPos]).outVertex()
route_points.append(from_point)
```

```
# write the results to a Shapefile
result = 'C:\\temp\\route.shp'
writer = VectorWriter(result,None,[],2,layer.crs())
fet = QgsFeature()
fet.setGeometry(QgsGeometry.fromPolyline(route_points))
writer.addFeature(fet)
del writer
processing.load(result)
```

2. If you are using your own network dataset instead of `network_pgr.shp`, which is provided with this book, adjust the coordinates of `from_point` and `to_point` for the route's starting and ending points.

3. Change the file paths for the result layer depending on your operating system.

4. Make sure that the network layer is loaded and selected in the QGIS layer list.

5. Save the script and run it.

How it works...

On line 8, we created a `QgsLineVectorLayerDirector` object (`http://qgis.org/api/classQgsLineVectorLayerDirector.html`), which contains the network configuration. The constructor (`QgsLineVectorLayerDirector(layer,-1,'','','',3)`) parameters are as follows:

  ▶ The network line layer

  ▶ The ID of the direction field: we set it to `-1` because this script does not consider one-ways

  ▶ The following three parameters are the values for the in link direction: reverse link direction, and two-way

  ▶ The last parameter is the default direction: `1` for the in link direction, `2` for the reverse direction, and `3` for the two-way

Line 10 creates the `QgsGraphBuilder` (`http://qgis.org/api/classQgsGraphBuilder.html`) instance, which will be used to create the routing graph on line 14.

On lines 11 and 12, we defined the starting and ending points of our route. To be able to route between these two points, they have to be matched to the nearest network link. This happens on line 13 in the `makeGraph()` function, which returns the so-called `tied_points`.

The actual route computation takes place on line 18 in the `QgsGraphAnalyzer.dijkstra()` (`http://qgis.org/api/classQgsGraphAnalyzer.html`) function.

The `while` loop, starting on line 22, is where the script moves through the tree created by Dijkstra's algorithm to collect all the vertices on the way and add them to the `route_points` list, which becomes the resulting route geometry on line 31.

The writer for output route line layer is created on line 29, where we pass the file path, `None` for default encoding, the `[]` for empty fields list, and the `2` for geometry type, which equals to lines as well as the resulting layer CRS. The following lines, 30 to 32, create the route feature and add it to the writer.

Finally, the last line loads the resulting shapefile, and this is displayed on the map, as illustrated by the following screenshot:

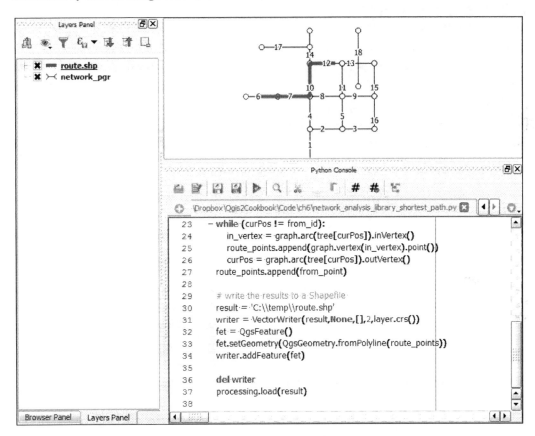

See also

You can read more about QGIS's network analysis library online in the PyQGIS Developer Cookbook at `http://docs.qgis.org/testing/en/docs/pyqgis_developer_cookbook/network_analysis.html`.

Routing point sequences

In the recipes so far, we routed from one starting point to one destination point. Another use case is when we want to compute routes that connect a sequence of points, such as the points in a GPS track. In this recipe, we will use the point layer to route processing script to compute a route for a point sequence. At its core, this script uses the same idea that was introduced in the previous recipe, *Calculating the shortest paths with the QGIS network analysis library*, but this computes several shortest paths one after the other.

Getting ready

To follow this recipe, `load network_pgr.shp` and `sample_pts_for_routing.shp`, which contains a point layer that should be routed from the sample dataset.

Additionally, you need to get the point layer to route script from `https://raw.githubusercontent.com/anitagraser/QGIS-Processing-tools/master/2.6/scripts/point_layer_to_route.py` and save it in the `Processing` script folder, which is set to `C:\Users\youruser\qgis2\processing\scripts` (on Windows), `/home/youruser/.qgis2/processing/scripts` (on Linux), and `/Users/youruser/.qgis2/processing/scripts` (on Mac) by default. Alternatively, save the point layer to route to the folder configured in the **Processing** menu under **Options | Scripts | Scripts folder**.

How to do it...

To compute the route between the input points, you need to perform the following tasks:

1. Load the network and the point layer.

2. If you are using your own data, make sure that both layers are in the same CRS. If they are in different CRS, you need to reproject them (for example, using the **Reproject layer** tool from the **Processing Toolbox** option) before you continue.

3. Start the point layer to route tool from the **Processing Toolbox** option.

4. Pick the **points** and **network** input layers, make sure that **Open output file after running algorithm option** is activated, and click on **Run** to start the route computation. The resulting route layer will be loaded automatically:

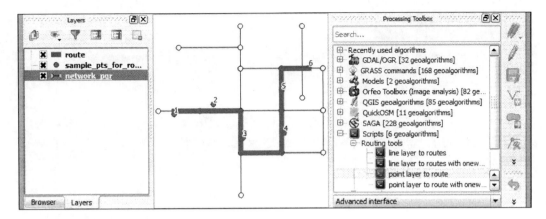

How it works...

The **point layer to route** tool uses the QGIS network analysis library. We already discussed the basic use of this library in the previous recipe, _Calculating the shortest paths with the QGIS network analysis library_. The main difference is that we now have to handle more than two points. Therefore, the script fetches all points from the input point layer and ties or matches them to the graph:

```
points = []
features = processing.features(point_layer)
for f in features:
    points.append(f.geometry().asPoint())
tiedPoints = director.makeGraph(builder, points)
```

For each pair of consecutive points, the script then computes the route between the two points just like we did in the _Calculating the shortest paths with the QGIS network analysis library_ recipe:

```
point_count = point_layer.featureCount()
for i in range(0,point_count-1):
    # compute the route between two consecutive points
```

The resulting route line layer contains one line feature for each consecutive point pair.

There's more...

Of course, you can also use the **point layer to route** tool to route between only two points as well.

See also

There is also a version of this script, which takes one-way information into account at `https://raw.githubusercontent.com/anitagraser/QGIS-Processing-tools/master/2.2/scripts/point_layer_to_route_with_oneways.py`.

Automating multiple route computation using batch processing

If you have multiple input point layers, you can use Processing's batch processing capabilities to speed up the process. In this recipe, we will compute routes for two input point layers at once, but the same approach can be applied to many more layers.

Getting ready

To follow this recipe, load `network_pgr.shp` and the two point layers, `sample_pts_for_routing.shp` and `sample_pts_for_routing2.shp`.

How to do it...

To get started, right-click on the **point layer to route** tool in the **Processing Toolbox** option and select **Execute as batch process**. Then perform the following steps:

1. In the **points** column, click the **...** button and use the **Select from open layers** option to select `sample_pts_for_routing` and `sample_pts_for_routing2`.

2. Select and remove the third line using the **Delete row** button at the bottom of the dialog.

3. In the **network** column, click the **...** button and use the **Select from open layers** option to select `network_pgr`. You can avoid having to pick the file twice by double-clicking on the table header entry (where it reads **network**). This will autofill all rows with the same network file path.

4. In the **routes** column, you need to pick a path for the resulting route files. In the **Save file** dialog, which opens when you click on the **...** button, you can specify one base filename and click on **Save**. The following **Autofill settings** dialog lets you specify if and how you want to have the rows filled. Use **Autofill mode Fill with numbers** and Processing will automatically append a running number to the filename that you specified. You can see an example in the following screenshot where we specified route as the base filename.

5. Click on **Run** to execute the batch process. Both routes will be computed and loaded automatically:

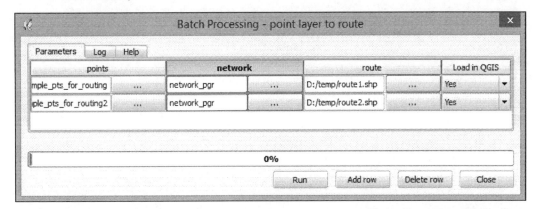

Matching points to the nearest line

In this recipe, we will use the QGIS network analysis library from Python console to match points to the nearest line. This is the simplest form of what is also known as map matching.

Getting ready

To follow this recipe, load `network_pgr.shp` from the sample data.

How to do it...

The following script will match three points, `QgsPoint(3.63715,3.60401)`, `QgsPoint(3.86250,1.58906)`, and `QgsPoint(0.42913,2.26512)`, to the network:

1. Open Python console and its editor and then load or paste the following `network_analysis_match_points.py` script:

```
import processing
from processing.tools.vector import VectorWriter
from PyQt4.QtCore import *
from qgis.core import *
from qgis.networkanalysis import *

layer = processing.getObject('network_pgr')
director = QgsLineVectorLayerDirector(layer,-1,'','','',3)
director.addProperter(QgsDistanceArcProperter())
builder = QgsGraphBuilder(layer.crs())
additional_points =
    [QgsPoint(3.63715,3.60401),QgsPoint(3.86250,1.58906),QgsPoi
    nt(0.42913,2.26512)]
```

```
tied_points = director.makeGraph(builder,additional_points)

result = 'C:\\temp\\matched_pts.shp'
writer = VectorWriter(result,None,[],1,layer.crs())
fet = QgsFeature()

for pt in tied_points:
    fet.setGeometry(QgsGeometry.fromPoint(pt))
    writer.addFeature(fet)

del writer
processing.load(result)
```

2. Make sure that the network layer is selected in the layer list.

3. Run the script. The results should be loaded automatically.

How it works...

This script uses the QGIS network analysis library's ability to match points to lines using the `makeGraph()` function. The resulting `tied_points` list contains the coordinates of the points on the network that are closest to the input `points`.

The `1` option on line 15 specifies that the output layer is of type point.

The `for` loop finally goes through all points in the `tied_points` list and creates point features, which are then added to the result `writer`.

Creating a routing network for pgRouting

This recipe shows you how to import a line layer into PostGIS and create a routable network out of it, which can be used by PostGIS's routing library, pgRouting. (For details about pgRouting, please visit the project website at `http://docs.pgrouting.org`.)

The installation of PostGIS with pgRouting won't be covered in detail here because instructions for the different operating systems can be found on the project's website at `http://docs.pgrouting.org/2.0/en/doc/src/installation/index.html`.

If you are using Windows, both PostGIS and pgRouting can be installed directly from the Stack Builder application, which is provided by the standard PostgreSQL installation, as described at `http://anitagraser.com/2013/07/06/pgrouting-2-0-for-windows-quick-guide/`.

Getting ready

To follow this exercise, you need a PostGIS database with pgRouting enabled. In QGIS, you should set up the connection to the database using the **New** button in the **Add PostGIS Layers** dialog. Additionally, you should load `network_pgr.shp` from the sample data.

How to do it...

These steps will create a routable network table in your PostGIS database:

1. Open **DB Manager** by navigating to **Database | DB Manager**.

2. In **Tree** on the left-hand side of the dialog, select the database that you want to load the network to.

3. Go to **Table | Import Layer/File** to load the `network_pgr` layer into your database, as shown in the following screenshot:

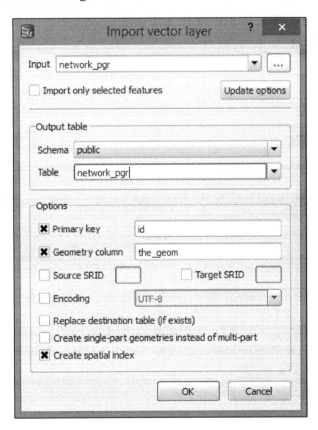

4. After `network_pgr` has been imported successfully, open the SQL window of DB Manager by pressing *F2*, clicking on the corresponding toolbar button, or in the **Database** menu.

5. pgRouting is a little picky when it comes to column data types. You will notice this when you see **Error, columns 'source', 'target' must be of type int4, 'cost' must be of type float8**. When we import `network_pgr` with QGIS's DB Manager, it creates the cost column as numeric. As pgRouting won't accept numeric, we will use **Table | Edit Table** in **DB Manager** to edit the cost column. Click on the **Edit column** button and change **Type** from **numeric** to **double precision** (which equals the required float8).

6. Now that the data is loaded and ready, we can build the network topology. This will create a new `network_pgr_vertices_pgr` table, which contains the computed network nodes:

```
SELECT pgr_createTopology('network_pgr',0.001);
```

7. Once this topology is ready, we can test the network by calculating a simple shortest path from the node number `16` to the node number `9`:

```
SELECT pgr_dijkstra('SELECT id, source, target, cost
   FROM network_pgr', 16, 9, false, false);
```

This will result in the following:

```
(0,16,6,1)
(1,17,7,1)
(2,5,8,1)
(3,6,9,1)
(4,11,15,1)
(5,9,-1,0)
```

How it works...

The preceding `pgr_dijkstra` query consists of the following parts:

▶ `'SELECT id, source, target, cost FROM network_pgr'`: This is a SQL query, which returns a set of rows with the following columns:

▶ `id`: This is the unique edge ID (type int4)

▶ `source`: This is the ID of the edge source node (type int4)

▶ `target`: This is the ID of the edge target node (type int4)

▶ `cost`: This is the cost of the edge traversal (type float8)

▶ `16, 9`: These are the IDs of the route source and target nodes (type int4)

- ▶ `false`: This is `true` if the graph is directed
- ▶ `false`: If `true`, the `reverse_cost` column of the SQL-generated set of rows will be used for the cost of the traversal of the edge in the opposite direction

The results of `pgr_dijkstra` contain the list of network links that our route uses to get from the start to the destination. The four values in reach result row are as follows:

- ▶ `seq`: This is the sequence number, which tells us the order of the links within the route starting from 0
- ▶ `id1`: This is the node ID
- ▶ `id2`: This is the edge ID
- ▶ `cost`: This is the cost of the link (can be distance, travel time, a monetary value, or any other measure that you chose)

See also

In the following recipe, *Visualizing pgRouting results in QGIS*, we will see how to use the results of `pgr_dijkstra` to visualize the route on a map.

If you are interested in more pgRouting SQL recipes, you will find a whole chapter on this topic in *PostGIS Cookbook* by Packt Publishing.

Visualizing the pgRouting results in QGIS

In the previous recipe, *Creating a routing network for pgRouting*, we imported a network layer, built the topology, and finally tested the routing. Building on these results, this recipe will show you how to visualize the routing results on a map in QGIS.

Getting ready

You should first go through the previous recipe, *Creating a routing network for pgRouting*, to set up the necessary PostGIS tables. Alternatively, you can use your own network tables, but be aware that you may have to alter some of the SQL statements if your table uses different column names.

How to do it...

To visualize the results in QGIS, we can use the DB Manager SQL window, as shown in the following screenshot. The extended query that we use here joins the routing results back to the original network table to get the route link geometries, which we want to display on the map:

1. Open DB Manager by navigating to **Database | DB Manager**.

2. In **Tree** to the left of the dialog, select the database that you want to load the network to.

3. Open the SQL window of DB Manager and configure it, as shown in the following screenshot:

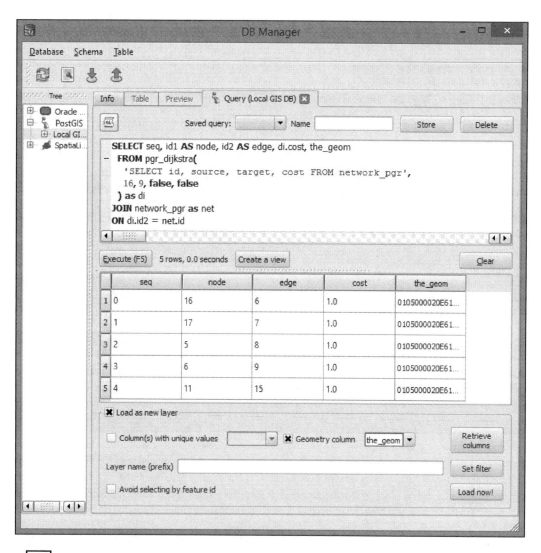

Note that there must not be a semicolon at the end of the SQL statement. Otherwise, loading the results as a new layer will fail.

4. Make sure that the **Geometry** column is selected correctly and click on the **Load now!** button to load the query result as a new layer, as shown in the following screenshot:

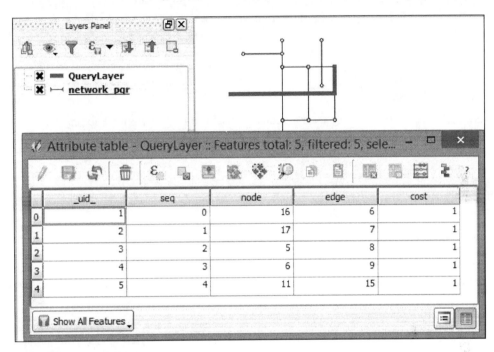

How it works...

As `pgr_dijkstra` only returns a list with the IDs of the route edges, we need to get the edge geometries from the original network table in order to display the route on the map. Therefore, we join the routing results with the network table on `id2` (which contains the edge ID) and the network table's `id` column.

See also

To make using pgRouting from within QGIS more convenient, the pgRoutingLayer plugin provides a GUI to access many of pgRouting's functions. You will find an introduction to this plugin in the *Using the pgRoutingLayer plugin for convenience* recipe.

Using the pgRoutingLayer plugin for convenience

The previous recipe, *Visualizing pgRouting results in QGIS*, showed you how to manually add pgRouting results to the map. In this chapter, we will use the pgRoutingLayer plugin to get more convenient access to the functions that pgRouting offers, including the most basic algorithms, such as Dijkstra's algorithm, which we have used so far, to more complex algorithms, such as `drivingDistance` and `alphashape`, which can be used to visualize catchment zones, also known as service areas.

Getting ready

You should first go through the previous recipe, *Creating a routing network for pgRouting*, to set up the necessary PostGIS tables. Alternatively, you can use your own network tables, but be aware that you may have to alter some of the SQL statements if your table uses different column names.

Additionally, install the pgRoutingLayer plugin from Plugin Installer. You will need to enable experimental plugins in **Settings** to view this.

How to do it...

The pgRoutingLayer plugin adds a new panel to the QGIS GUI, which allows convenient access to the available routing functions. The following steps show you how to use this plugin:

1. First, you should select a database from the **Database** field that contains your routing network table. The drop-down list contains all the configured PostGIS connections.

2. Next, you can select a function from the **Function** field that you want to use. Let's try Dijkstra's algorithm first; select the `dijkstra` function. You will recognize the parameters from the previous recipes where we wrote the pgRouting SQL query manually.

3. Specify the parameters for the network table (`edge_table`) and the **geometry**, **id**, **source**, **target**, and **cost** columns, as shown in the following screenshot:

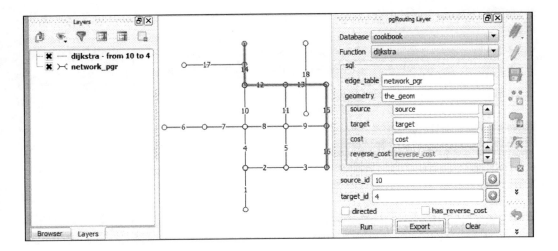

4. Now, you can use the green **+** buttons beside the **source_id** and **target_id** input fields to select the source and target nodes in the map.

5. When everything is configured, you can click on the **Run** button to compute and display the route.

6. Next, you can switch functions and compute a service area. Select the `alphashape` function. The rest of the input fields adapt automatically to the selected function.

7. Now, you can use the green **+** button right beside the **source_id** input field to select the starting or center node of the service area.

8. Then, select the size of the service area by specifying the **distance** limit.

9. Finally, click on the **Run** button to compute and display the service area, as shown in the following screenshot:

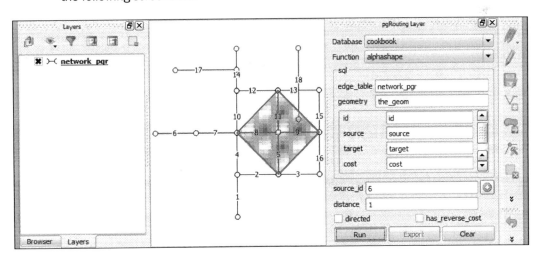

How it works...

When we click on the **Run** button, the query results are visualized as a temporary overlay on the map. If you want to save the output permanently, you can click on the **Export** button. Currently, the **Export** button is only available for the routing functions but not for the service area functions.

See also

For a detailed documentation on the pgRouting algorithms, refer to the project documentation website at `http://docs.pgrouting.org/2.0/en/doc/index.html`.

Getting network data from the OSM

A popular data source for real-world routing applications is **OpenStreetMap** (**OSM**). This recipe shows you how to prepare OSM data for usage with pgRouting using the osm2po command-line tool to convert OSM data to an insert script for PostGIS. Finally, we will test the data import using the pgRoutingLayer plugin.

Getting ready

Download osm2po from `http://osm2po.de` and unpack the download. Note that osm2po requires Java to be installed on your machine.

You also need a pgRouting-enabled database to follow this recipe.

Additionally, you should have the pgRoutingLayer plugin installed and enabled because we will use this to test the OSM data import.

You can use the `wake.pbf` OSM file from our sample data, or download your own data from services such as `http://download.geofabrik.de`.

How to do it...

Open the command line to perform the following steps. If you are working on Windows, we recommend using the osgeo4W Shell:

1. Go to the `osm2po` folder and open `osm2po.config` in a text editor. Look for the following configuration line and remove the # at the beginning of the line to activate the pgRouting export:

   ```
   postp.0.class = de.cm.osm2po.plugins.postp.PgRoutingWriter
   ```

2. Now use osm2po to convert the OSM `.pbf` file to SQL. Adjust the file paths for your system, as follows:

```
D:\osm2po-5.1.0>java -jar osm2po-core-5.1.0-signed.jar prefix=wake
"C:\tmp\OSM_NorthCarolina\wake.pbf"
```

3. When osm2po is finished, you should see the following:

```
INFO Services started. Waiting for requests at
http://localhost:8888/Osm2poService
```

4. You should now find a folder with the name of the prefix (that is, `wake`) inside the `osm2po` folder. This contains a log file, which in turn provides a command-line template to import the OSM network to PostGIS:

```
INFO commandline template:
psql -U [username] -d [dbname] -q -f
"D:\osm2po-5.1.0\wake\wake_2po_4pgr.sql"
```

5. Using this template, we can easily import the `.sql` file into an existing database, as follows:

```
D:\osm2po-5.1.0\wake>psql -U [username] -d cookbook -q -f D:\
osm2po-5.1.0\wake\wake_2po_4pgr.sql
```

6. Now, the data is ready for use in QGIS. When we connect to the cookbook database, we can see the `wake_2po_4pgr` table:

7. Finally, we can use the **pgRouting Layer** plugin to test the OSM data import by calculating a service area of **0.1** hours (the **distance** value) around the **43679** (**source_id**) source node number:

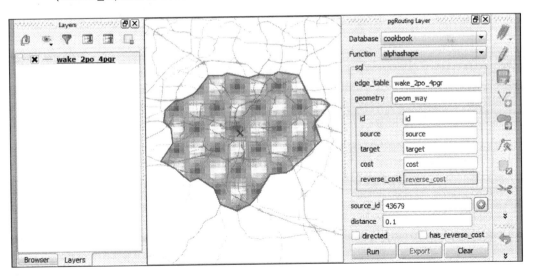

How it works...

The network table created by osm2po contains, among others, the following useful columns:

- ▸ km: This is the length of the network edge
- ▸ kmh: The is the speed on the edge, depending on the street class and the values specified in the osm2po configuration
- ▸ cost: This is the travel time computed using km/kmh

7
Raster Analysis I

In this chapter, we will cover the following recipes:

- ▶ Using the raster calculator
- ▶ Preparing elevation data
- ▶ Calculating a slope
- ▶ Calculating a hillshade layer
- ▶ Analyzing hydrology
- ▶ Calculating a topographic index
- ▶ Automate analysis tasks using the graphical modeler

Introduction

Raster analysis is a classic area in GIS analysis. This chapter shows you some of the most important and common tasks of raster analysis. Elevation data is commonly stored as raster layers, and in this format, it is particularly suitable to run a large variety of analysis. For this reason, terrain analysis has traditionally been one of the main areas of raster analysis, and we will show you some of the most common operations that are related to **Digital Elevation Models** (**DEM**), from simple analysis, such as slope calculation, to more complex ones, such as drainage network delineation or watershed extraction.

Using the raster calculator

The raster calculator is one of the most flexible and versatile tools in QGIS. This allows you to perform algebraic operations based on raster layers, and compute new layers. This recipe shows you how to use it.

Getting ready

Open the `catchment_area.tif` file. The file should look like the following screenshot:

How to do it...

1. Open the **Processing Toolbox** option and find the algorithm called **Raster calculator** by searching for it using the search box. Double-click on the algorithm item to execute it, as shown in the following screenshot:

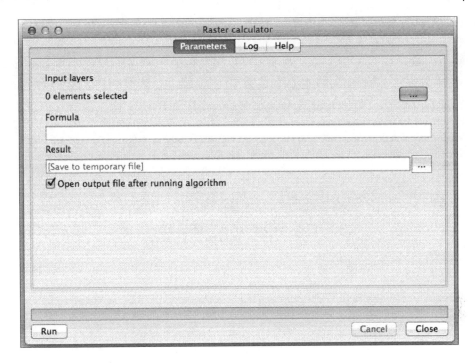

2. Click on the button in the **Input layers** field to open the layer selector. There is only one layer available: the `catchment_area` layer. Select this layer.

3. In the **Formula** field, enter `ln(a)`.

4. Click on **Run** to run the algorithm. The resulting layer will be added to the QGIS project, as follows:

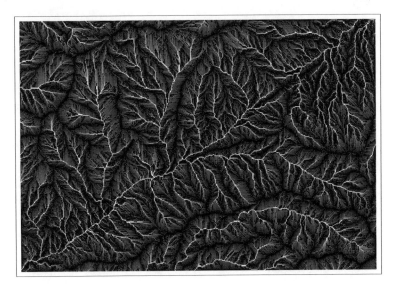

How it works...

The layers selected in the layer selector are referred to using a single letter in alphabetical order (a for the first one, b for the second one, and so on). In this case, we selected just one layer, so we can refer to it as a in the formula.

The formula calculates a natural logarithm of the values in the catchment area layer. The distribution of values in this layer is not homogeneous because it contains a large number of cells with low values and just a few of them with very large values. This causes the rendering of the layer to be not very informative with most of the colors in the color ramp not even being used.

The resulting layer is much more informative because applying the logarithm alters the distribution of values, resulting in a more explicit rendering.

There's more...

QGIS contains a raster calculator module outside of Processing. You can find this by navigating to **Raster | Raster calculator...**:

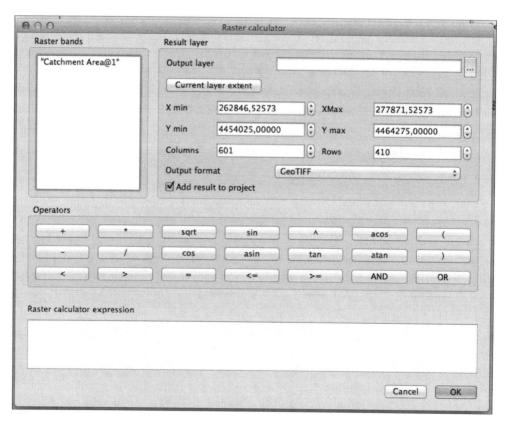

This interface resembles an actual calculator, and it is more intuitive and user friendly. On the other hand, this lacks many of the functions that are available in the Processing raster calculator (the logarithm that we have computed, for instance, is not available). This also cannot be used in automated processes, such as scripts or graphical models, which are only available for the Processing algorithms.

On the other hand, the QGIS built-in calculator supports multiband layers, while the Processing one is limited to single-band ones.

See also

▶ The QGIS raster calculator is described in more detail in the QGIS manual at `http://docs.qgis.org/2.8/en/docs/user_manual/working_with_ raster/raster_calculator.html`

Preparing elevation data

In this recipe, we will show you how to perform terrain analysis in QGIS. Terrain analysis algorithms assume certain characteristics in the DEMs that are used as inputs, so it is important to know them and prepare these DEMs if they are needed. This recipe shows you how to do this.

Getting ready

Open the `dem_to_prepare.tif` layer. This layer contains a DEM in the EPSG:4326 CRS and elevation data in feet. These characteristics are unsuitable to run most terrain analysis algorithms, so we will modify this layer to get a suitable one.

How to do it...

1. Reproject the layer to the EPSG:3857 CRS, using the **Save as...** entry in the context menu that appears by right-clicking on the layer name.

2. Open the resulting reprojected layer.

3. Open the Processing raster calculator and select the reprojected layer as the only raster input in the **Input layers** field. Enter a `*` `0.3048` in the **Formula** field. Run the algorithm.

How it works...

Most of the algorithms that we are going to use assume that the horizontal units (the unit used to measure the size of the cell) are the same as the units used in the elevation values that are contained in the layer. If the layer does not meet this requirement, the result of the analysis will be wrong.

Our input layer uses a CRS with geographic coordinates (degrees). As elevation cannot be measured in degrees, the layer cannot have the same units for horizontal and vertical distances, and it is not ready to be used for terrain analysis.

By reprojecting the layer to the EPSG:3857 CRS, we get a new layer in which coordinates are expressed in meters. This is a unit that is more suitable for the type of analysis that we plan to run. Actually, after the reprojection, the units are meters only near the equator, but this gives us enough precision for this case. If more precise calculations are needed, a local projection system should be used.

The next step is converting the elevation values in feet to elevation values in meters. Knowing that 1 foot = 0.3048 meter, we just have to use the calculator to apply this formula and convert the values in the reprojected layer.

There's more...

There are other things that must be taken into account when running a terrain analysis algorithm to ensure that results are correct.

One common problem is dealing with different cell sizes. An assumption that is made by most terrain analysis algorithms (and also most of the ones not related to terrain analysis) is that cells are square. That is, their horizontal and vertical values are the same. This is the case in our input layer (you can verify this by checking the layer properties), but it may not be true for other layers.

In this case, you should export the layer and define the sizes of the cells of the exported layer to have the same value. Right-click on the layer name and select **Save as...**. In the save dialog that will appear, enter the new sizes of the cells in the lower part of the dialog:

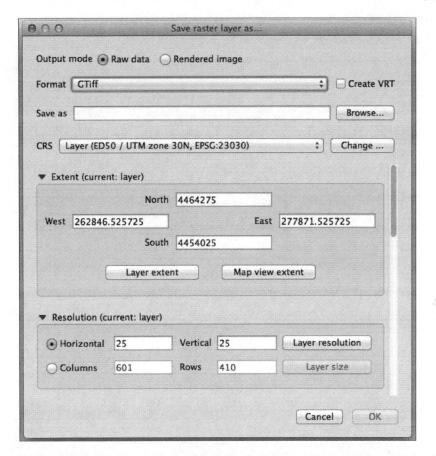

Calculating a slope

Slope is one of the most basic parameters that can be derived from a DEM. It corresponds to the first derivative of the DEM, and it represents the rate of change of the elevation. It is computed by analyzing the elevation of each cell and comparing this with the elevation of the surrounding ones. This recipe shows you how to compute slope in QGIS.

Getting ready

Open the DEM that we prepared in the previous recipe.

How to do it...

1. In the **Processing Toolbox** option, find the **Slope** algorithm and double-click on it to open it:

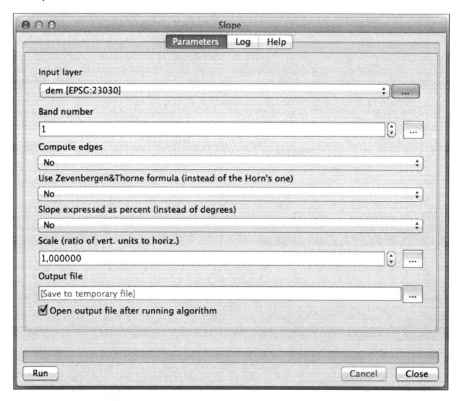

2. Select the DEM in the **Input layer** field.
3. Click on **Run** to run the algorithm.

The slope layer will be added to the QGIS project.

How it works...

Slope is calculated from a DEM elevation model by analyzing the cells around a given one. This analysis is performed by the slope algorithm from the GDAL library.

There's more...

There are several ways of using the slope algorithms in QGIS. Here are some comments and ideas about this.

Using a ratio for elevation values

If the units of elevation are not the same as the horizontal units, you can convert them, as we did in the previous recipe, using the raster calculator. However, the slope module contains an option to convert them on-the-fly by entering the conversion factor in the Scale field. Note that this option is not available in other terrain analysis modules that we will use, so it's still good practice to create a layer with the correct units, which can be used without any further processing.

Other slope algorithms

The Processing framework contains algorithms that rely on several external applications and libraries. These libraries sometimes contain similar algorithms, so there is more than one option for a given analysis.

If you switch the presentation mode of the toolbox from **simplified** to **advanced** using the lower part of the drop-down list and then type **slope** in the search box, you will see something like the following screenshot:

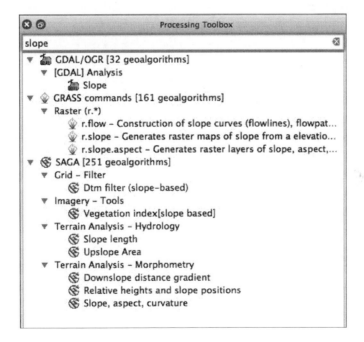

Calculating the slope

Try using the GRASS or SAGA algorithm to calculate the slope. Each of them has different parameters and options, but all of them perform similar calculations and create slope layers.

Apart from Processing, you can also perform analysis using the Raster Terrain Analysis plugin.

See also

▶ The *Using the raster calculator* recipe in the beginning of this chapter

Calculating a hillshade layer

A hillshade layer is commonly used to enhance the appearance of a map and display topography in an intuitive way, by simulating a light source and the shadows it casts. This can be computed from a DEM by using this recipe.

Getting ready

Open the DEM that we prepared in the *Preparing elevation data* recipe.

How to do it...

1. In the **Processing Toolbox** option, find the **Hillshade** algorithm and double-click on it to open it:

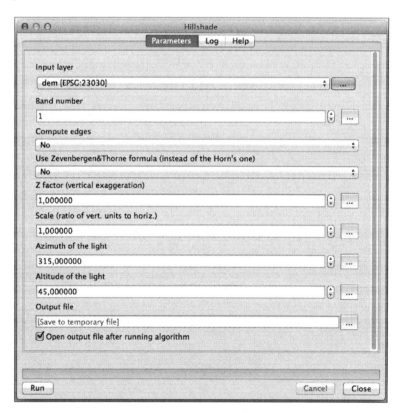

2. Select the DEM in the **Input layer** field. Leave the rest of the parameters with their default values.

3. Click on **Run** to run the algorithm.

The hillshade layer will be added to the QGIS project, as follows:

How it works...

As in the case of the slope, the algorithm is part of the GDAL library. You will see that the parameters are very similar to the slope case. This is because slope is used to compute the hillshade layer. Based on the slope and the aspect of the terrain in each cell and using the position of the sun that is defined by the **Azimuth** and **Altitude** fields, the algorithm computes the illumination that the cell will receive. This is based on a focal analysis, so shadows are not considered and are not a real illumination value, but they can be used to render and to display the topography of the terrain.

You can try changing the values of these parameters to alter the appearance of the layer.

There's more...

As in the case of slope, there are alternative options to compute the hillshade. The SAGA one in the **Processing Toolbox** option has a feature that is worth mentioning.

The SAGA hillshade algorithm contains a field named **method**. This field is used to select the method that is used to compute the hillshade value, and the last method that is available. **Raytracing** differs from the other ones as it models the real behavior of light, making an analysis that is not local but that uses the full information of the DEM instead because it takes into account the shadows that are cast by the surrounding relief. This renders more precise hillshade layers, but the processing time can be notably larger.

Enhancing your map view with a hillshade layer

You can combine the hillshade layer with your other layers to enhance their appearance.

As you used a DEM to compute the hillshade layer, it should be already in your QGIS project along with the hillshade itself. However, this will be covered by the hillshade because of the new layers produced by Processing are added on top of the existing ones in the layers list. Move it to the top of the layer list so that you can see the DEM (and not the hillshade layer) and style it to something like the following screenshot:

Lets see the steps to enhance the map view with a hillshade layer:

1. In the **Properties** dialog of the layer, move to the **Transparency** section, and set the **Global transparency** value to **50%**, as shown in the following screenshot:

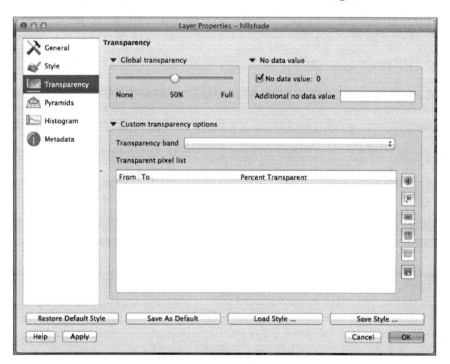

2. Now, you should see the hillshade layer through the DEM, and the combination of both of them will look like the following screenshot:

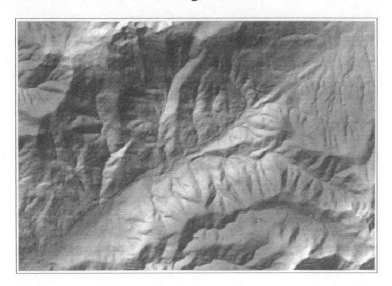

Another way of doing this is using the blending modes in QGIS. You can find more information about this in the recipe, *Understanding the feature and layer blending modes* of *Chapter 10, Cartography Tips*, or in the QGIS manual at `http://docs.qgis.org/2.8/en/docs/user_manual/working_with_vector/vector_properties.html#style-menu`.

Analyzing hydrology

A common analysis from a DEM is to compute hydrological elements, such as the channel network or the set of watersheds. This recipe shows you the steps to do these analysis.

Getting ready

Open the DEM that we prepared in the *Preparing elevation data* recipe.

How to do it...

1. In the **Processing Toolbox** option, find the **Fill Sinks** algorithm and double-click on it to open it:

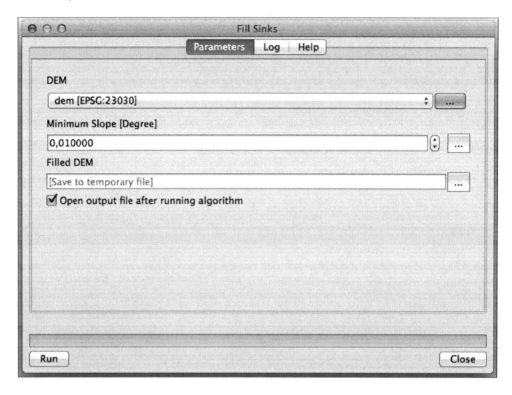

2. Select the DEM in the **DEM** field and run the algorithm. This will generate a new filtered DEM layer. From now on, we will just use this DEM in the recipe and not the original one.

3. Open **Catchment Area** and select the filtered DEM in the **Elevation** field:

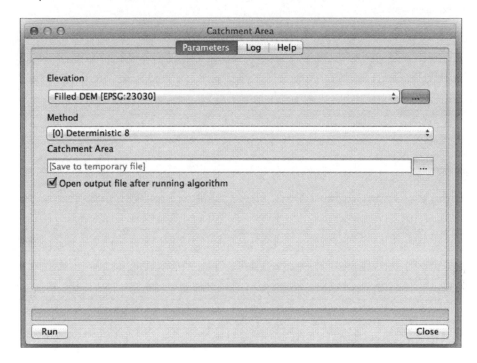

4. Run the algorithm. This will generate a catchment area layer:

5. Open the **Channel network** algorithm and fill it in, as shown in the following screenshot:

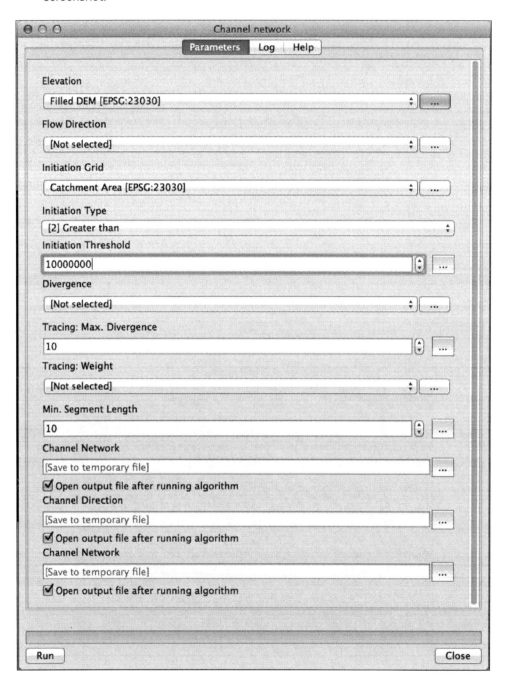

6. Run the algorithm. This will extract the channel network from the DEM, based on the catchment area, and it will then generate it as both a raster and vector layer:

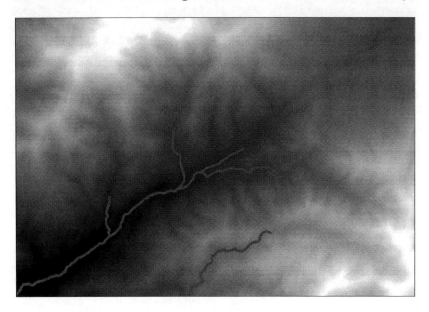

7. Open the **Watershed basins** algorithm and fill it in, as shown in the following screenshot:

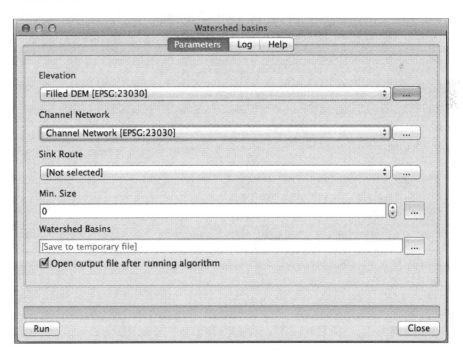

8. Run the algorithm. This will generate a raster layer with the watersheds calculated from the DEM and the channel network. Each watershed is a hydrological unit that represents the area that flows into a junction, which is defined by the channel network:

How it works...

Starting from the DEM, the preceding steps follow a typical workflow for hydrological analysis:

▶ First, the sinks are filled. This is a required preparation whenever you plan to perform a hydrological analysis. The DEM may contain sinks where a flow direction cannot be computed, which represents a problem to model the movement of water across these cells. Removing these sinks solves this problem.

▶ The catchment area is computed from the DEM. The values in the catchment area layer represent the area that is upstream of each cell. That is, the total area in which if water is dropped, it will eventually pass through the cell.

▶ Cells with high values of the catchment area will likely contain a river, while cells with lower values will have overland flow. By setting a threshold on the catchment area values, we can separate the river cells (the ones above the threshold) from the remaining ones and extract the channel network.

▶ Finally, we compute the watersheds associated with each junction in the channel network that was extracted in the last step.

There's more...

The key parameter in the preceding workflow is the catchment area threshold. If a larger threshold is used, fewer cells will be considered as river cells, and the resulting channel network will be sparser. As the watershed is computed based on the channel network, this will result in a lower number of watersheds.

You can try this yourself with different values of the catchment area threshold. Here, you can see the result for threshold is equal to 1,000,000 in the following screenshot:

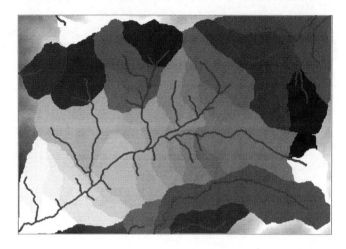

The channel network has been added to help you understand the structure of the resulting set of watersheds.

Here, you can see the result for a threshold of 50,000,000 in the following screenshot:

Note that in this last case, with a higher threshold value, there is only one single watershed in the resulting layer.

The threshold values are expressed in the units of the catchment area which, as the size of the cell is assumed to be in meters, are in square meters.

Calculating a topographic index

As the topography defines and influences most of the processes that take place in a given terrain, the DEM can be used to extract many different parameters, which give us information about these processes. This recipe shows you how to calculate a popular one, which is called the Topographic wetness index, which estimates the soil wetness based on the topography.

Getting ready

Open the DEM that we prepared in the *Preparing elevation data* recipe.

How to do it...

1. Calculate a slope layer using the **Slope, aspect, curvature** algorithm from SAGA in the **Processing Toolbox** option. Calculate a catchment area layer using the **Catchment area** algorithm from the **Processing Toolbox** option. Note that you must use a sink-less DEM, such as the one that we generated in the previous recipe with the **Fill sinks** algorithm.

   Open the **Topographic wetness index** algorithm from the **Processing Toolbox** option and fill it in, as shown in the following screenshot:

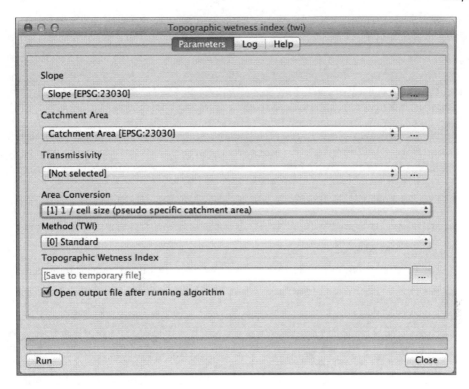

2. Run the algorithm. This will create a layer with the topographic wetness index, indicating the soil wetness in each cell:

How it works...

The index combines slope and catchment area, two parameters that influence the soil wetness. If the catchment area value is high, this means that more water will flow into the cell, thus, increasing its soil wetness. A low value of slope will have a similar effect because the water that flows into the cell will not flow out of it quickly.

This algorithm expects the slope to be expressed in radians. This is the reason why the **Slope, aspect, curvature** algorithm has to be used because it produces its slope output in radians. The other **Slope** algorithm that you will find, which is based on the GDAL library, creates a slope layer with values expressed in degrees. You can use this layer if you convert its units using the raster calculator.

There's more...

Other indices that are based on the same input layers can be found in different algorithms in the **Processing Toolbox** option. The Stream Power Index and the LS factor both use the slope and catchment area as inputs as well, and they can be related to potential erosion.

Automating analysis tasks using the graphical modeler

Most analysis tasks involve using several algorithms. Repeating the same analysis with a different dataset or different input parameters requires using them one by one, making this task tedious and error-prone. You can automate analysis workflows using the Processing graphical modeler, which allows you to define a workflow graphically and wrap it in a single algorithm. This recipe introduces the main ideas about the modeler and creates a simple model as an example.

Getting ready

No special preparation is needed in QGIS for this recipe, but make sure that you have read the previous recipe about computing a topographic index. This recipe will create a model based on the workflow in that recipe, so it is important that you understand it.

How to do it...

1. Open the graphical modeler by navigating to **Processing | Graphical modeler**:

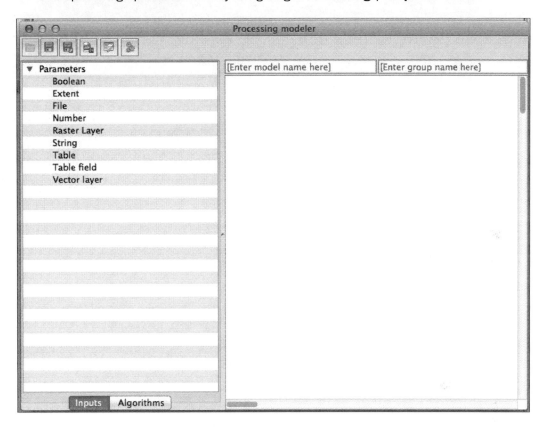

2. Double-click on the **Raster Layer** item to add a raster input. In the dialog that will appear to define the input, name it DEM and set it as mandatory:

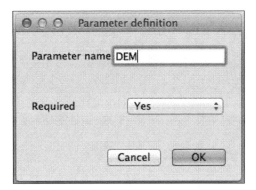

3. Click on **OK** to add the input to the canvas:

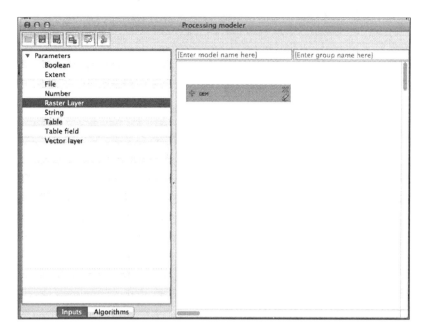

4. Move to the **Algorithms** tab. Double-click on the **Slope, aspect, curvature** algorithm and set the algorithm definition, as shown in the following screenshot:

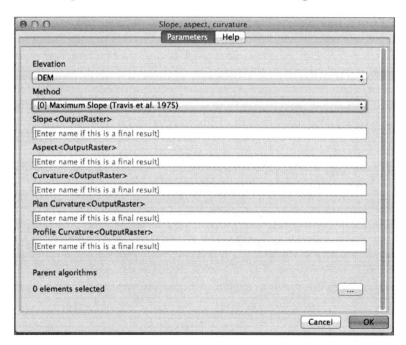

5. Close the dialog by clicking on the **OK** button. This will be added to the modeler canvas, as follows:

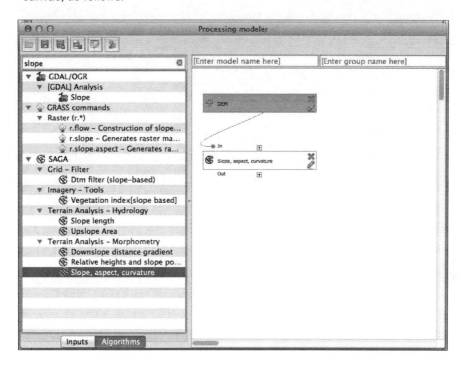

6. Add the **Catchment area** algorithm to the model by double-clicking on it in the algorithm list and filling in the dialog, as shown in the following screenshot:

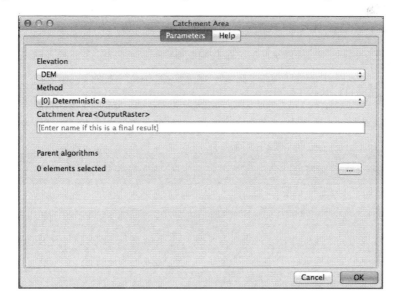

7. Finally, add the **Topographic wetness index** algorithm, defining it as shown in the following screenshot:

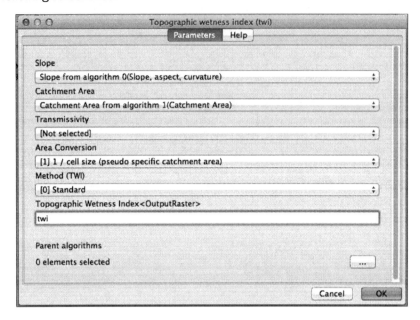

8. The final model should look like the following screenshot:

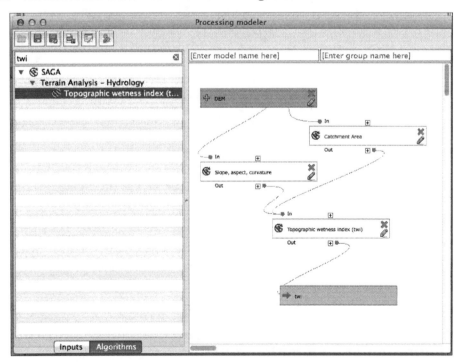

9. Enter a name and a group to identify the model and save it by clicking on the **Save** button. Do not change the save location folder, because Processing will only look for it in the default location, you can however change the name of the model. Close the modeler dialog. If you now go to the **Processing Toolbox** option, you will find a new algorithm in the **Models** section, which corresponds to the workflow that you have just defined:

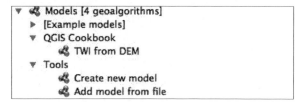

How it works...

The model automates the workflow and wraps all the steps into a single one.

By saving the model in the models folder, Processing will see this when updating the toolbox and will include it along with the rest of algorithms so that it can be executed normally.

See also

▶   More information about the graphical modeler can be found in the Processing chapter of the QGIS manual at `http://docs.qgis.org/2.8/en/docs/user_manual/processing/modeler.html`

8
Raster Analysis II

In this chapter, we will cover the following recipes:

- ▸ Calculating NDVI
- ▸ Handling null values
- ▸ Setting extents with masks
- ▸ Sampling a raster layer
- ▸ Visualizing multispectral layers
- ▸ Modifying and reclassifying values in raster layers
- ▸ Performing supervised classification of raster layers

Introduction

Following the previous chapter, this chapter introduces some additional techniques for raster analysis. This chapter will show you how to work with images, how to modify raster values and classify them, and how raster layers can be used along with vector layers, thus extending the set of tools that were introduced in the recipes in the previous chapter.

Calculating NDVI

The **Normalized Differential Vegetation Index** is a very popular vegetation index that gives us useful information about the presence or absence of live green vegetation.

Getting ready

NDVI is calculated using a band with red spectral reflectance values, and another one with near-infrared reflectance values. In the sample dataset, you will find two image files named `red.tif` and `nir.tif` that can be used to compute NDVI. A project named `ndvi.qgs` is available, which contains these two layers and a landsat image corresponding to this same area. Open this project.

How to do it...

1. Open the **Processing Toolbox** menu and find the algorithm called **Vegetation index[slope based]**. Double-click on the algorithm item to execute it:

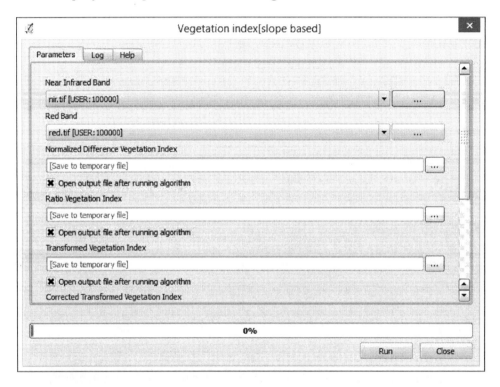

2. Select the `red.tif` layer in the **Red Band** field and the `nir.tif` layer in the **Near Infrared Band** field. Click on **Run** to run the algorithm.

3. The algorithm will produce a set of layers with different vegetation indices, NDVI is among them:

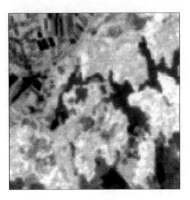

How it works...

All vegetation indices that are computed by the algorithm are based on the relation between red and near-infrared reflectances. Leaf cells scatter solar radiation in the near-infrared reflectance and absorb radiation in the red reflectance, which can be used to predict the location of healthy green vegetation based on these two values.

NDVI is computed with the formula given in the following section.

There's more...

As the formula of the NDVI is rather simple, you can calculate it without using a specific algorithm, just by going to the raster calculator. You can use the one integrated in the Processing Framework or the QGIS built-in on. You can see how you should fill the parameters in the QGIS Raster calculator to compute the NDVI, based on the two proposed sample layers in the following screenshot:

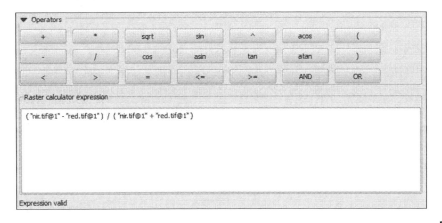

Extracting bands

The vegetation indices algorithm requires the red and infrared values to be in two separate layers, each of them with a single band. However, it's common to have both of them in a multiband image. To be able to use these bands, you must separate them, extracting them into two separate files.

This can be done using the GDAL translate algorithm. The project contains a multiband image named landsat.tif with the red band in band number 3 and infrared band in band number 4:

1. Open the **Translate** algorithm in the **Processing Toolbox** menu.

2. Fill its parameters, as shown in the following screenshot, to export the infrared band:

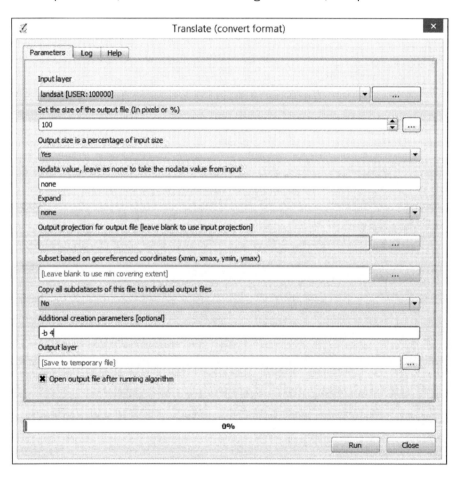

3. Run this again, as shown in the following screenshot, to export the red band:

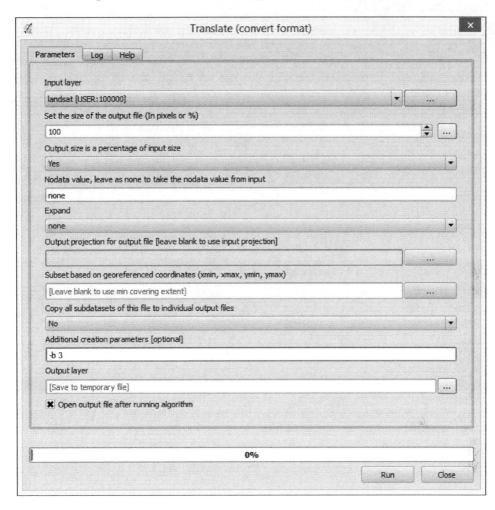

The Translate algorithm uses the GDAL library underneath. You can also use this library as an independent tool from the console. At the lower part of the algorithm dialog, you will find a text field where you will see the equivalent console call to your current algorithm configuration.

Handling null values

Null values are a particular type of values that are used to indicate cells where the value for a given layer is not defined. Understanding how to use them is important to avoid wrong results when performing analyses but also to use them as a tool to get better and more correct results. This recipe explains some of the fundamental ideas about null values in raster layers.

How to do it...

The `watershed.tif` layer contains the area of a watershed. Cells inside the watershed are cells from which water will eventually flow into the outlet point of the watershed. The remaining cells belong to a different watershed. To mask the DEM with the watershed mask, follow these steps:

1. Open the `watershed.tif` layer.

2. Open the identify tool and check whether the cells that belong to the watershed have a value of 1, and the ones outside, have a value of `no data`.

3. Try clicking inside and outside the watershed; in your **Identify Results** dialog, you will see the results, as shown in the following screenshot:

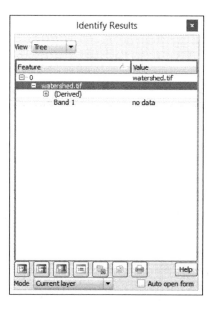

4. Now, let's calculate some statistics of the raster layer. Open the **Raster layer statistics** algorithm in the **Processing Toolbox** menu.

5. Select the watershed layer in the **input layer** field and click on **OK** to run the algorithm. The result is a short text output that looks like the following screenshot:

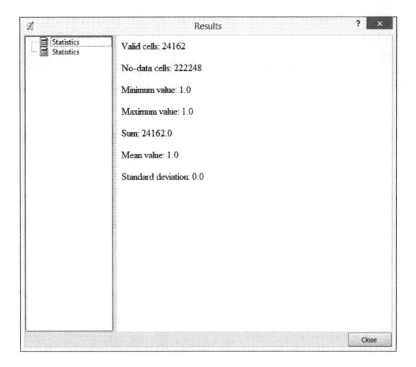

Only the cells with a value of 1 have been considered, and the average value in the layer is equal to 1.

The layer has 610 columns and 401 rows, but the total number of valid cells is much lower than 610 x 410. These are the cells that have been used to compute the statistics.

How it works...

Raster layers always cover a rectangular region. However, in some circumstances, the land object that the layer represents might not be rectangular. This might be due to a purely geophysical reason (imagine a layer with water temperature that contains non-water cells), political ones (a layer with a DEM of a given country with no data available for a neighboring country), or many others. In any case, a value is needed for these cells to indicate that no data is available. An arbitrary value is selected and used. As such, this is usually a value that is not a logical and/or feasible value for the variable that is stored in the layer.

In the case of the example layer, the value used is -99999, which is the default value set for no-data values. This means that, when the identify tool shows **no data**, it has actually selected a value of -99999 in this case.

Algorithms in the Processing framework systematically ignore no-data cells, and do not use their values. You can clearly see this in the preceding example. A large part of the cells in the layer have a value of 1 (the ones that belong to the watershed), but many of them have a value of -99999. The average value of the cells should then be different from 1, but as -99999 is defined as the no-data value, all cells with this value are ignored. The average of the layer is, therefore, equal to 1.

There's more...

Null values should be considered not only when performing an analysis, but also when we just want to render a layer that contains them.

Controlling the rendering of null values

Null values are also considered separately when rendering a raster layer. You can choose to select them using a given color (as set by the current color palette), or to not render them at all. To make all cells with null values transparent, open the layer properties and go to the **Transparency** section. Make sure that the **No data value** checkbox is checked, as shown in the following screenshot:

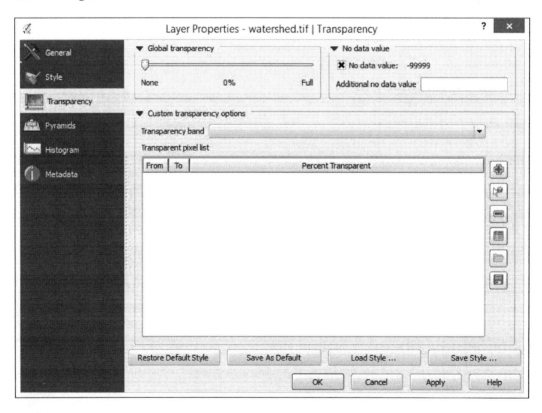

Setting extents with masks

The extent of a layer can be set using a second layer, which acts as a mask. This recipe shows you how to do this.

How to do it...

To mask the DEM with the watershed mask, follow these steps:

1. Open the `watershed.tif` layer and the `dem.tif` layer.
2. Open the **Raster Calculator** algorithm present in the **Processing Toolbox** menu.
3. In **Main input layer**, select the DEM, and in the **Additional layers** field, select the watershed layer.
4. In the **Formula** field, enter the formula, *a*b*.
5. Click on **Run** to run the algorithm. You will get a masked DEM, as follows:

How it works...

When using the raster calculator, all operations involving a no-data value will result in another no-data value. This means that, when multiplying the DEM layer and the mask layer, in the cells that contain no-data values in the mask layer, the value in the resulting layer will be a no-data value, no matter which elevation value is found in the DEM layer for this cell.

As cells inside the watershed in the mask layer have a value of 1, the result is a layer with elevation values for watershed cells and no-data values for the remaining ones.

There's more...

Here are some additional ideas about masks.

Restricting analysis to a given area

Once we have masked the area of interest (in this case, the watershed), all analysis that we perform will be restricted to this. For instance, let's calculate the average elevation of the watershed:

1. Open the **Basic statistics for raster layers** algorithm.

2. Select the masked DEM in the **Input layer** field and click on **Run** to run the algorithm. You will get the statistics on the **Results** window:

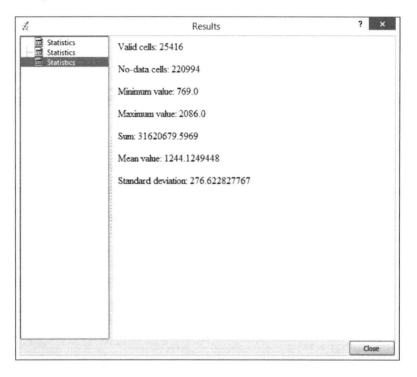

These values have been computed using only valid cell values and ignoring the no-data ones, which means that they refer to the watershed and not the the full extent of the raster layer.

Removing superfluous no-data values

Sometimes, you might have more no-data values that are needed in a raster layer, as in the case of the proposed watershed layer. To reduce the extent of the layer and just have the minimum extent that covers the valid data, you can use the **Crop to data** algorithm:

1. Open the **Crop to data** algorithm in the **Processing Toolbox** menu.

2. Enter the masked DEM in the **Input layer** field and click on **Run** to run the algorithm. The resulting layer should look like this when you disable transparency for no-data values:

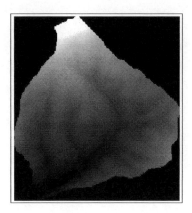

 Note that, if you have opted to render no-data cells as transparent pixels, you will see no visual difference between the original and the cropped layer.

Masking using a vector mask

Masking a raster layer can also be done using a polygon vector layer. The watershed.shp file contains a single polygon with the area of the watershed that we have already used to mask the DEM. Here is how to use this to mask that DEM without using the raster mask:

1. Open the **Clip** grid with the **polygon** algorithm.

2. Select the DEM in the **Input** field.

3. Select the vector layer in the **Polygons** field.

4. Click on **Run** to run the algorithm. The clipped layer will be added to the QGIS project.

In this case, the clip algorithm automatically reduces the extent of the output layer to the minimum extent defined by the polygon layer, so there is no need to run the **Crop to data** algorithm afterwards.

Sampling a raster layer

Data from a raster layer can be added to a points layer by querying the value of the layer in the coordinates of the points. This process is known as sampling, and this recipe explains how to perform it.

Getting ready

Open the `dem.tif` raster layer and the `dem_points.shp` vector layer:

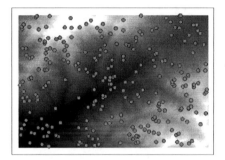

How to do it...

1. In the **Processing Toolbox** menu, find the **Add grid values to points** algorithm and double-click on it to open it:

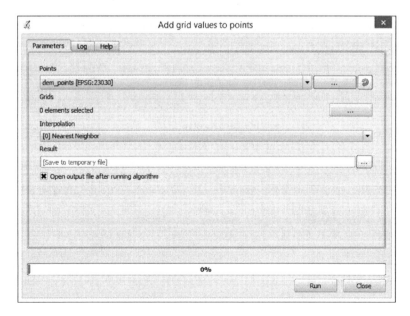

2. Select the DEM in the **Grids** field.

3. Select the point layer in the **Points** field.

4. Click on **Run** to run the algorithm.

A new vector layer will be created. This contains the same points as the input layer, but the attribute table will have an additional field with the name of the selected raster layer and the values corresponding to this layer in each point:

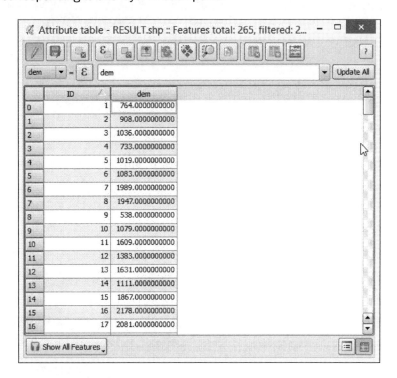

How it works...

The coordinates of the points are taken, and the value of the pixel in which the layer falls is added to the resulting points layer.

This method assumes that the value of a cell is constant in all the area covered by this cell. A different approach is to consider that the value of the cell represents its value only in the center of the cell and perform additional calculations to compute the value at the exact sampling point using the values of the surrounding cells as well. This can be done using several different interpolation methods, which can be selected in the **Interpolation method** selector, changing the default value, which only uses the value of the cell where the sampling point falls.

Layers are assumed to be in the same CRS and no reprojection is performed. If this is not the case, the value added to the vector layer might not be correct.

There's more...

Here, you can find some ideas about how to combine a raster and vector layer in different situations.

Other raster-vector data transfer operations

Data coming from a raster layer can also be added to other types of vector layers. In the case of a vector layer with polygons, the **Grid statistics for polygons** algorithm can be used, as follows:

1. Open the `watershed.shp` file that we used in the previous recipe.

2. Open the **Grid** statistics in the **Polygons** field.

3. Select the raster layer to clip in the **Grids** field.

4. Select the polygon layer with the mask in the **Polygons** field.

5. Select the statistics to be calculated from the remaining parameters. For instance, to calculate just the mean elevation, leave the **Mean** field selected and unselect the others.

6. Click on **Run** to run the algorithm.

The resulting layer is a new polygon layer with the watershed and an additional field in the attributes table, containing the mean elevation value for each polygon.

If more statistics are selected, the result will have a larger number of additional fields added, one for each new parameter computed and each selected grid.

Visualizing multispectral layers

Multispectral layers can be rendered in different ways depending on how bands are used. This recipe shows you how to do this and discusses the theory behind it.

Getting ready

Open the `landsat.qgs` project.

How to do it...

1. The Landsat image, when opened with the default configuration, looks something like the following screenshot:

2. Double-click on the layer to open its properties and move to the **Style** section:

    1. Select the band number 4 in the **Red band** field.

    2. Select the band number 3 in the **Green band** field.

    3. Select the band number 2 in the **Blue band** field.

    Your style configuration should be like the following:

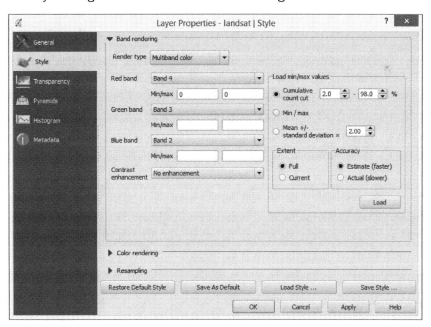

3. Click on **OK**.

The image should now look like the following:

How it works...

Colors representing a given pixel are defined using the RGB color space, which requires three different components. A normal image (such as the one you will get from a digital camera) has three bands containing the intensity for each one of these three components: red, green, and blue.

Multispectral bands, such as the one used in this recipe, have more than three bands and provide more detail in different regions of the electromagnetic spectrum. To visualize these, three bands from the total number of available bands have to be chosen and their intensities have to be used as intensities of the basic red, green, and blue components (although they might correspond to a different region of the spectrum, even outside the visible range). This is known as a *false color* image.

Depending on the combination of the bands that are used, the resulting image will convey a different type of information. The combination chosen is frequently used for vegetation studies, as it allows you to separate coniferous from hardwood vegetation as well as providing information about vegetation health.

The combination is applied, in this case, to a Landsat 7 image, which is taken with the ETM+ sensor. The wavelengths covered by each band are as follows (in micrometers):

- **Band 1**: 0.45 - 0.515
- **Band 2**: 0.525 - 0.605
- **Band 3**: 0.63 - 0.69
- **Band 4**: 0.75 - 0.90

> ▶ **Band 5**: 1.55 - 1.75
> ▶ **Band 6**: 10.40 - 12.5
> ▶ **Band 7**: 2.09 - 2.35

There's more...

Different combinations are frequently used for Landsat layers. One of them is the following:

> ▶ Select the band number 3 in the **Red band** field
> ▶ Select the band number 2 in the **Green band** field
> ▶ Select band number 1 in the **Blue band** field

This is a natural color combination, as the bands used for the **R**, **G**, and **B** components actually have the wavelengths corresponding to the colors **red**, **green**, and **blue**:

If you are using an image that is not a Landsat 7 one, each band will have a different meaning, and using the same combination of band numbers will yield different results. The meaning of each band must be checked in order to understand the information displayed by the rendered image.

See also

> ▶ Landsat data is freely available. If you want to download Landsat data corresponding to a given region, visit `http://landsat.gsfc.nasa.gov/`. Here, you can find more information about where and how you can download it.

Modifying and reclassifying values in raster layers

A very useful technique to work with raster data is changing their values or grouping them into categories. In this recipe, we will see how to do this.

Getting ready

Open the DEM file that we used in previous recipes.

How to do it...

We will classify the elevation in three groups:

- Lower than 1,000m
- Between 1,000 and 2,000m
- Higher than 2,000m

To do this, follow these steps:

1. Open the **Change grid values** algorithm from the **Processing Toolbox** menu. Set the **Replace condition** parameter to **Low Value <= Grid Value < High Value**.

2. Click on the button in the **Lookup table** parameter and fill the table that will appear, as shown in the following screenshot:

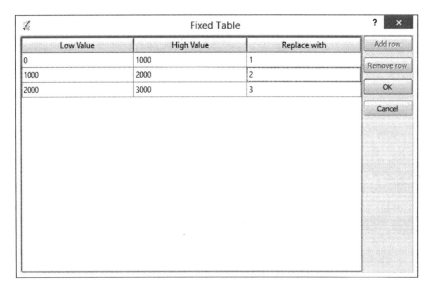

Low Value	High Value	Replace with	
0	1000	1	Add row
1000	2000	2	Remove row
2000	3000	3	OK
			Cancel

3. Run the algorithm. This will create the reclassified layer:

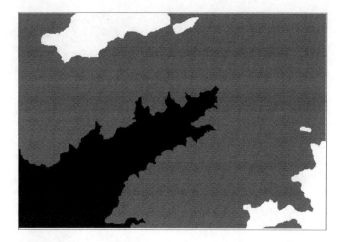

How it works...

Values for each cell are compared with the range limits in the lookup table, considering the specified comparison criteria. Whenever a value falls into a given range, the class value specified for this range will be used in the output layer.

There's more...

Other strategies can be used to automate a reclassification, especially when this involves dividing the raster layer values into classes with some constant property. Here, we show two of these cases.

Reclassifying into classes of equal amplitude

A typical case of reclassification is dividing the total range of values of the layer into a given number of classes. This is similar to slicing it, and if applied on a DEM, such as our example data, this will have a result similar to that of defining contour lines with a regular interval (although the result is a not vector layer with lines in this case, but a new raster layer).

To reclassify in equal intervals, follow these steps:

1. Open **Raster calculator** from the **Processing Toolbox** menu.

2. Select the DEM as the only layer to use.

3. Enter the formula, *int((a-514)/(2410-514) * 5)*.

The reclassified layer will look like the following:

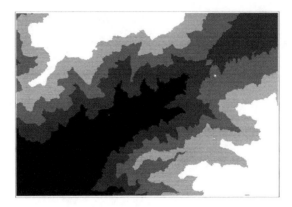

The numerical values in the formula correspond to the minimum and maximum values of the layer. You can find these values in the properties window of the layer.

To create a different number of classes, just use another value instead of 5 in the formula.

Reclassifying into classes of equal area

There is no tool to reclassify into a set of *n* classes, as each of them occupies the same area, but a similar result can be obtained using some other algorithms. To show you how this is done, let's reclassify the DEM into five classes of the same area:

1. Open the **Sort grid** algorithm and enter the DEM as the input layer. Click on **Run** to execute the algorithm.

    The resulting layer has the cells ordered according to their value in the DEM, so the cell with a value of 1 represents the cell with the lowest elevation value, 2 is the second lowest, and so on.

2. Reclassify the ordered layer into five classes of equal amplitude using the procedure described earlier. The final layer should look like the following:

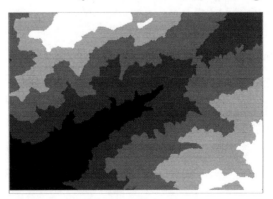

See also

▶ The **Processing Toolbox** menu contains additional classification algorithms, most of them based on SAGA. One algorithm that has a different approach is **Cluster analysis for grids**. This will create a given number of classes in such a way that it minimize the variances in the groups, trying to make them as homogeneous as possible. This is also known as unsupervised classification.

Performing supervised classification of raster layers

In the previous recipes, we saw how to change the values of a raster layer and create classes. When you have several layers, classifying might not be that easy, and defining the patterns to perform this classification might not be obvious. A different technique to be used in this case is to define zones that share a common characteristic and let the corresponding algorithm extract the statistical values that define them so that this can later be applied to perform the classification itself. This is known as **Supervised classification**, and this recipe explains how to do this in QGIS.

Getting ready

Open the `classification.qgs` project. It contains an RGB image and a vector layer with polygons.

How to do it...

1. The image has to be separated into individual bands. Run **Split RGB bands** using the provided image as the input, and you will obtain three layers named R, G, and B.
2. Open the **Supervised classification** algorithm from the **Processing Toolbox** menu.

3. Fill in its parameter window, as shown in the following screenshot:

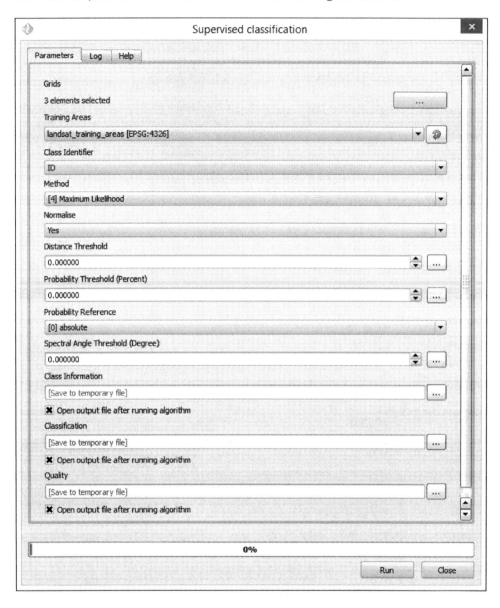

4. In the first field, you should select the three layers resulting from the last step (R, G, and B).

5. Click on **OK** to run the algorithm. Two layers and a table will be created. The layer named **Classification** contains the classified raster layer:

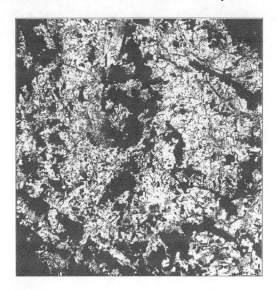

How it works...

The supervised classification needs a set of raster layers and a vector layer with polygons that define the different classes to create. The identifier of the class is defined in the **Class** field in the attributes table. If you open the attributes tables, you will see that it looks something like the following:

	ID	BOTYP
0	1	Forest
1	2	Wheat
2	3	Urban
3	4	Crop
4	5	Crop-clear

There are five different classes, each of them represented by a feature and with a text ID along with a numerical ID. The classification algorithms analyzes the pixels that fall within the polygons of each class and computes statistics for them. Using these statistics assigns a class to each pixel in the image, trying to assign the class that is statistically more similar among the ones defined in the vector layer. The numerical ID is used to identify the class in the resulting raster layer.

There's more...

There are other ways of performing a supervised classification in QGIS. One of them, which allows more control over the different elements in the process, is to use the **QGIS semi-automatic classification** plugin.

Other more sophisticated classification methods can be used from the **Processing Toolbox** menu. They can be found in the **Advanced** interface of the toolbox, under the **Orfeo Toolbox** group, as shown in the following screenshot:

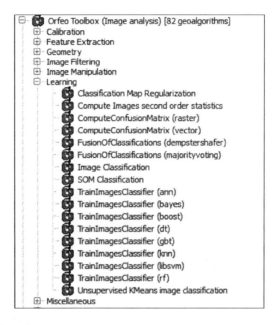

See also

▸   You can download and install this using the QGIS plugin manager. For more information about how to use the plugin, you can check its website at `http://fromgistors.blogspot.fr/p/semi-automatic-classification-plugin.html`.

9

QGIS and the Web

In this chapter we will cover the following recipes:

- ▶ Using web services
- ▶ Using WFS and WFS-T
- ▶ Searching CSW
- ▶ Using WMS and WMS Tiles
- ▶ Using WCS
- ▶ Using GDAL
- ▶ Serving web maps with the QGIS server
- ▶ Scale-dependent rendering
- ▶ Hooking up web clients
- ▶ Managing GeoServer from QGIS

Introduction

QGIS is a classic desktop **geographic information system** (**GIS**). However, these days only working with local data just isn't enough. You want to be able to freely use data from the web without spending days downloading this data. At the same time, you want to be able to put maps online for a much wider audience than a paper map or PDF. This is where web services come in. QGIS can be both a web service client and a web server, providing you with lots of options to use and share geographic data. This chapter covers the basics of using open web services for geographic data and a few methods to put your maps online.

Using web services

There are quite a few different types of web-based map service that can be loaded in QGIS. Each type of web service provides data; often, this is the same data in different ways. This recipe is about helping you figure out what type of web service you want to consume, and conversely what type of web service you may want to create for others to use.

Getting ready

This recipe is all about thinking, so you don't need anything in particular to start. It does help if you have a project in mind and some type of data you are interested in using or creating. Most, if not all, of these methods require an Internet connection or a local server, providing these services. Of course, if you have the data locally, you should probably just load it directly.

To help with the following section, here's a list of acronyms:

- **CSW**: This is **Catalog Service for the Web**
- **WFS**: This is **Web Feature Service**
- **WFS-T**: This is **Web Feature Service, Transactional**
- **WCS**: This is **Web Coverage Service**
- **WMS**: This is **Web Map Service**
- **WMTS**: This is **Web Map Tile Service**
- **TMS**: This is **Tile Map Service**
- **XYZ**: This is an "X Y Z" Service (there really isn't a formal name for this one because it's not an official standard)

How to do it...

1. Start by answering the following questions with regards to using data over web services:
   - Do you already know where to find the data that you want?
   - Do you need to edit or apply custom styling to this data?
   - Do you care if the data is vector or raster?
   - Do you need the data at its original resolution or quality?
   - Do you need data at specific resolutions or in a specific projection?

2. Use the following decision matrix to pick out which services are appropriate to your use case:

Criteria	CSW	WFS	WFS-T	WCS	WMS	Tiles (WMTS, XYZ, TMS)
Do you already know where to find the data you want?	No	Yes	Yes	Yes	Yes	Yes
Do you need to edit or apply custom styling to the data?		Yes	Yes	Yes	No	No
Do you care if the data is vector or raster?		Vector	Vector	Raster	Raster	Raster
Do you need the data at its original resolution or quality?		Yes	Yes	Yes	No	No
Do you need data at specific resolutions or in a specific projection?		Yes	Yes	Yes	Yes	No
Recipe number in this chapter.	3	2	2	5	4	4, 6

Now that you've found the appropriate recipe for the web service that you want to use, jump to this recipe later in this chapter. If you're still not sure, read on for more hints on how to pick the correct service. This recipe applies both to how you use web services and how to decide what web services to offer (if you put up a web service for other people to use).

Generally speaking, from left (WFS) to right (Tiles) the speed of the service increases. Tiles serve data the fastest to end users but with the most limitations.

How it works...

For each of the services, there is a QGIS tool (built-in or plugin). This tool stores your list of web servers and connection settings for each service. When you go to load a layer from a chosen server for a particular protocol an up-to-date list of layers is requested from the server (that is, the GetCapabilities XML). You then get to pick off this list the layers that you would like to add to the map canvas (and depending on service type, the projection, and the file type).

There's more...

Vector is generally slower, as more data needs to be transmitted as the data grows. Raster formats are a fixed number of pixels onscreen, so it's always approximately the same amount of data per screen load.

WMS, WMTS, WFS, and WCS are sometimes referred to as W*S as a collective group of related services that behave similarly.

Each situation will have additional considerations. For example, if you need a specific projection, you probably can't use a Tile service because these are usually only in very specific projections (Web/Spherical Mercator). Or perhaps, you want to print large paper maps. Then, you probably want WFS or WCS in order to get the full resolution possible over your entire region.

One of the most common mistakes is to think that you need vector data when you actually just need a background tile that incorporates vector data. A great example of this is road data. If you don't actually need to style, select, or individually manipulate road data, and then a Tile or WMS type layer will be much faster.

See also

▸   For more information, read the standards at the OGC website, `http://opengeospatial.org`

Using WFS and WFS-T

Web Feature Services (**WFS**) is an OGC standard method to access and, in some cases, edit (WFS-T) vector data over the Internet. When you need full attribute tables, local style control, or editing, WFS is the way to go. Like most other web services, the biggest advantage over a local layer is that you don't have to copy or load the whole layer at once.

 If you just need to view the layer, often WMS or a Tile service (described in other recipes within this chapter) are more efficient.

Getting ready

You need the URL of a WFS service to use and a working Internet connection. We will use the public Mapserver demo website (`http://demo.mapserver.org/`).

 To try WFS-T, which involves editing, you will need to get access to a service (typically, password protected) or make one yourself. Do you need a WFS-T test server? This is a great case where OSGeo-Live comes in handy, as you can run your own WFS-T server in a virtual machine at `http://live.osgeo.org`.

How to do it...

1. Find a WFS service that you want to use and copy the GetCapabilities URL. For this example, we will use the Mapserver demo website, `http://demo.mapserver.org/`.

> As with other web services, it's more efficient if you load your local layers and zoom to their extent first. This enables you to not waste time loading data from web services for extents outside your area of interest.

2. Open the add WFS dialog by clicking on the following icon:

3. Create a **New** connection.

4. Assign **Name** of your choosing and paste in the **URL** field for the WFS service, (`http://demo.mapserver.org/cgi-bin/wfs?SERVICE=WFS&VERSION=1.0.0&REQUEST=GetCapabilities`):

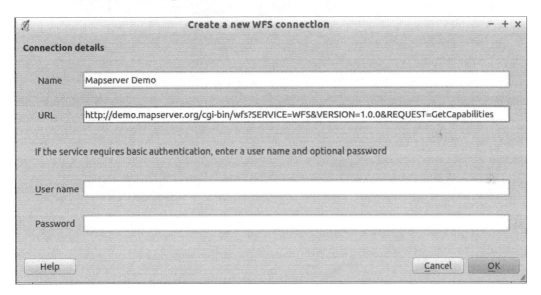

> On future usage of the same service, this will already be in your list of services, so you only have to add it once.

5. Save your edits by clicking on the **OK** button.

6. Now select the service from the drop-down menu.

7. Query for a list of layers by clicking on the **Connect** button.

8. Select the layer or layers that you want to add to the map; either `continents` or `cities` works for this example:

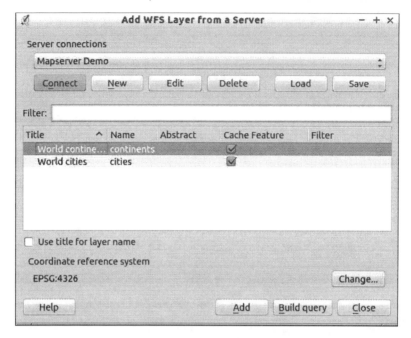

9. When your selection is complete, use the **Add** button to place the layer in the map.

10. Rearrange the render order of the map by dragging layers up and down in the list.

11. Pan and zoom to make fresh requests for WFS data to be loaded to the view.

 WFS layers can be restyled with standard layer properties. Also, the information tool and the attribute table will appear as other vector layers.

How it works...

For each web service, there is a main URL. When you browse to this URL and add the `GetCapabilities` parameter (QGIS does this for you), the returned result is an XML file, which describes the services that are offered by the server. The client, QGIS, parses the list of layers for you to choose from, and once you pick the layer(s), uses the additional information in the XML to look up the data at the specific URL.

Data requests are limited to the visible bounding box of the map canvas. This limits the amount of data that is requested. At least this is how it should work. However, features that go off screen will likely be included in their entirety to maintain geometry integrity. So, expect that loading large vector layers over WFS has the potential to be extremely slow.

There's more...

WFS-T services typically require passwords and are designed to work over the Internet. If you are working within a local network, you may consider just using PostGIS layers. Either way, it should also be noted that versioning and conflict resolution are not automatic, requiring the service backend to be configured to support such features.

Searching CSW

CSW is a catalog web service. Its main function is to provide discoverability of geographic data and link you to usable data either by download or by any other of the web services that are mentioned in this chapter.

Getting ready

This recipe uses the MetaSearch plugin. It requires the pycsw and owslib libraries installed in your system's Python. Refer to the *Adding plugins with Python dependencies* recipe of *Chapter 11, Extending QGIS,* for help on installing pycsw and owslib if you don't know how to do this.

How to do it...

1. Open the MetaSearch plugin by navigating to **Web | MetaSearch | MetaSearch**.

> If you don't see the **Web** menu, check the plugin manager and ensure that MetaSearch is enabled (checkmark).

2. Pick a service from the dropdown on the right: **UK Location Catalogue Publishing Service**.

> If you don't see any services in the drop-down list, click on the **Services** tab and use the **Add default services** button.

3. Type a search term in box on the left: Park.

4. (Optional) Set an extent to limit the search. In this case, use **Map Extent**.

> Global searches often return too many results, or they cause the connection to time out while waiting for all the results. As with other web services, it is advisable to load a reference layer and zoom to the area of interest first before trying to search them. The third tab, **Settings**, allows you to adjust the timeout. Increase this if you're getting too many timeout errors.

5. Click on the **Search** button and wait for the results:

    1. Double-click on any of the results to see additional details.

    2. If a selected result is available as a loadable layer, one or more of the service buttons at the bottom of the screen will be enabled. To understand more about how to use each of these choices, refer to the other recipes in this chapter on WMS, WFS, and WCS:

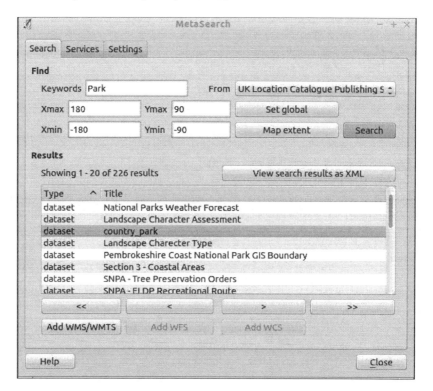

How it works...

MetaSearch queries websites that provide catalogs in the CSW standard, which is defined by the OGC. Once your request parameters are sent, the receiving website queries its online database for matches. If matches are found, metadata about the results is sent back to the client, in this case, QGIS.

CSW currently includes options to search by keyword and spatial extent. Future versions may enable setting time frames.

There's more...

If you pick opening an additional service that is based on the results, Metasearch will create a temporary service registration and open the correct service dialog. Unfortunately, at this time, you need to then scroll through the available layers to find the one that you want and actually add it to the map.

> Additional future CSW searches will ask if you want to override the existing connection. You must say yes. If you find yourself using the same W*S service, consider copying the GetCapabilities URL and making a new permanent entry in the correct service dialog.

You can add more catalogs to search on the **Services** tab within the plugin. You will need to find the CSW GetCapabilities URL on the website that you want to query. Most of the common geoportal-type websites now support CSW, including (but not limited to) Geonode, Geonetwork, and the ESRI Geoportal.

CSW is a relatively new standard when compared to some of the others, and it seems to be hard to find services that consistently work and actually offer WMS, WCS, or WFS of the layers in their catalog.

See also

▸ The *Adding plugins with Python dependencies* recipe of *Chapter 11, Extending QGIS*, for help on installing pycsw and owslib if you don't know how

Using WMS and WMS Tiles

Web Map Services (**WMS**), one of the first OGC web services created, provides a method for dynamic raster generation served over the Web. They are a compromise between the flexibility of WFS and the speed of Tile services.

Getting ready

There are several iterations of WMS, and QGIS supports most of them. To use a WMS, you need to give QGIS the GetCapabilities URL of the service that you want to view data from.

How to do it...

1. Find a WMS service that you want to use and copy the GetCapabilities URL. In this recipe, we can use the Geoserver demo website (`http://demo.opengeo.org/geoserver/web/`).

 As with other web services, it's more efficient if you load your local layers and zoom to their extent first. This enables you to not waste time loading data from web services for extents outside your area of interest.

2. Open the **Add WMS** dialog.

3. Create a **New** connection.

4. Assign a **Name** of your choosing and paste in the **URL** (`http://demo.opengeo.org/geoserver/ows?service=wms&version=1.3.0&request=GetCapabilities`):

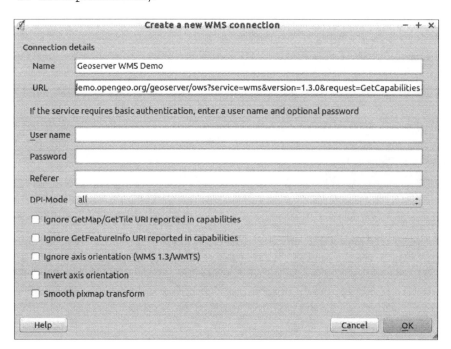

On future usage of the same service, this will already be in your list of services, so you only have to add it once.

5. Save your edits by clicking on **OK**.

6. Now select the service from the drop-down list.

7. Query for a list of layers using the **Connect** button.

8. Select the layer or layers that you want to add to the map:

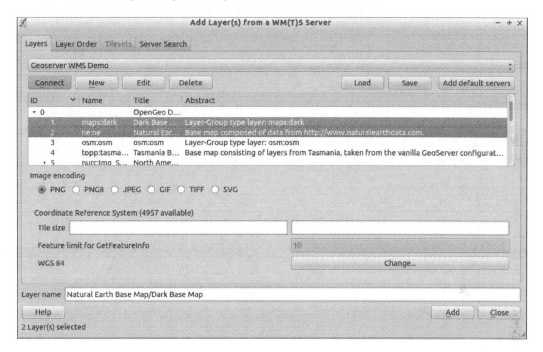

 You can select one or more layers. If you select multiple layers, they will be merged and only appear as a single layer in the QGIS Layers list. The **Layer Order** tab lets you arrange the WMS layers within the combined layer. This is important when one of the layers is opaque and has 100% continuous data, allowing you to put other data on top of it visually.

9. There are several other options, including image type and projection:

   ❑ For an image type, PNG is a good default as it supports lossless compression and transparency. If you don't need transparency and are okay with a little data loss, JPG can be used for smaller files, so they are faster to load.

       □   When picking projection, if you can use the original projection of the data (if you know it), you will get the least resampling. Otherwise, pick something that matches the other data that you plan to use in conjunction with the WMS.

 Not all image types and projections are available; this depends on what the server offers. If one image type doesn't seem to work, try a different one before reporting a bad server.

10. When your selection is complete, use the **Add** button to place the layer in the map.

11. Rearrange the render order of the map by dragging layers up and down in the list.

12. Pan and zoom to make fresh requests for WMS data to be loaded to the view.

How it works...

When you pan and zoom the map, a request with the bounding box of the viewable extent and scale is sent to the service. The server then renders an image that matches the request and passes it back to the client (in this case, QGIS).

There's more...

Some WMS services now also support tiling under the **Web Map Tiling Service** (**WMTS**) protocol. From the client's perspective, this not really different from WMS in usage. On the server side, after each request the results are cached so that if the same extent and scale is requested, the cached version can be delivered instead of creating the results from scratch. For you, the end user, this should result in faster loading if a service provides WMTS.

When configuring a WMTS, use the WMTS URL instead of the WMS URL. One example would be the Geoserver demo site's WMTS:

```
http://demo.opengeo.org/geoserver/gwc/service/
wmts?REQUEST=GetCapabilities
```

Once successful, this will take you to the **Tilesets** tab, where you can pick which layer and projection of the available options you want to load. As the Tiles are premade or cached, you will usually not have the option to combine multiple layers at once and will need to load them one at a time:

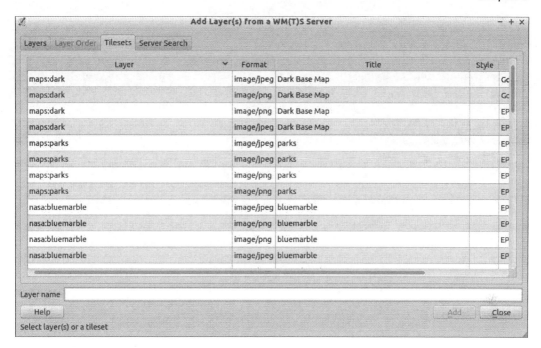

 WMS-C is an earlier version of the WMTS standard. In usage, it's pretty much the same, though the URL pattern may look more similar to the WMS.

See also

▶ See the QGIS documentation for more information about the WMS capabilities of QGIS at `http://docs.qgis.org/2.8/en/docs/user_manual/working_with_ogc/ogc_client_support.html#ogc-wms`

Using WCS

A **Web Coverage Service** (**WCS**) differs greatly in use case from the other services, but it behaves very similarly. The goal of WCS is to allow users to extract a region of interest from a large raster data that is hosted remotely. Unlike a WMS or Tiled set, WCS is a clip of the original data in full resolution and usually in the original projection. This format is ideal if you need the raster data for analysis purposes and not just visualization.

Getting ready

For this recipe, you need a WCS to connect to. Check with your data providers to see whether they offer WCS. For this recipe, we can use the OpenGeo Geoserver Demo site at `http://demo.opengeo.org/geoserver/web/`.

How to do it...

1. Open a web browser and go to `http://demo.opengeo.org/geoserver/web/`.

2. On the right-hand side, you'll see a list of web services that are available; right-click on **WCS 1.1.1** and copy the link.

3. In QGIS, open the WCS dialog.

4. Select **New** to create a new server entry.

5. In the boxes, perform the following:

    1. Provide a name so that you remember which service this is.

    2. Paste the URL that you copied earlier in the URL box (`http://demo.opengeo.org/geoserver/ows?service=wcs&version=1.1.1&request=GetCapabilities`):

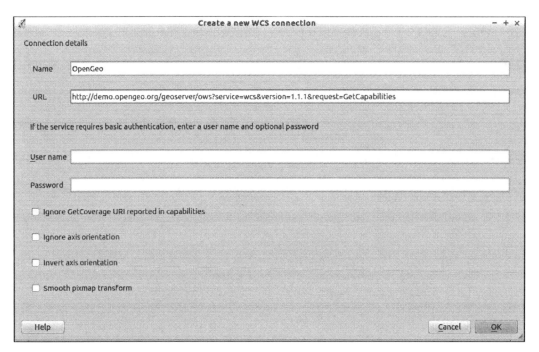

6. Click on the **OK** button.

7. Now, you'll be back on the **Add Layer(s) from a WCS Server** dialog:

    1. Click on the **Connect** button.

    2. After the list is populated, select a layer to add to the map. Click on the **Add** button. Try the Blue Marble layer.

    3. Now, click on the **Close** button to return to your map:

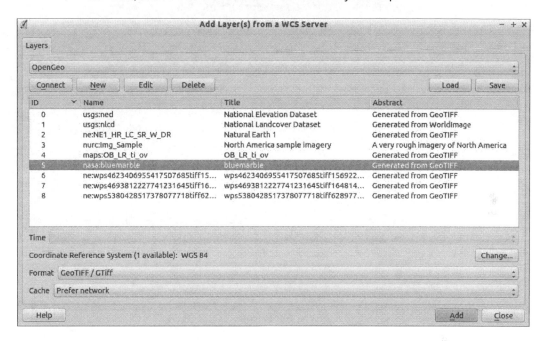

8. You should now see the Blue Marble layer loaded.

> If you zoom in to the level of a US State or a European country, you will see the image start to pixelate. Blue Marble is a low resolution image put together by NASA that roughly shows what the whole world looks like from space, cloud free. It is meant as a general view of the whole world and does not contain fine details.

9. (Optional) Use the **Save As** option to download a portion or the entire WCS layer at its full original resolution.

How it works...

WCS, like other web services, sends a bounding box request to the server, which in turn delivers the raster data to QGIS. Unlike WMS, no rendering is done on the server side, the raw original raster data is sent. This could mean the following:

▶ There was no resampling of the image before it was sent

▶ You can apply your own styling to the data that is delivered

Keep in mind that requesting the full extent of a high resolution raster will result in a large amount of data transfer. This is unlike Tiles or WMS, which at most return the exact number of pixels in the viewable area at the resolution that is requested.

As with other web services, it is recommended that you zoom in to your area of interest before loading a WCS.

There's more...

Another bonus of WCS over WMS is that because WCS delivers the original data, it is not limited to a 3-band RGB image. You can use WCS to view and download Multi or Hyperspectral data (4+ bands common in remote-sensing applications).

Currently, QGIS only supports 1.0.x and 1.1.x, not WCS 2.x; at least not yet!

Using GDAL

The QuickMapsServices and OpenLayers plugins, as described in the *Loading BaseMaps with the QuickMapServices plugin* and *Loading BaseMaps with the OpenLayers plugin* recipes in *Chapter 4, Data Exploration*, are awesome as they put a reference layer in your map session. The one downside, however, is that it is a hassle to add new layers. So, if you come across or build your own Tile service and want to use it in QGIS, this recipe will let you use almost any Tile service.

Getting ready

You will need a web browser, text editor, and the URL of a web-based XYZ (sometimes called TMS) service—one that allows you to make requests without an API key. We're going to use the maps at http://www.opencyclemap.org/.

Viewing the JavaScript source (a good tool for this is **Firebug**, or other web-developer tools for the browser), we can view the source URLs for the tiles.

How to do it...

1. Open `http://www.opencyclemap.org/` in a web browser.

2. Now, figure out the URL for the tiles by looking at the source code:

   1. Look in `map.js` and you'll see the layer definition:

      ```
      var cycle = new OpenLayers.Layer.OSM("OpenCycleMap",
        ["https://a.tile.thunderforest.com/cycle/${z}/${x}/${y}.
        png",
        "https://b.tile.thunderforest.com/cycle/${z}/${x}/${y}.
        png",
        "https://c.tile.thunderforest.com/cycle/${z}/${x}/${y}.
        png"],
        { displayOutsideMaxExtent: true,
          attribution: cycleattrib, transitionEffect: 'resize'}
      );
      ```

   2. Or, you can look at the image files your browser downloads. If you put `https://a.tile.thunderforest.com/cycle/13/1325/3143.png` into a browser, it will load that one tile.

3. The pattern is pretty straight forward:

   ```
   <server name>/<layer>/<zoom>/<tile index X>/<tile index
   X>.<image format>
   ```

   > In this particular case, the Tile Index pattern is the TMS style; refer to `http://www.maptiler.org/google-maps-coordinates-tile-bounds-projection/`.

4. To turn this into a layer in QGIS, open up a text editor and paste in the following definition. This definition tells GDAL which driver to use and the server URL pattern with z, x, and y as variables. Save the file as `opencyclemap.xml`:

   ```
   <GDAL_WMS>
     <Service name="TMS">
       <ServerUrl>http://c.tile.thunderforest.com/cycle/${z}/${x}/
         ${y}.png</ServerUrl>
     </Service>
     <DataWindow>
       <UpperLeftX>-20037508.34</UpperLeftX>
       <UpperLeftY>20037508.34</UpperLeftY>
       <LowerRightX>20037508.34</LowerRightX>
       <LowerRightY>-20037508.34</LowerRightY>
       <TileLevel>18</TileLevel>
       <TileCountX>1</TileCountX>
   ```

```
      <TileCountY>1</TileCountY>
      <YOrigin>top</YOrigin>
    </DataWindow>
    <Projection>EPSG:3785</Projection>
    <BlockSizeX>256</BlockSizeX>
    <BlockSizeY>256</BlockSizeY>
    <BandsCount>3</BandsCount>
    <Cache />
  </GDAL_WMS>
```

5. You can now load the layer using the Raster dialog or the browser:

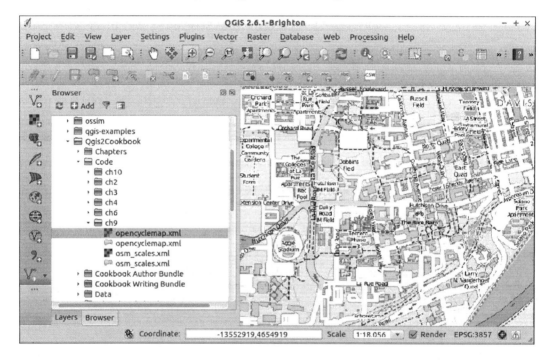

Note that there are two listings for `opencyclemap.xml`; only the one with the square-shaped icon will work (that is, a raster), as tiles are a raster format.

How it works...

The XML file defines the parameters of the service; however, because XYZ-style servers don't follow a standard, the URL pattern varies slightly for each server and the servers do not have a GetCapabilities function that describes available layers. By telling GDAL how to handle the URL, you are wrapping a nonstandard format into a typical GDAL layer, which QGIS can easily be loaded as a raster.

There's more...

One additional tip when using Spherical Mercator (EPSG:3785) is that you can set a custom list of scales (**Zoom Levels**) in QGIS. The following set of scales can be loaded per QGIS project, and will change the dropdown at the bottom right. These scales match the scales that most servers will provide, so you get the best viewing experience:

1. Go to **File** | **Project Properties**.
2. Select the **General** tab.
3. Check the **Project Scales** checkbox.
4. Load the `scales.xml` file that is provided:

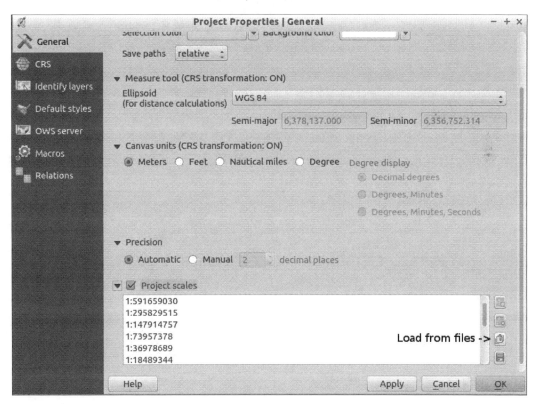

This technique is not limited to just tile services. Many other formats that GDAL works with can be wrapped for easier usage in QGIS. This is a similar method to **Virtual Raster Tables** (**VRT**) layers mentioned in the *Creating raster overviews (pyramids)* recipe in *Chapter 2, Data Management*.

Lastly, you may ask why a new plugin using this method doesn't replace the OpenLayers plugin. Such an idea has been under discussion for a while; the key sticking point is that accessing some layers, such as Google, Bing, and so on, with this method may violate the Terms of Service as they do not keep the Copyright, Trademark, and Logo in the correct place. Also, caching and printing such layers may not be legal. In general, avoid using proprietary data when possible to reduce licensing issues.

See also

▸   This recipe and method has actually been known and discussed in many QGIS venues. The most frequently cited example is available at `http://www.3liz.com/blog/rldhont/index.php?post/2012/07/17/OpenStreetMap-Tiles-in-QGIS`.

▸   The full explanation of options for GDAL can be found at `http://www.gdal.org/frmt_wms.html`.

Serving web maps with the QGIS server

QGIS and the Web is not all about consuming data, it can also be used to serve data over the Web for others to view online or consume in other web clients (such as QGIS). Keep in mind that setting up your own web service is not the easiest way to make a web map (refer to the *Hooking up web clients* recipe in this chapter). This is, however, a great way to transition all the hard work that you've put into a QGIS project file into something other people can see and use.

Getting ready

For this recipe, you need a working installation of the QGIS server. This involves running a standard web server (such as Apache or Nginx). There are many ways to set up the server, so please see the official documentation at `http://hub.qgis.org/projects/quantum-gis/wiki/QGIS_Server_Tutorial`.

Once you have the QGIS server running, then you just need a QGIS project with the configuration outlined in this recipe.

How to do it...

1. Open QGIS.

2. Load up and style some layers:

   ❑ You need at least one vector layer to offer a WFS.

   ❑ You need at least one raster layer to offer a WCS.

   ❑ WMS can be any combination of layers, you can choose to server each as an independent layer or as a combined layer.

3. Edit the **Project** properties in **File | Project Properties**:

   1. Open the **OWS server** tab.

   2. Check the **Service Capabilities** box to enable GetCapabilities.

   3. Fill out some of the boxes so that end users know what your server is about, who runs it, and how to contact you:

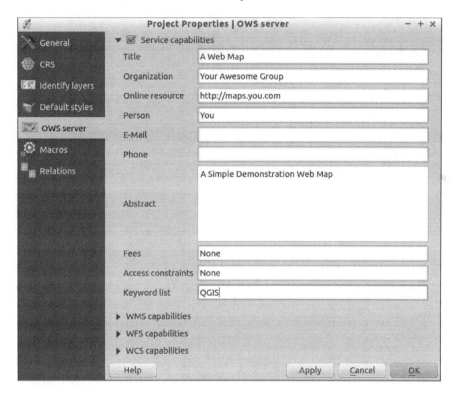

4. Now examine the **WMS capabilities** section:

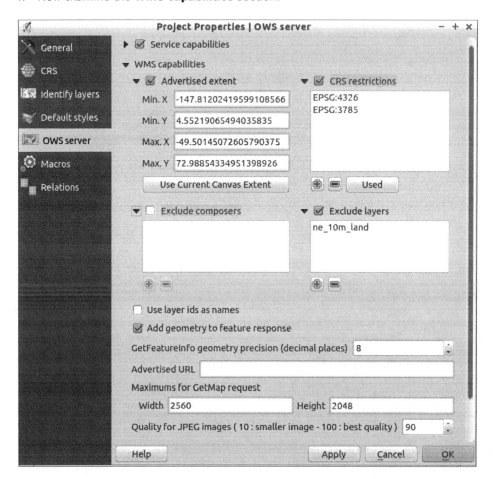

 Most of these features are optional optimizations. Pick and choose what suits your needs.

5. Here, you can set the maximum extent that clients should expect.

6. The **CRS restrictions** option lets you limit what projections are allowed.

7. **Exclude Layers** allows you to have layers in your project that don't show up on the web.

8. **Add geometry to feature response** is an optional enhancement if you are building a web map and you want to be able to work with the actual vectors (if it is a vector to begin with).

9. **GetFeatureInfo** precision is about how close a user has to click to query a location. If you have a lot of data, you probably want this number to be small; but if you have only a few features, making this bigger makes it easier for end users.

10. Set **Maximums for GetMap request** if you want to reduce the load on your server by limiting how much data a user can request at once. This is a good idea for a public server. 2560 x 2048, as shown in the screenshot, is enough pixels for an HD-resolution screen to be filled in a single request.

11. Next, take a look at the **WFS capabilities** section:

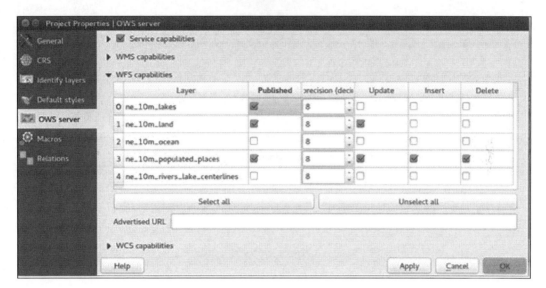

 Only enable WFS if you want users to be able to request vector data as vectors. This can be more intensive than WMS on your bandwidth. Also, do not enable WFS-T features unless you secure your server to only permitted users.

1. Check the **Published** box next to any vector layers that you want to be usable over WFS.

2. To enable WFS-T, check the **Update, Insert**, and **Delete** checkboxes. As they are separate, you can choose to only allow new data (**Insert**), only allow edits to existing data (**Update**), or only allow removal of data (**Delete**). **Insert** would be the safest option as it prevents editing or deletion of existing data.

12. Finally, take a look at **WCS capabilities**:

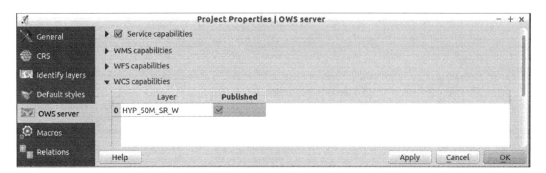

 This an all or none feature. Don't enable this unless you want users to be able to download the original raster data.

13. When you are done setting options, click on the **OK** button.

14. Now, save the project in a place where the QGIS server has access to it.

 In Apache, this is usually a folder such as /var/www/.

15. Once saved, you can test access from any OGC-compliant web client:

    1. For a simple test, use a fresh QGIS project and the **Add WMS** dialog.

    2. The GetCapabilties URL will look something like http://localhost/cgi-bin/qgis_mapserv.fcgi?map=/usr/local/share/qgis/QGIS-NaturalEarth-Example.qgs.

 The key part of this URL that is somewhat unique to QGIS server is the map parameter, which is followed by the full system path to the QGIS project file.

This may seem odd, but adding your QGIS server as a WMS in QGIS is a great way to test whether it's working.

How it works...

The QGIS server is a middleman that takes in web service requests and translates them into QGIS internal calls, returning the requested data or rendered images, which are delivered to the end user via the web server.

There's more...

The QGIS server contains many options that allow you to control which types of service to offer, which layers to offer over each service, and how to style these services. Alternatives to the QGIS server include MapServer and GeoServer (refer to the *Managing GeoServer from QGIS* section in this chapter).

See also

▶ For more details, refer to the main documentation for the QGIS server at http://hub.qgis.org/projects/quantum-gis/wiki/QGIS_Server_Tutorial.

▶ Once you create a service, test it by adding your service to a QGIS project. Refer to the previous recipes in this chapter for how to add WMS, WFS, or WCS services.

Scale-dependent rendering

While they are not specifically for web services, being able to change the styling and presence of data based on the scale of the map can have a huge impact on the speed and readability of web services. Unlike printed maps, web maps are viewed at multiple scales. This variation in scales often requires different cartography to keep the map legible and usable.

Getting ready

You'll need a QGIS project, preferably one with a high data density or differing levels of information. A good example is road data, where you have major, minor, local, and other variants of road classification. caryStreets.shp converted from CAD in a previous chapter is a good example.

How to do it...

1. Open QGIS and load caryStreets.shp.

2. Now, open the attribute table and look for an attribute to filter in. In caryStreets.shp, there are several potential columns to use, such as StreetType, Major_Road, and Main_Road.

 StreetType appears to be classes, whereas the other two columns appear to be True or False flags. Any of these are decent candidates for filtering rules.

3. Now, open the **Properties** section for the layer:

    1. Switch to the **Style** tab to edit the symbology.

    2. Change the top-right dropdown to **Rule Based Rendering**.

    3. Create a new rule (green plus sign).

4. In the pop up dialog set **Label** to **Major Roads** and **Filter** to **"Major_Road" = 't'**.

5. (Optional) You can use the expression builder to build the filter statement and test it. Click on the **...** button to open the dialog.

 You could create two copies of Major with different scale ranges so that as you zoom in, the major roads become thicker at the same time that minor roads are enabled.

This is what your layer looks like before and after you create the first rule:

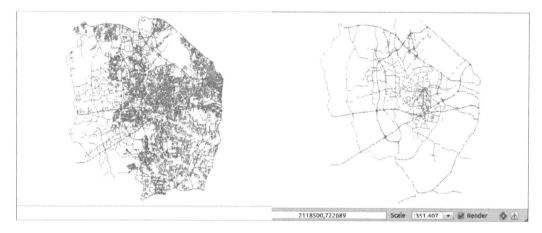

6. Now, add another rule for minor roads by filtering for **"Major_Road" = 'f'**.

7. This time, you're going to enable the **Scale range** option.

8. Set **Minimum (exclusive)** to **1:100,000**. For any scale bigger than this, the features will be hidden. For **Maximum (inclusive)**, type in **1:0**, which will disable the **Max filter**.

9. Pick a different line type and/or color for the minor roads:

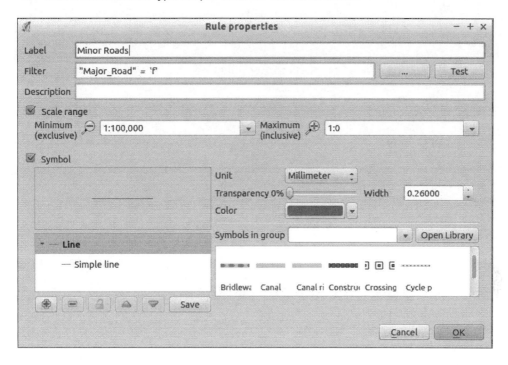

10. You should now have two rules, one for major roads and one for minor roads:

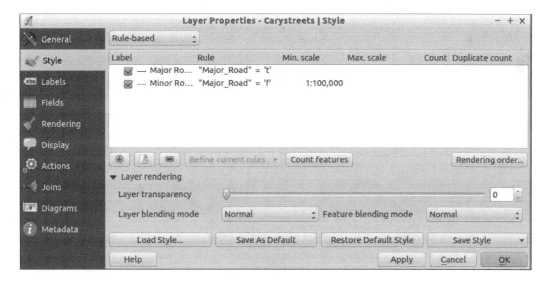

You don't have to open the **edit rule** dialog; you can directly modify parts of the rules in the **Rule Based Rendering** page.

11. Go back to the map and zoom in to **1:50,000**, then zoom out to **1:250,000**. The minor roads should appear and disappear as you change past the **1:100,000** scale:

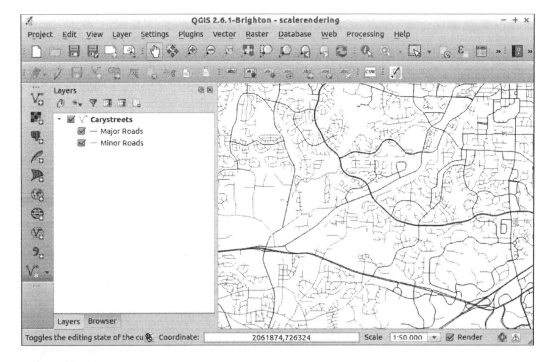

How it works...

The goal with scale-dependent rendering is generally to make your map readable at many different zoom levels. By setting the **Min** and **Max** scales for each layer or subfeatures within a layer, you can declutter a map for readability. The rendering engine just checks the scale against each rule before deciding what to render.

There's more...

Scale-dependent rendering can be used in several ways. This can be used to change the styling based on zoom or hide or reveal data based on the zoom level. However, it's also not limited to just changing styles or layers. You can also perform scale-dependent labeling, which is part of data-driven labeling described in the *Configuring data-defined labels* recipe in *Chapter 10, Cartography Tips*, of this book.

Scale rules also work on raster layers; however, this only allows you to turn a raster on and off. It doesn't allow you to change its appearance.

If you have a QGIS server set up from earlier in this chapter, the scaling rules should apply to your web services (WMS and WFS).

 You probably don't want to use something as complex as a street layer via WFS in a web browser because it's almost guaranteed to crash. Stick to pushing such complex layers as Tiles or WMS.

See also

The Rule Based Rendering has a lot of features crammed into it. However, this is not yet a comprehensive guide to everything that it can do, so you'll need to explore and perform Internet searches for now.

Hooking up web clients

Sometimes, the best way to share a map is to build a website with a map embedded in it. There are many methods to accomplish this goal, ranging from a simple dump of a few layers to a highly-interactive map, which is based on web services. There are many web clients that will work with standard OGC services. This recipe will show you how to build a simple web map using Leaflet—a popular JavaScript library that is used to create web maps.

Getting ready

You will need the qgis2leaf plugin and some sample data. The `schools_wake.shp` (Points) and `census_wake_2000.shp` files make for a good example.

How to do it...

1. Install and enable the qgis2leaf plugin.

 Make sure to check out the qgis2web plugin, which is a newer variant that works similarly but has some different options.

2. Load up some layers to make a map composition.

 Make a copy of your layer and eliminate unnecessary columns that you don't need to show on the web map. Reducing the size of the attribute table will make it easier to read popups with information and speed up web page loading.

3. Style the map as you want it to appear online.

 Styling can be really tricky. Leaflet and other web map libraries don't support 100% of the same options as QGIS. Try making a few maps, changing settings, and re-exporting these maps a few times to figure out how to get it the way that you want. It may not look good in QGIS but look good in the export.

4. (Optional) Configure labels. In this example, label the School names.

 Only black labels are currently supported. Though you can probably customize the CSS and JavaScript (js) after the export if you need labels in a different style.

5. Open the qgis2leaf plugin from its icon on the toolbar or from the **Web** menu:

    1. Click on the **GetLayers** button to add the layers from your map to the export list.

    2. There are lots of options here, and they are optional. Go ahead and check **Create Legend**. If you made labels, also check **Export Labels and labels on hover**.

 Create Cluster is a fantastic option if you have a lot of points on the map. This will group points into a circle with a number indicating how many points are near there. As you zoom in, they will split apart into smaller groups, until at some zoom, all the points are in their original spot.

    3. For the frame size, you can pick a size of the page that you want the map to take up (in pixels). However, fullscreen works well if the map is the only thing that you care about.

    4. Go ahead and add a tile-based base layer; **Stamen Terrain** is an interesting choice. Keep in mind that you can only have one of these on at a time, but you can toggle between them.

5. Pick an output folder location and fill in the remaining map information describing how you want it to show up in the results.

6. Export the project:

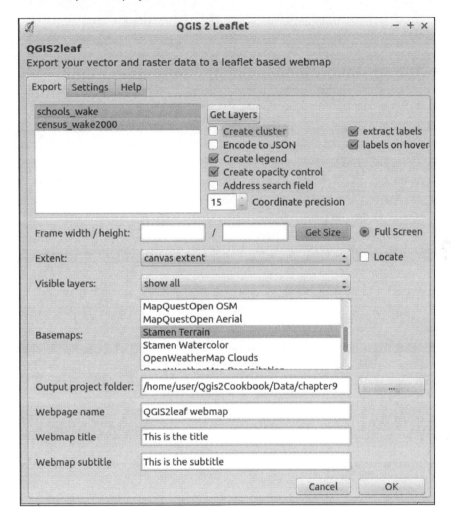

6. After exporting, the map should open in your web browser. If it doesn't, open your operating system file explorer (or web browser) and navigate to the output folder. You should see a new folder called export_year_month_day_hour_minute_ seconds (for example, export_2015_02_19_11_34_05). Inside this folder is index.html. Open this file with a web browser to see your map:

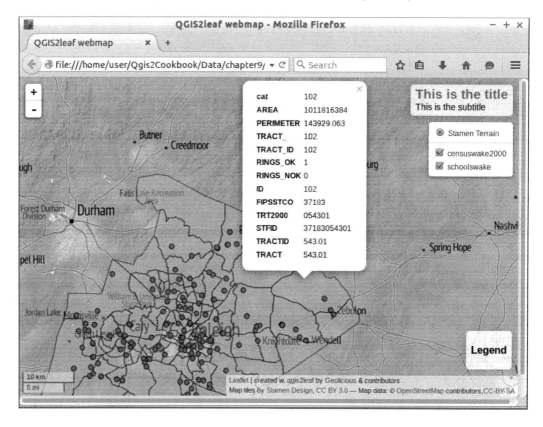

7. Note that all the vectors are clickable, and the popup will display the attribute table information. If you turned on labels and hover, then hovering over a point will display the name.

How it works...

The qgis2leaf plugin converts your map into something that is compatible with the web. Generally, this means converting vector data to the GeoJSON format and generating an HTML page (web page) with some JavaScript to create and populate the map.

Raster layers are trickier, and if you can, try to stick to using Tile or WMS services to serve them. Refer to the next section to see how to use Tiles or WMS.

 If you need host tiles locally, try using the QTiles plugin to generate them.

There's more...

The next logical step is to make the map dynamic based on a web service. To do this, you can swap static files for web services:

1. Add a WMS layer to the map (you can use the previous recipe in this chapter on QGIS server if you have it running). Add an external source WMS, such as the USGS NAIP Airphoto. (Here's the GetCapabilities URL, `http://isse.cr.usgs.gov/arcgis/services/Orthoimagery/USGS_EROS_Ortho_NAIP/ImageServer/WMSServer?request=GetCapabilities&service=WMS`).

2. Re-export with the same settings:

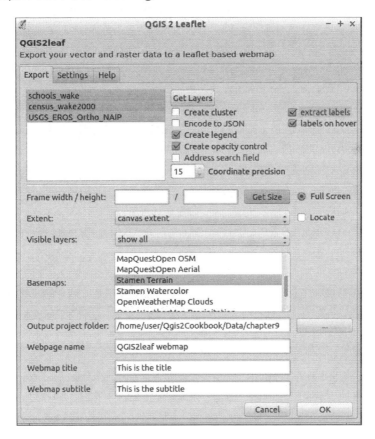

Now that you've created the Leaflet map, if you wanted to get into JavaScript programming, all of the code that you need is in the directory produced, either directly in `index.html` or in the `js` folder. In particular, you can see exactly how layers are styled and added to the map.

You don't have to use Tiles or WMS for raster layers but this is recommended. If you do want to use a local file, be warned there is a bug currently where some exports fail unless your raster is converted to a `.jpg` format image in EPSG:4326 projection.

See also

▶ Don't forget to look at the documentation for the Leaflet JavaScript library on how to customize your results after the export at `http://leafletjs.com/`.

▶ As mentioned before, qgis2Leaf is only one of many possible ways to create a web map. Export to OpenLayers 3 (`https://plugins.qgis.org/plugins/ol3/`) is very similar but uses the OpenLayers JavaScript library. Lizmap (`http://www.3liz.com/en/lizmap.html`) and QGIS Web Client (`https://github.com/qgis/QGIS-Web-Client`) are two more popular options that add more elaborate prebuilt interfaces but require a little more setup.

Managing GeoServer from QGIS

QGIS does not only serve as a frontend for the QGIS server, but it can also serve as a frontend for other similar servers. GeoServer is one of the most popular ones, and you can configure it from QGIS, upload layers, or even edit the style of a GeoServer layer using the QGIS symbology tools.

Getting ready

For this recipe, you will need the GeoServer Explorer plugin. This can be installed using Plugin Manager.

You will also need a running instance of GeoServer. We will assume that you have a local one running on port 8080, but you can replace the corresponding URL with the one of the GeoServer instance that you have available, whether local or remote.

How to do it...

1. Open the **GeoServer Explorer** by navigating to **Web | GeoServer | Geoserver Explorer**. The explorer will appear on the right-hand side of the QGIS window.

2. Click on the **GeoServer Catalogs** item in the explorer tree, and then select the **New catalog** button.

3. Complete the fields in the dialog that will appear to define a new catalog and click on **OK**:

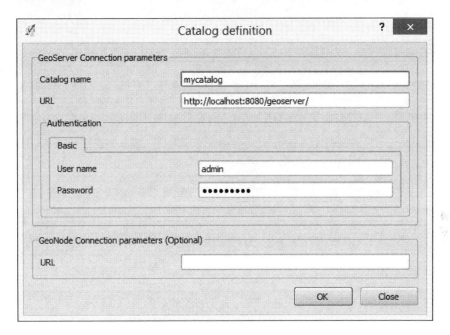

4. The new catalog will be added to the explorer tree, and you can now browse its content.

5. Open the `zipcodes_wake.shp` layer and style it.

6. In the QGIS Layer List, drag the entry corresponding to the `zipcode_wake.shp` layer and drop it on the catalog item in the GeoServer Explorer. The layer will be uploaded and added to the default workspace of the catalog.

7. You can check whether the layer is now in the catalog by opening a web browser and going to the GeoServer web interface at `http://localhost:8080/geoserver/web/`.

How it works...

The GeoServer Suite plugin communicates with GeoServer using its REST API. By linking QGIS with the GeoServer REST API, it allows you to easily configure many elements that, otherwise, should be configured manually, such as the styling of layers.

There's more...

The Geoserver Explorer plugin has a lot of features to work with GeoServer. Here are some additional ideas so that you can explore them. For more information, check out the plugin help at `http://boundlessgeo.github.io/qgis-geoserver-plugin/`.

Editing a remote style

Once the layer is in the GeoServer catalog, you can edit its style without having to upload the layer again. Just open the **Styles** branch in the explorer tree under the corresponding catalog and double-click on the style to edit, or select the **Edit...** item in the context menu that is shown when right-clicking on the element:

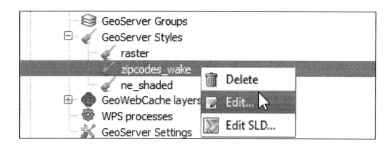

The QGIS symbology dialog will be opened, and you can edit the style in there. Once you close the dialog, the style will be uploaded and updated in the catalog.

Support for multiple formats

The GeoServer REST API only supports shapefiles for vector layers, but you can drag and drop any layer in any format that is supported by QGIS. This plugin will take care of converting it before uploading, in case this is needed.

See also

Don't have a Geoserver instance, it's pretty easy to setup for testing. See `http://geoserver.org/` for details.

10
Cartography Tips

In this chapter, we will cover the following recipes:

- ▶ Using Rule Based Rendering
- ▶ Handling transparencies
- ▶ Understanding the feature and layer blending modes
- ▶ Saving and loading styles
- ▶ Configuring data-defined labels
- ▶ Creating custom SVG graphics
- ▶ Making pretty graticules in any projection
- ▶ Making useful graticules in printed maps
- ▶ Creating a map series using Atlas

Introduction

Cartography has changed quite a bit in the past decade as more people transition to purely electronic map products on a device or on the Web. While some types of visualizations are better suited to different media, many of the underlying tools and techniques can actually be applied across the board. This chapter covers a variety of tools that enable you, the QGIS user, to maximize the readability and beauty of your maps.

Using Rule Based Rendering

In the past, if you wanted to apply a wildly different style to more than one type of data in the same source, the only way to do this was to duplicate or subset a layer. With Rule Based Rendering, you now just have to create rules that are applied on-the-fly. This opens a huge door on cartographic possibilities with different features in the same layer not only having different colors but also different fill types, transparency, line type, and all manner of other customizations. Extending from categorized symbology, rules also allow for mixing and inheritance, allowing for intermediate categories or some shared properties and reducing the amount of work to create elegant symbology.

Getting ready

Rule Based Rendering is built-in to vector symbology. So, you'll need a good complicated vector layer to fully utilize its potential. A road layer is often a good use case, but for this example we'll go slightly simpler with `busroutesall.shp`.

How to do it...

1. Load the `busroutesall.shp` layer.
2. Right-click on the layer name in the **Layers** window, select **Properties**, then pick **Style** on the left-hand side of the new window.
3. Change the symbology drop-down type to **Rule-Based**.
4. Pick the attributes that you want to use to differentiate between groups of features:
    1. In this case, let's edit the initial rule (double-click on the rule or the **Edit** icon between **+** (add) and **-** (remove).
    2. Rules can be based on attribute table values or geometry properties, including on-the-fly calculated values. First let's style routes shorter than 2,000 map units apply here. In the **Filter** box type `$length < 2000` (Do you want to see all the options? Then, open the filter tool with the **...** button). Name your rule and click on **OK**. Back in the main **Style** dialog, apply the rule to see the results in Canvas. Make sure to use the **Test** button to verify that your rule works:

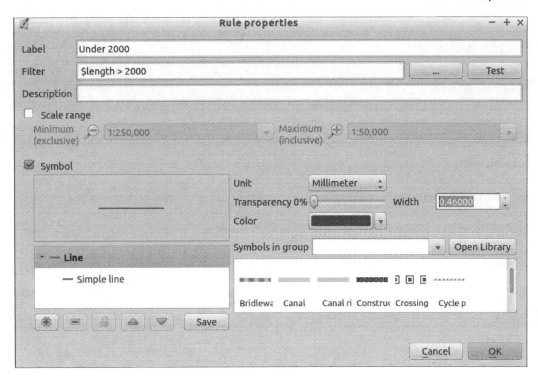

 You can apply more than one rule to objects, the rendering being a combination of the rules and the rendering order.

5. Now to make it more interesting, let's add another rule that's the inverse:

   1. Add a new rule with the green **+** button below the rule list.

   2. For the filter, use `$length > 2000` (don't forget to test this).

   3. Pick some other symbology that differs quite a bit so that it's easy to tell them apart (such as a different line type). Click on **OK** and then click on **Apply** to see to the two rules in action.

6. Now, things get really interesting. Let's add a subrule by either right-clicking on a rule or by highlighting a rule and clicking on the **Refine current rules** dropdown:

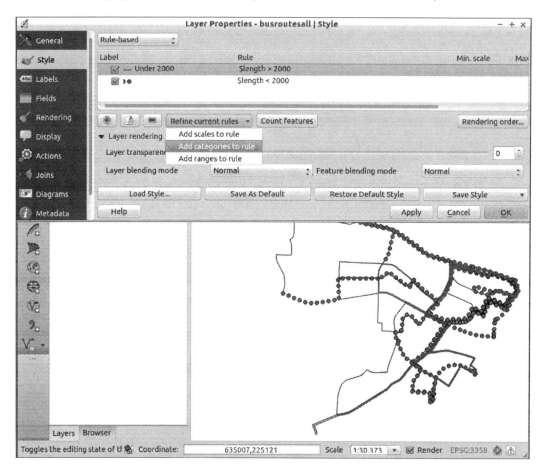

7. Select **Add categories to rule**:

    1. In the subdialog, select **Route**.

    2. Pick a color ramp and/or line style, click on **Classify**, and then click on **OK**:

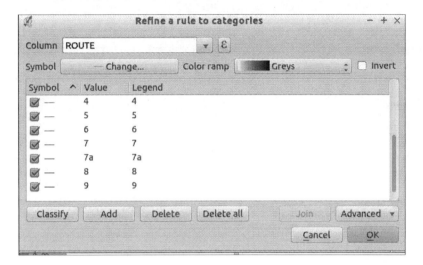

    3. Before you click on **Apply**, edit the main rule and uncheck the **Symbol** box (otherwise, the **Rule** and **Sub Rules** list will be additive, which can be useful in some cases).

8. Now, when you look at the **Rule** list, you will see subrules under their parents.

9. Finally, let's add a third top-level rule that is not based on the length:

1. Make a rule filter on the ROUTE name that contains a. The rule will look like: `"Route" LIKE '%a'`.

2. Pick a line symbol that will make these routes stick out even with their current coloring and click on **Apply**:

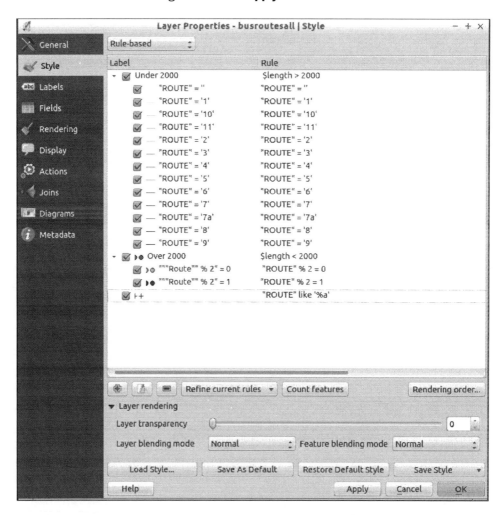

10. Play around some more; there are all sorts of things you can do, from partial string matching to splitting by even or odd numbers (`"ROUTE" % 2 = 0` is even-numbered).

11. Finally, the map looks like the following:

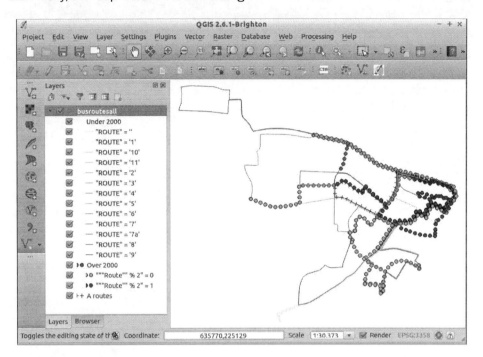

How it works...

Each rule is processed in the rendering order specified from top to bottom, the last rule being drawn last and, therefore, on top. The rules are added to any existing style that is already applied to feature. You can change the rendering order by changing the rule order or by applying a render order. The filters work just like attribute filters in the field calculator or the table search. All of the symbology options are available to vectors and can be applied to one or many rules. You can group rules by scale-rendering rules too.

There's more...

There are way too many possible ways to use Rule Based Rendering than can be described here. You can create rendering groups that inherit rules from their parent and apply their own. Each feature given a unique ID could have a completely different look. The big improvement over using traditional single symbol, categorized, or graduated symbology is that you don't have to edit every possible group, and you can more easily stack rules, mixing and matching all the original methods.

There are some catches. Not everything you do with Rule Based Rendering is possible with web services; so, before you go too crazy, consider your output format and test your ideas before spending too much time on this.

Handling transparencies

Transparency is a lack of pigment or color, such that you can see through one feature to the feature beneath. You can think of this as being similar to tinted or stained glass; some light is allowed to pass through and reflect off what's inside. When used right, transparency can help emphasize or de-emphasize features in a map composition. It can also be used to blend two layers to look as if they are one layer.

Getting ready

This recipe demonstrates transparency for both vectors and rasters, so we'll need an example of each. The `lakes.shp` and `elevlid_D782_6.tif` layers will work well for demonstration purposes. Load both of these layers in a fresh project, putting `lake.shp` on top.

How to do it...

1. With a vector layer loaded, open **Properties** and the **Style** tab.

2. On the right-hand side of the dialog, you will see a **Transparency** slider at 0% (this means 100% solid or opaque).

3. Adjust the slider to the right and apply the changes to see them in the map:

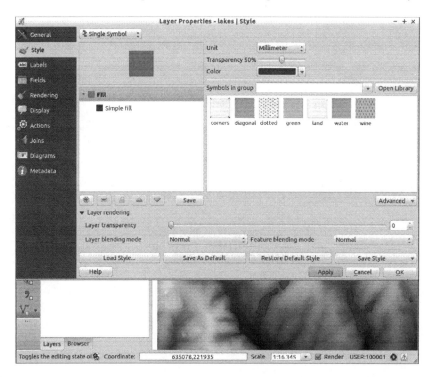

Using a bold or dark color will make it easier to notice the change. You will also notice that the **Simple fill** option shows the original color.

4. Now to demonstrate this on a raster, first reset the lakes back to 0%.

5. Swap the order in the Layers list so that `elevlid` is on top.

6. Now, open **Properties** of `elevid` and the **Transparency** tab.

7. The **Global transparency** option will change the value evenly for the whole raster. Set it to 50% and apply it. You should now be able to see the lakes layer, which was hidden below:

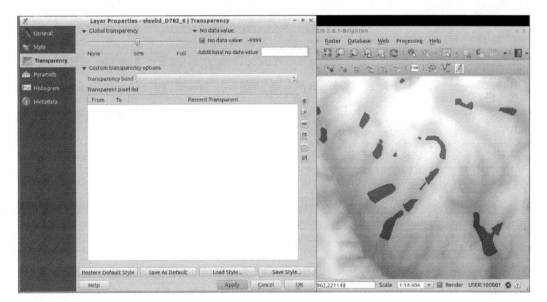

 No data value is always 100% transparent no matter what **Global transparency** is set to. Use this to easily eliminate values that you don't want to show up at all.

8. (Optional) You may have noticed that below the **Global transparency** slider is **Custom transparency options**. This will allow you to make particular values more transparent than others. You can either assign specific values to specific transparencies, or you can add a band to the raster (or use a multiband raster), which specifies the amount of transparency to apply to the rest of the raster (some data formats, such as GeoTiff, call this an Alpha Transparency band):

   ❏ Reset the global back to 0% (otherwise, this is applied in too)

   ❏ Use the green **+** sign to add some values

- From 100 To 125, 25% transparent
- From 125 To 150, 75% transparent
- Click **Apply** and notice the lower elevation lakes are harder to see:

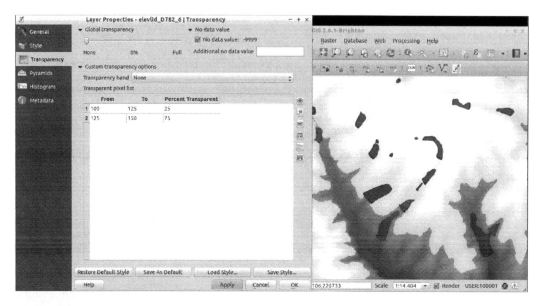

How it works...

This is really a computer graphics thing, but the simplest explanation is that you're telling the computer to combine a percentage of two different layers in the same location instead of the top layer's value covering. Based on the math of the original colors and their transparency, a blended color is calculated for each pixel on the screen.

This doesn't begin to explain all the possible variations of appearance that can be achieved by mixing multiple layers and multiple transparencies, only tinkering can show you this.

There's more...

One classic example of transparencies is to mix hillshades and airphotos. You can place either layer on top and then adjust the transparency to let the other show through. Generally, you would place the hillshade underneath in this case (but either can work). The end result is a landscape that appears to have 3D relief, but it looks like an airphoto.

Another classic example is to create a mask layer with a hole cut out around the region that you want to emphasize. You now place the mask layer on top. Before adding transparency, it blocks everything but the hole. Then, you slowly add transparency so that you can see surrounding regions, but they are muted and stand out less. For this technique, try a black, gray, or white fill for the mask layer. Each will have a slightly different look.

When styling vectors, you can apply different transparencies to different features in the same layer if you use Rule Based Rendering. Each rule can have a different transparency value and the entire layer can have yet another transparency modifier in the **Layer Rendering** section.

Lastly, keep in mind that not all output formats handle transparency well. In particular, be careful using color gradients with transparencies when exporting to PDF. Generally, PNG handles transparency, SVG may work or at least allow to you to edit the transparency after export, unlike image formats.

Understanding the feature and layer blending modes

In this recipe, we will look at the different layer and feature blending modes. Using these tools, we can achieve special rendering effects, which you may already know from other graphics programs.

Getting ready

To follow this recipe, you just need to load `stamen.png` and `effect.png` from our sample data. Make sure that stamen (left-hand side in the following screenshot) is the lower layer and effect (right-hand side in the following screenshot) is the upper layer. To test the feature blending modes, load `blending.shp`:

(Background maps "Watercolor" and "Toner" by Stamen Design, under CC BY 3.0. Data by OpenStreetMap, under CC BY SA).

How to do it...

Using the two raster layers, we can try the different blending modes. Of course, this works for vector layers, as well:

1. Double-click on the `effects` layer to open **Layer Properties**.

2. You can find the blending settings by going to **Layer Properties | Style | Color Rending** together with other helpful controls for **Brightness**, **Contrast**, **Saturation**, and more, as shown in the next screenshot:

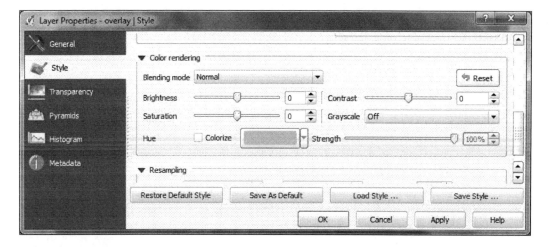

3. Change the **Blending mode** and click on **Apply** to see the results.

4. Similarly, for vector layers, such as our blending layer, we find the blending mode settings by going to **Layer Properties | Style | Layer rendering**, as shown in the following screenshot:

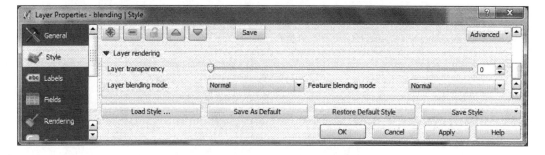

The main difference is that, for vector layers, we can control how features are blended together, and how the result is then blended to the underlying layers using the **Feature blending** and **Layer blending** modes, respectively. The feature blending mode is applied on a per-feature-basis.

The following screenshot shows the differences between feature and layer blending:

Feature and/or layer blending in action (from left to right): feature blending only, layer blending only, feature and layer blending combined (background maps "Watercolor" and "Toner" by Stamen Design, under CC BY 3.0. Data by OpenStreetMap, under CC BY SA).

The following is an explanation of the preceding screenshots:

▶ The leftmost image shows that **Feature blending** mode is set to **Multiply,** while **Layer blending** mode is set to default, **Normal**. This results in a map where the vector features are rendered on top of each other using the **Multiply** mode before the whole layer is overlaid on top of the lower layer(s).

▶ The center image instead shows **Normal Feature blending** mode combined with **Multiply Layer blending** mode. You can see how the features can block each other out because they are drawn on top of each other.

▶ Finally, the rightmost image shows both **Layer blending** mode and **Feature blending** modes being set to **Multiply**. In this combination, the **Multiply** rule is applied on both the feature and the layer level and, therefore, we can see features and the underlying background layer(s) shining through the features in the upper layer.

How it works...

Based on the selected blending mode, the pixel colors (in the RGB mode) of the lower and upper layers are mixed as described next. For illustration and quick reference, the following figure shows the results of all 12 blending modes (from left to right and top to bottom), except for the **Normal** setting, which does not mix the colors but only uses the alpha channel of the upper layer to blend with the layer below it:

▶ **Lighten**: The **Lighten** mode selects the maximum of each RGB component from the foreground and background pixels. Be aware that the results tend to be jagged and harsh.

▶ **Screen**: The **Screen** mode paints light pixels from the upper layer over the lower layer, but it skips the dark pixels.

- ▶ **Dodge**: The **Dodge** mode will brighten and saturate the lower layer based on the lightness of the upper layer. This means that brighter colors in the upper layer cause the saturation and brightness of the lower layer to increase. This works best if the top pixels aren't too bright; otherwise, the effect is quite extreme.

- ▶ **Addition**: The **Addition** mode adds the pixel values of both layers. If the result exceeds 1 (in the case of RGB), the respective areas are displayed in white.

- ▶ **Darken**: The **Darken** mode creates a result that retains the smallest RGB components of both layers. Therefore, this is the opposite of the Lighten mode and, just as with Lighten, the results tend to be jagged and harsh.

- ▶ **Multiply**: The **Multiply** mode multiplies the values of both layers, thus resulting in a darker picture.

- ▶ **Burn**: The **Burn** mode causes darker colors in the upper layer to darken the lower layer. **Burn** can be used to tweak and colorize underlying layers.

- ▶ **Overlay**: The **Overlay** mode combines the **Multiply** and **Screen blending** modes. As a result, light parts become lighter and dark parts become darker.

- ▶ **Soft light**: The **Soft light** mode is very similar to **Overlay**, but it uses a combination of **Burn** and **Dodge**. This is supposed to emulate shining a soft light on an image.

- ▶ **Hard light**: The **Hard light** mode is also very similar to **Overlay**. It is supposed to emulate projecting a very intense light on an image.

- ▶ **Difference**: The **Difference** mode subtracts the values of the upper layer from the lower layer (or the other way around) to always get a positive value. Blending with black (which has an RGB value of 0,0,0) produces no change.

- ▶ **Subtract**: The **Subtract** mode subtracts the values of one layer from the other. In the case of negative values, black is displayed:

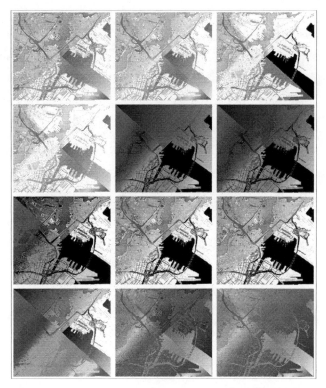

Overview of the 12 blending modes (background maps "Watercolor" and "Toner" by Stamen Design, under CC BY 3.0. Data by OpenStreetMap, under CC BY SA): first row: Lighten, Screen, and Dodge; second row: Addition, Darken, and Multiply; third row: Burn, Overlay, and Soft light; fourth row: Hard light, Difference, and Subtract.

Saving and loading styles

What's better than making an awesome style for your feature layers? Being able to easily share and reuse them. Both vector and raster styles can be saved and reused—however, in slightly different ways.

Getting ready

For this recipe, you need two similar vector layers and a set of two similar raster layers. In the example data that is provided, use two of the bus route shapefiles and two of the elevation rasters (for example, `elevlid_D782_6.tif`).

How to do it...

First we'll start by copying and pasting styles for vector layers:

1. Load up two bus route shapefiles and two elevlid rasters.

2. The simplest method is to copy styles for vectors or rasters. Just right-click on the layer name in the list and select **Copy Style** from the **Style** menu. Then, right-click on the layer that you want to apply this to and select **Paste Style** from the **Style** menu. You can only copy styles between layers of the same type (for example, **Point to Point**):

   Try to copy and paste the style of one bus route to the second bus route using the right-click menus:

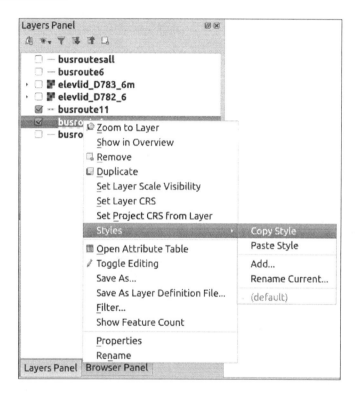

3. Now to export styles for later use, right-click on a layer and navigate to **Properties |
   Symbology**.

4. In the bottom-right, there is a **Save Style** button in the **Style** menu. The output
   choices are **QGIS Layer Style File...** (aka .qml) or **SLD File...**. Both formats are
   XML text files, **QGIS Layer Style...** is recommended for maximum compatibility:

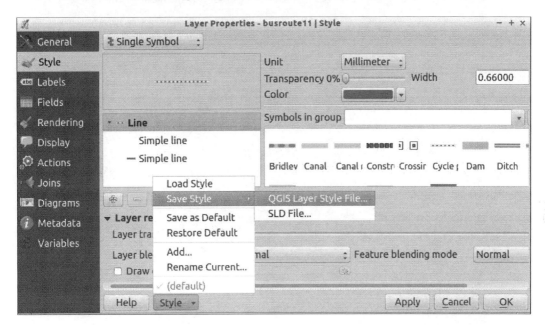

5. SLD is compatible with some other web map systems, but it will not capture your
   QGIS style 100% except in the simplest cases (not all the same options exist in SLD).
   QML is the native QGIS style file. Note the **Load style** option for later usage.

6. Go ahead and apply a new style to one of the bus route layers.

7. Then, save the symbology to **QGIS Layer Style File** (qml).

8. In the property dialog of the second bus route file, click **Load Style...** and pick the file
   that you just saved.

> You can open this file in a text editor and make customizations or,
> for example, batch-find and replace values.

Rasters are slightly trickier in that you can save a symbology file, but you can also save a color table. The color table is a text file that lists raster value ranges and associated color codes. It's a much simpler format to hand-edit than XML (QGIS Layer Style File), but does not retain things like transparency or classification settings:

1. Go ahead and apply a new color gradient to one of the elevlid layers.

2. Save just the color table to a `.txt` file with the disk button (above the color table on the right end of the button row; refer to the screenshot).

3. In the property of the second elevid file, load the color table and pick the file that you just saved.

4. Apply the changes to your layer style:

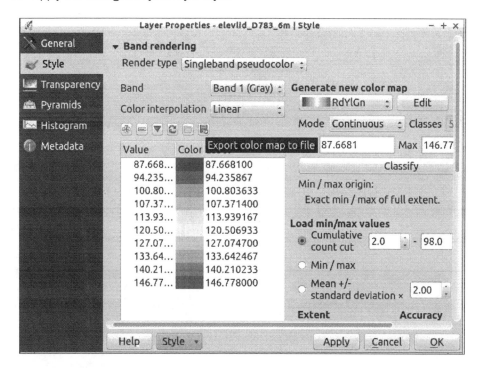

 Note that the same **Style** menu is available as was in the vector properties. You can use this to save and load QGIS Layer Style File (.qml) just as we did earlier.

How it works...

Normally the style information for a layer is saved in the `.qgs` (if you save your project) project file. The various export methods just package up the style information for a layer into a separate file in a generic manner (not associated with the original data). This lets you apply similar styles to similar data sources.

Vector symbology is stored in a special XML file that ends in the `.qml` extension. You can read or edit the file if you want, and it can be produced via scripts or copied and pasted to create mashups of multiple styles.

Raster symbology can also be stored in a `.qml` file. However, there's an additional option to export the classification ranges and colors to a simple text file, one value or range of values and one color code per line.

There's more...

The second format **SLD** (**Style Layer Descriptors**) is very common in web services. While not all features of QGIS styling have equivalents in SLD, it's still a good starting point to share your style across software platforms such as Mapserver or Geoserver.

Configuring data-defined labels

If there was a list of top features of QGIS, data-defined labels would be high on that list. They offer the ease of automatic labeling with the customization of freehand labeling. You can mix and match automatic and custom edits, storing the values in a table for later reference.

Getting ready

There are a couple of useful plugins for data-defined labeling which will add the extra attribute fields that you need to either an existing layer or make a new layer just for labels. Download and install **Layer to labeled layer** and **Create labeled layer**.

How to do it...

1. Open QGIS and load `census_wake2000.shp`.

2. Create a copy of the layer using the **Save As** dialog, and save the layer as `census_wake2000_label.shp`. (You don't always have to do this but this process does modify the table, so it's a good idea to make a backup.)

3. Highlight `census_wake2000_label.shp` in the layer list.

4. Run the **Layer to labeled layer** plugin (**Plugins | Layer to Labeled layer** plugin):

   1. Set **Label Field** to STFID.

   2. Click on **OK**:

5. If you look at the attribute table now, you will see a whole bunch of new fields, starting with the **Lbl** prefix, which are NULL:

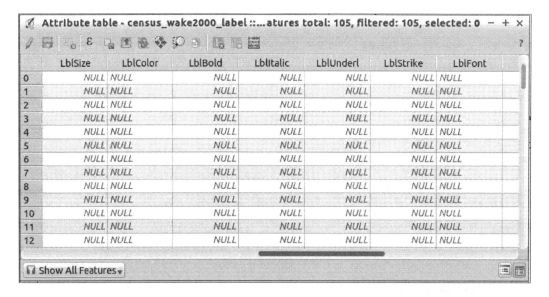

6. Now, ensure that you have the **Label** toolbar open (**View | Toolbars | Label**):

7. Either in the layer (by navigating to **Properties | Labels**) or using the first button on **Label Toolbar, Layer Labeling Options**, open the label management dialog.

8. Throughout the dialogs, you will see markers next to each field. A yellow one indicates a data-defined attribute, a white marker is the same setting for all:

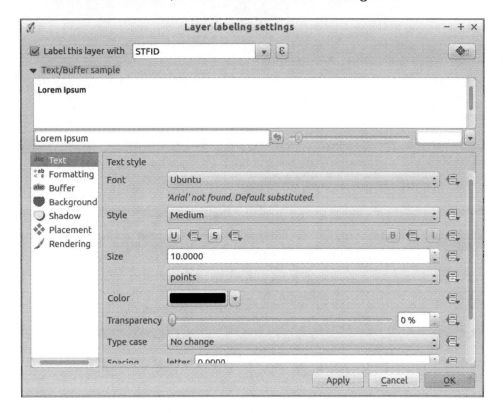

 If you want to control additional attributes at this point, add a new field to the layer. Then, return to this dialog and select the white icon to pick the name of the field to use.

9. Now, you are ready to make custom edits to various labels and have the table store the settings. Depending on the setting, there are a couple of ways to make the edits. Note that you must toggle editing on the layer before you can change the labels:

1. You can edit the field directly in the table either by hand, or you can use the field calculator to automate repetitive patterns (for example, give all major roads the same **Font** and **Color** label).

2. For some attributes, such as X,Y and rotation, you can also edit by hand in the map using the **Label Toolbar** option.

Example: moving and rotating a label

1. Toggle editing by clicking on the following icon:

2. On the **Label Toolbar** menu, select the **Move Label** button. Now, click on a label and drag it to a new location, releasing the mouse button when you are done moving the label. Note that you must ensure that the X and Y fields in step 38 are set for this tool to be usable:

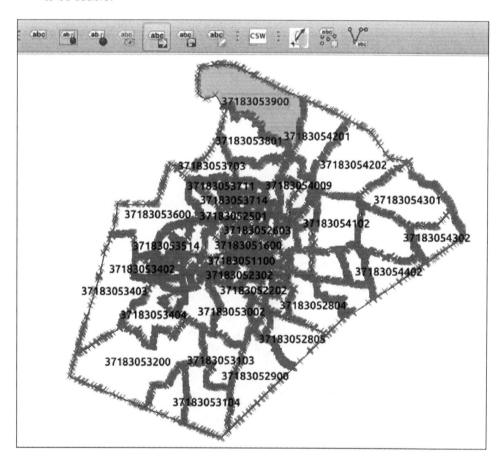

If you check the attribute table you will see that in the **LblX** and **LblY** fields, the values have now been saved for the labels that you moved.

3. Now, try the **Rotate Label** button. See if you can make some of the labels fit inside their polygons using the move and rotate:

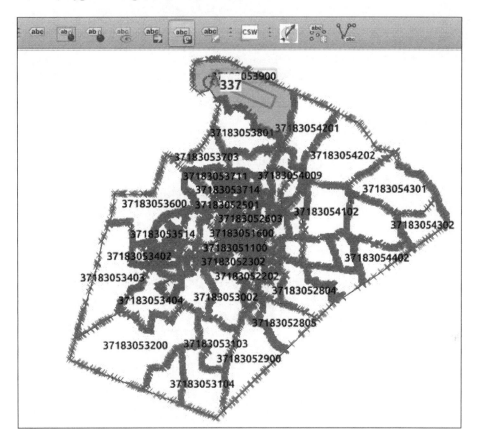

You can also use the **Change Label** button to edit the other properties of a specific label that you select. This is really nice when you just need some fine-tuning.

4. Save your edits and toggle editing off to keep your changes.

How it works...

The basic premise is that you keep an extra set of attributes in a table often as additional fields to your existing table.

 You could add fields to your attribute table by hand, and assign them to label properties. Using the **Layer to Labeled Layer** plugin does this for you.

These fields if you set them are used in determining the location, size, font, color, angle, and so on, of the label for the given row. If you don't set them, then the automatic settings from the labeling engine are kept.

There's more...

Data-defined labels are powerful in that you can combine automated, calculated, and custom-edited values. They are automated from the built-in labeling engine and calculated using the field calculator to populate the data-defined fields (for example, with `if` statements or calculations that are based on other attributes). Lastly, by just making these little hand tweaks, you can fix a few not-quite labels that misbehave.

Note that you don't have to use data-defined labeling on an existing layer. You can create just a label layer with the **Create labeled layer** plugin. In other software, user-defined labeling is often called Annotation layers. QGIS also has annotation layers. These are layers where you click to add a label to the map and then write and style it however you want. The biggest problem is that these layers are not associated with the data that they label. You can't easily give them to someone else, and if a label name or style changes, you have to chase down and hand-edit every fix. In QGIS, data-defined labeling solves almost all the shortcomings of annotation layers because it actually saves to a shapefile with all its properties as fields.

Creating custom SVG graphics

This recipe is all about making your map unique by creating custom icons, north arrows, or even fill patterns.

Getting ready

You will need a vector illustration program (for example, Inkscape or Adobe Illustrator).

Don't have one? There are several free and open source options available on all platforms. Many people in the QGIS community use Inkscape (`http://inkscape.org`), but you can also use LibreOffice Draw or OpenOffice Draw. The most common proprietary software equivalent is Adobe Illustrator.

You will also need a text editor, such as TextEdit (Mac), Notepad, Notepad++ (Windows).

How to do it...

1. Open up your vector illustration program.

2. Set the canvas to a reasonable size to work with. Square ratios tend to work well because the icon will eventually be used to mark points in QGIS; 100x100 pixels is fine.

3. Draw a simple shape such as a square, circle, or star. Make sure you go most of the way towards the edges and fill the whole page.

Remember that you will be using this drawing at sizes closer to 8-32 pixels; it's just really annoying to work at these scales. when creating and editing illustrations

4. Save the drawing as an `.svg` file.

5. Now, open the `.svg` file in a text editor, search and find the style line of your object, and replace it with the following lines:

```
stroke-width="param(outline-width) 1"
stroke="param(outline) #000"
fill="param(fill) #FFF"
```

If working with a complex icon, set your line to a specific color code that is different from all other colors in the drawing. Make a note of the color code so that you can use it to search the .svg file in your text editor.

The before-after scenario when this code has been incorporated is shown in the following table:

Before	After
```<rect```	```<rect```

```
<rect
   style="color:#000000;display
   :inline;overflow:visible;vis
   ibility:visible;opacity:1;fi
   ll:"param(fill)
   #000000";fill-
   opacity:1;stroke:"param(outl
   ine) #ff0000";stroke-
   width:"param(outline-width)
   4";stroke-
   miterlimit:4;stroke-
   dasharray:none;stroke-
   opacity:1;marker:none;enable
   -background:accumulate"
     id="rect3336"
     width="301.61023"
     height="308.96658"
     x="30.651445"
     y="725.00476" />
```

```
<rect
   stroke-width="param(outline-
   width) 1"
   stroke="param(outline) #000"
   fill="param(fill) #FFF"
     id="rect3336"
     width="301.61023"
     height="308.96658"
     x="30.651445"
     y="725.00476" />
```

6. Save your changes.

7. Now, start up QGIS and load a point layer.

8. Go to **Properties | Style**.

9. In the symbology options, there are two levels of objects that make a symbol: the marker and then a sublevel of actual symbols that combine to make it.

10. Select the subobject, which is usually labeled **Simple Marker** by default.

11. Now, change the dropdown in the upper-right to SVG Marker.

12. Below the box displaying the symbol options look for the **...** button and select to load an SVG from file. Use this to select the .svg file that you previously created.

13. Once imported, you should be able to change the fill color of the symbol (if you performed Step 5):

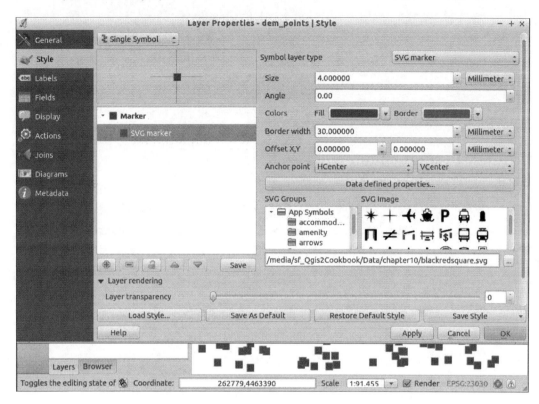

 You may need to adjust the size and widths in large amounts for changes to be apparent. Make use of the **Apply** button to see the changes in the map but keep the dialog open for easy adjustment.

How it works...

The special text that you add to the `.svg` file is a marker or placeholder. QGIS looks for these particular words and then utilizes them to insert symbol changes on-the-fly as the SVG is read into the program.

There's more...

While this recipe demonstrated a very simple SVG, this method applies to more complicated symbols.

Also note that in **Settings | Options | System**, you can set paths to folders of SVGs so that all of them will be available in the symbology dialogs all the time.

See also

QGIS also lets you customize fill patterns using SVG symbols. The QGIS *Training Manual* has a good example of this at `http://docs.qgis.org/2.8/en/docs/training_manual/basic_map/symbology.html#hard-fa-creating-a-custom-svg-fill`.

Making pretty graticules in any projection

A graticule is a set of reference lines on a map that help orient a map reader. They are often set at, and labeled, with the coordinates. The tricky part about using graticules, however, is projections. If you don't make them correctly, instead of smooth curves between the line intersections, you get awkward unusual shapes (mostly straight lines). The default QGIS graticule creator is not projection-friendly, so in this recipe, you'll see an add-on processing algorithm that does this. This recipe is about ensuring you get nice, smooth, and properly-labeled graticules.

Getting ready

You don't really need much for this recipe other than a bounding box and a coordinate interval that you want to space the lines at. Usually, these will be in Latitude, Longitude WGS 84 (EPSG:4326), and decimal degrees, respectively, since the whole point of a graticule is to add reference lines that help orient a user.

How to do it...

1. Start by downloading a **Processing Toolbox** algorithm specifically for this task called **Lines Graticule**:

    1. Open the **Processing Toolbox**.

    2. Go to **Scripts | Tools | Get scripts from on-line scripts collection**:

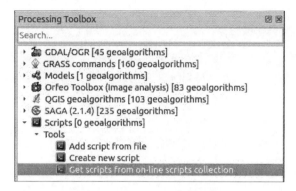

3. In the **Not Installed** section, check the box for the **Lines Graticule** algorithm.

4. Click on the **OK** button to install the algorithm.

 Every time that you use a tool, it's good to check for updates.

You will see something like the following screenshot:

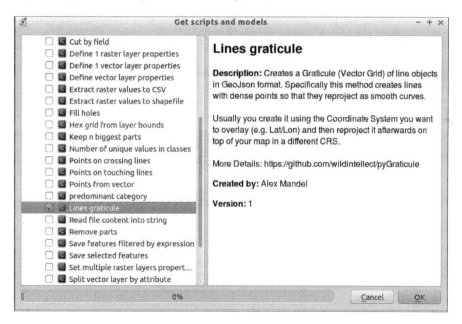

2. Now that you've downloaded the algorithm, open it by navigating to **Scripts | Vector** (it's called **Lines graticule** though the code is actually pygraticule.py):

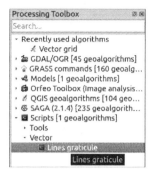

3. You can fill in the parameters by hand if you know them or use the **...** button to get values from your existing project.

4. For now, you can use the defaults that will make a graticule for the whole world. The outputs are determined by outfile and graticule. These parameters are optional, you can choose to pick one, both, or neither. If you want a GeoJSON file, set the outfile. If you want a shapefile, set the graticule (if you want the results to autoload afterwards, make sure that the second output is set to temporary or a real file, just not blank). Refer to the **Help** tab for details about each parameter. There are two really important values to control the graticule:

    1. The **spacing** value denotes how often to draw a line (when doing world-scale maps, 20 or 30 degrees works well).

    2. The **density** value denotes how often to put nodes:

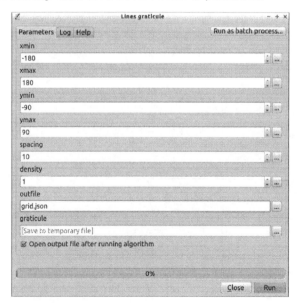

The more nodes, the smoother the curves; however, you get a bigger file that takes longer to make. Picking the right density may require trial and error to find the largest density before you notice the lines stop curving smoothly for a given map scale.

5. Once you've chosen your settings, click on **Run**.

6. After it runs, a vector layer should get loaded with the results. This won't look all that exciting, just straight lines making a grid.

7. The real magic is to now enable projection on-the-fly with one of the many decent world-wide projections such as "World Robinson (EPSG:54030):

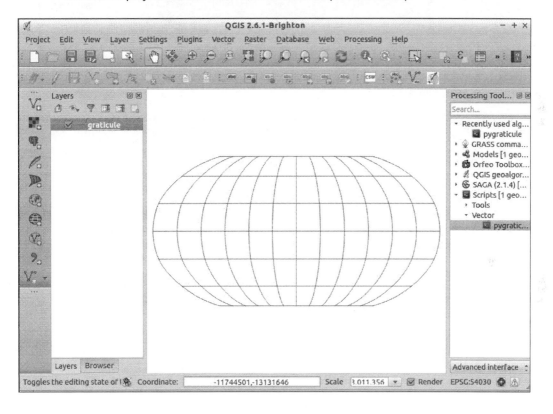

8. (Optional) If it doesn't look like the image, but instead still has straight lines that are oddly spaced, you need to disable the QGIS rendering simplification:

    1. Pick the layer from **Properties | Rendering**.

    2. Make sure that **Simplify geometry** is disabled:

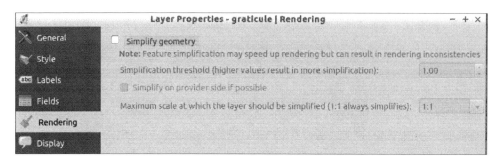

9. (Bonus) Generate a vector grid from **Vector | Research tools**. The difference looks like the following:

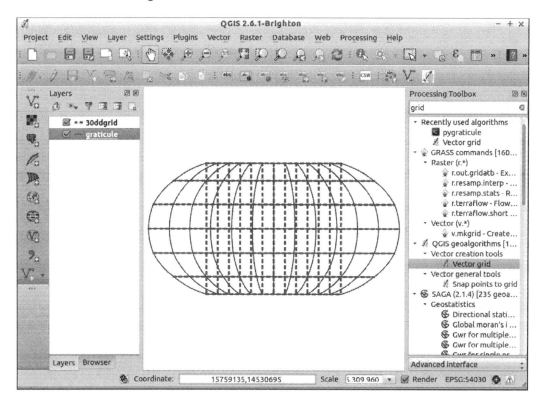

How it works...

Graticules are basically line layers (though sometimes they are also polygons). If you draw a grid with nodes only at the points where two lines intersect, you can easily see how distorting the grid will lead to blocky shapes. The key to smooth graticules is adding additional line nodes in between the intersections (that is, increase the node density).

It's important to note that, when using projections that don't cover the whole world (for example, polar or stereographic projections), pick bounding box values that fall within the projection limits; otherwise, you may get errors when trying to reproject.

There's more...

The primary advantages of graticules in the main map canvas are that you can use them as references while working in QGIS, include them in web and digital maps, and have full control of the labels and symbology. The method used here differs from other graticule (grid) tools in QGIS because it focuses on putting Latitude/Longitude lines with smooth curves as references into any projection. Other grid tools focus more on making regular squares across a map to subdivide a region.

The main advantages of the print composer method (next recipe) are its ability to make multiple coordinate systems easily and to add tick marks around the outside edge of a map. Tick marks are what you commonly see on navigation-oriented maps, such as USGS Topo quads, and other printed maps.

See also

Lines graticule (aka Pygraticule) can also be used as a pure Python script; for updates and more information, refer to `https://github.com/wildintellect/pyGraticule`.

To learn how to write your own processing toolbox algorithms, refer to the *Writing processing algorithms* recipe in *Chapter 11, Extending QGIS*.

Making useful graticules in printed maps

A graticule is a set of reference lines on a map that help orient a map reader. They are often set at and labeled with the coordinates. For traditional printed maps that are intended for navigation and surveying tasks where you want to mark the geographic coordinates, sometimes in multiple coordinate systems. This recipe is about adding such reference lines to a Print Composer map.

Getting ready

You will need a map, typically of a small area (several miles or km across). For this recipe, `elevlid_D782_6.tif` works well.

How to do it...

1. Load `elevlid_D782_6.tif`.

2. Turn on **Projection on-the-fly** by selecting **UTM Zone 17 N, WGS 84 (EPSG:32617)**.

3. Now create **New Print Composer**.

4. In **Print Composer**, select **Add New Map**, and then draw a rectangle on the canvas.

5. Now that you have the map, in the dialogs on the right-hand side of the screen select the **Item Properties** tab.

6. Scroll down or collapse sections until you see the **Grids** section.

7. Use the green plus (**+**) symbol to add a new grid.

8. Now, edit **Interval X** and **Interval Y** to 1,000 map units. (Make sure to tab to the next field or click on **Enter** for the values to stick.):

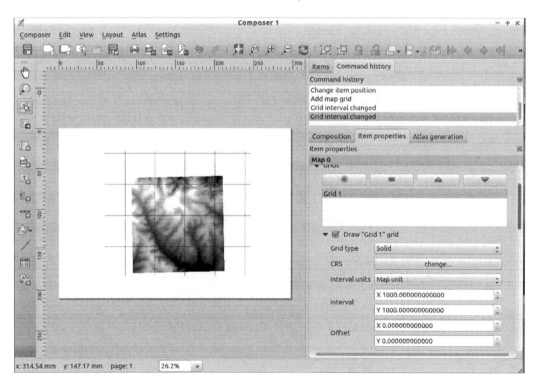

The current map units are UTM-based, meters, which means the lines will be 1,000 meters or 1 km apart.

9. Just below the **Interval** section, change **Line Style** and make the lines red so that they are easier to see.

10. Now, scroll down even further to the **Draw coordinates** section and check the box to enable labels for the grid lines:

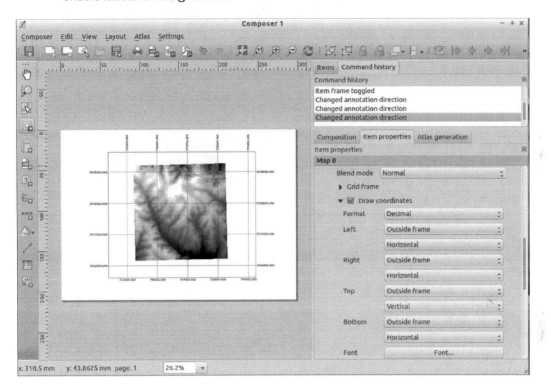

11. Once this is enabled, change the top and bottom orientation to vertical, and change the font color to red.

12. Now, to create a second grid, scroll back up to the **Grids** section and click the green plus sign (**+**) again to add a second grid.

13. This time, change the **CRS (Coordinate Reference System)** to **WGS 84 (EPSG:4326)**, which is the most common Latitude and Longitude system that people use.

14. Make this grid be spaced 0.01 map units (that is, degrees in this case) and change the style to blue to contrast with the other grid.

15. Now, scroll down and add **Draw coordinates**. Also, make the top and bottom vertical-oriented so that they avoid the first grid. You can also change the font color to match the lines:

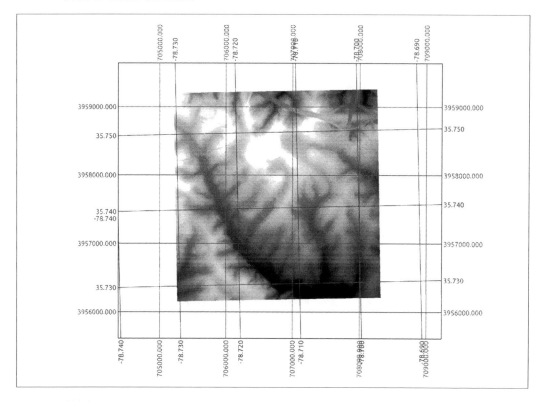

How it works...

Reference graticules are evenly spaced lines with marked coordinates. Based on your settings the composer calculates the positioning of the lines from the map data coordinates. The key to making useful graticules in the print composer is to select intervals that are often enough to provide reference but not so often that they cover a large portion of the map. It's also important to pick intervals that have nice rounded numbers, so that it's easy to calculate the value half way between two lines.

There's more...

There are two ways to make grids/graticules in QGIS: the print composer for printed maps or as a layer in QGIS for printed web maps as an internal usage.

The main advantages of the print composer method are the ability to do multiple coordinate systems easily and to add tick marks around the outside edge of a map. Tick marks are what you commonly see on navigation oriented maps, such as USGS Topo quads.

The primary advantages of graticules in the main map canvas are that you can use them as references while working with QGIS and have full control of the labels and symbology. Refer to the *Making pretty graticules in any projection* recipe in this chapter for how to make graticules in the main map interface.

Creating a map series using Atlas

In this recipe, we will use the **Print Composer Atlas** functionality to automatically create a PDF map book with a series of maps.

Getting ready

To follow this recipe, load `zipcodes_wake.shp` and `geology.shp` from our sample data. In the following screenshots, the `zipcodes_wake` layer was styled with a simple white border, while the geology layer is styled with random colors.

How to do it...

The **Print Composer Atlas** feature will create one map for each feature in the so-called **Coverage** layer. In this recipe, the zipcodes layer will serve as a **Coverage** layer, and we will create one map for each zipcode feature:

1. Click on the **New Print Composer** button or press *Ctrl + P* to get started. You will be prompted to set a title for the new composer. This can be left empty if you want QGIS to generate a title automatically.

2. Click on the **Add new map** button and drag open a rectangle on the composer page to create a map item for the main map.

3. To activate the Atlas functionality, we enable the map item's **Controlled by atlas** checkbox. The following screenshot shows the fully configured map's item properties. In the **Controlled by atlas** section, we can select which zoom mode Atlas should use:

    1. **Margin around feature**: This is the most flexible option, which tells Atlas to zoom to the feature while keeping the specified margin percentage around the feature.

    2. **Predefined scale (best fit)**: This tells Atlas to use the one predefined project scale (configurable in **Project Properties | General | Project scales**) where the feature best fits in.

3. **Fixed scale**: This keeps the same scale for all maps of the series; the scale is configured in the map's **Main properties**, that is, 100,000 in the following screenshot:

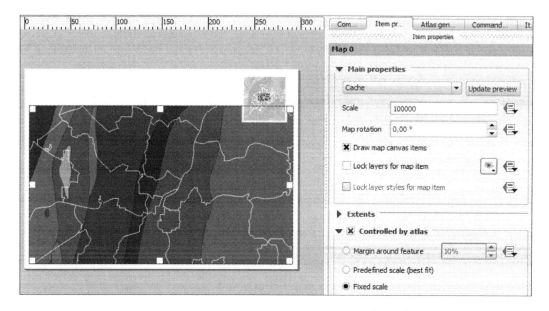

4. Next, we add a label for the title using the **Add new label** button. This title label will display the zip code polygon feature's NAME value which will be automatically updated by Atlas for each map in the series. To achieve this, we insert the following expression in the input field of the label item's **Main properties**:

```
[%attribute( @atlas_feature, 'NAME' ) %]
```

5. To finalize the Atlas configuration, we need to go to the **Atlas generation** tab. There, we first have to enable the **Generate an atlas** checkbox. This activates the **Configuration** section, where we can pick the **Coverage** layer and set it to the zipcodes_wake layer, as shown in the following screenshot.

6. To preview the Atlas output, we can now click on the **Preview Atlas** button. This button is only active if the **Generate an atlas** checkbox in the **Atlas generation** tab is enabled. Once the preview mode is active, you can step through the map series using the arrow buttons right besides the **Preview Atlas** button.

7. When we are happy with the preview, we can export the map series. The output behavior is controlled by the configuration in the **Atlas generation** tab's **Output** section, which you can also see in the following screenshot. Atlas supports exporting to separate image, SVG, or PDF files. Activate the **Single file export when possible** option to combine all maps into one PDF and click on the **Export Atlas as PDF** button, as shown in the following screenshot:

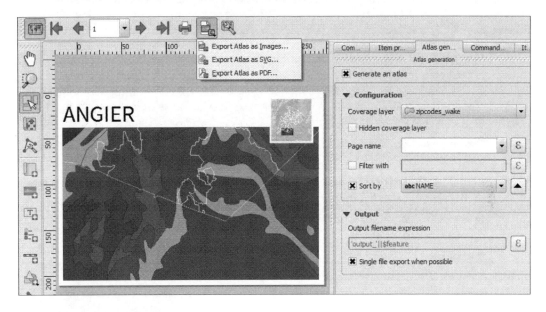

How it works...

The Atlas feature provides access to a series of variables related to the current feature. We already used this to display the NAME value of the current feature in the title label using the [%attribute(@atlas_feature, 'NAME') %] expression. Besides @atlas_feature, you have access to the following variables:

▶ @atlas_feature: This is the feature ID of the current Atlas feature. This makes it possible to use this information in rules to, for example, hide or highlight features based on their ID.

▶ @atlas_geometry: This is the geometry of the current Atlas feature and can be used in rules to, for example, only show features of other layers if their geometry intersects the Atlas feature geometry.

▶ @atlas_featurenumber: This is the number of the current Atlas feature.

▶ @atlas_totalfeatures: This is the total number of features in the Atlas coverage layer.

There's more...

Overview maps are a great way to provide context to more detailed main maps. To add an overview map (as shown in the upper-right corner of the composition in the following screenshot), you need to add a second map item to the composition. To turn this map item into an overview map, go to **Item properties | Overviews** and click on the button with the green plus sign. This will add an `Overview 1` entry and enable the **Draw "Overview 1" overview** configuration GUI:

- ▸ **Map frame**: The **Map frame** drop-down list enables us to define the main map that should be referenced by the overview map. By default, the map items are named `Map 0`, `Map 1`, `Map 2`, and so on, depending on the order they were added to the composition. Therefore, we will select the `Map 0` entry if the main map was the first item that was added to the composition.

- ▸ **Frame style**: The **Change ...** button can be used to choose a style for the overview frame. Usually, this will be a simple fill with transparency.

- ▸ **Blending mode**: These are supported by overview frames, as explained in detail in the *Understanding the feature and layer blending modes* recipe.

- ▸ **Invert overview**: Enable the **Invert overview** checkbox if you want to apply the overview frame style to the areas outside the extent of the main map.

- ▸ **Center on overview**: Enable the **Center on overview** checkbox if you want the overview map to automatically pan to center on the extent of the main map.

11

Extending QGIS

In this chapter, we will cover the following topics:

- ▶ Defining custom projections
- ▶ Working near the dateline
- ▶ Working offline
- ▶ Using the QSpatiaLite plugin
- ▶ Adding plugins with Python dependencies
- ▶ Using the Python console
- ▶ Writing Processing algorithms
- ▶ Writing QGIS plugins
- ▶ Using external tools

Introduction

QGIS can do many things on its own. However, as with all software, there are limits to its default abilities. The great news is there are many ways to extend QGIS to do even more through built-in customization options, existing add-on plugins, creating new analysis algorithms, creating your own plugins, and using external software that compliments QGIS. This chapter covers just a few of the common customizations and plugins that haven't been mentioned in other chapters, and how you can get started with making your own add-ons to share with others.

Defining custom projections

Map projections stump just about everybody at some point in their GIS career, if not more often. If you're lucky, you just stick to the common ones that are known by everyone and your life is simple. Sometimes though, for a particular location or a custom map, you just need something a little different that isn't in the already vast QGIS projections database. (Often, these are also referred to as **Coordinate Reference System (CRS)** or **Spatial Reference System (SRS)**.)

I'm not going to cover what the difference is between a Projection, Projected Coordinate System, and a Coordinate system. From a practical perspective in QGIS, you can pick the one that matches your data or your intended output. There's lots of little caveats that come with this, but a book or class is a much better place to get a handle on it.

Getting ready

For this recipe, we'll be using a custom graticule, a grid of lines every 10 degrees (10d_graticule.json.geojson), and the Natural Earth 1:10 million coastline (ne_10m_coastline.shp).

How to do it...

1. Determine what projection your data is currently in. In this case, we're starting with EPSG:4236, which is also known as Lat/Lon WGS84.

2. Determine what projection you want to make a map in. In this example, we'll be making an Oblique Stereographic projection centered on Ireland.

3. Search the existing QGIS projection list for a match or similar projection. If you open the **Projection** dialog and type Stereographic, this is a good start.

4. If you find a similar projection and just want to customize it, highlight the proj4 string and copy the information. **NAD83(CSRS) / Prince Edward Isl. Stereographic (NAD83)** is a similar enough projection.

> If you don't find anything in the QGIS projection database, search the Web for a proj4 string for the projection that you want to use. Sometimes, you'll find Projection WKT. With a little work, you can figure out which proj4 slot each of the WKT parameters corresponds to using the documentation at https://github.com/OSGeo/proj.4/wiki/GenParms. A good place to research projections is provided at the end of this recipe.

5. Under **Settings**, open the **Custom CRS** option.

6. Click on the **+** symbol to add a new definition.

7. Put in a name and paste in your projection string, modifying it in this case with coordinates that center on Ireland. Change the values for the `lat_0` and `lon_0` parameters to match the following example. This particular type of projection only takes one reference point. For projections with multiple standard parallels and meridians, you will see the number after the underscore increment:

```
+proj=sterea +lat_0=53.5 +lon_0=-7.8 +k=0.999912
+x_0=400000 +y_0=800000 +ellps=GRS80 +towgs84=0,0,0,0,0,0,0
+units=m +no_defs
```

The following screenshot shows what the screen will look like:

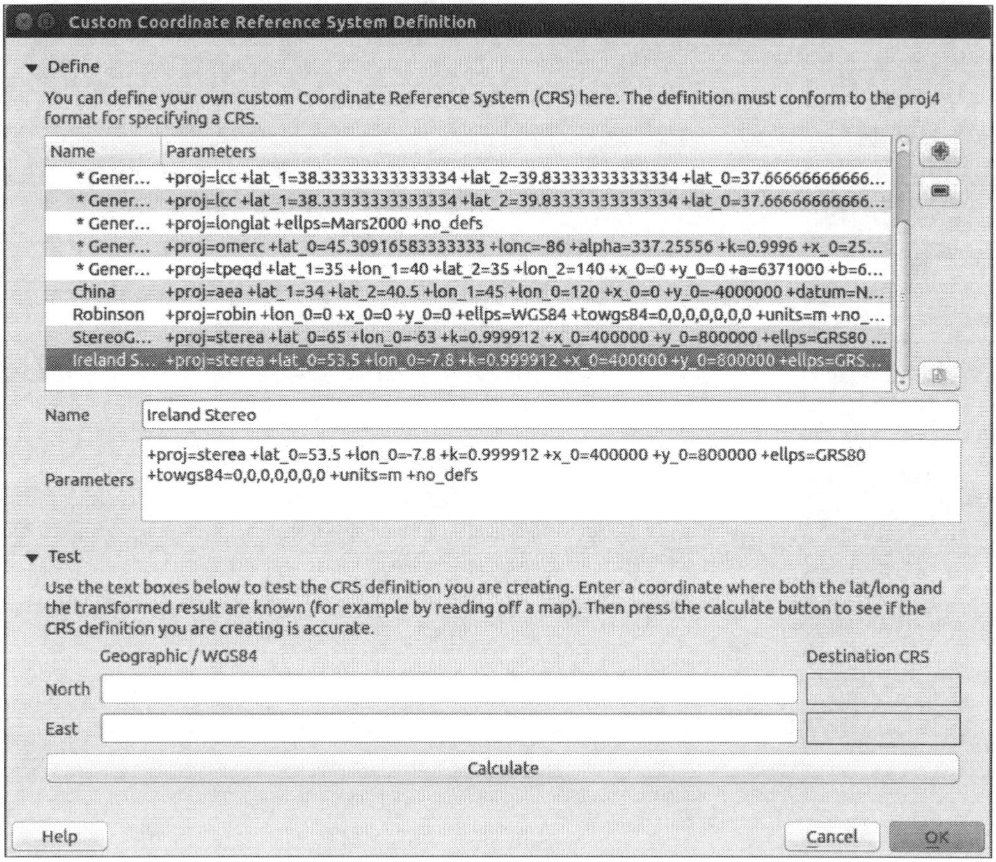

8. Now, click on another projection in the list of custom projections. There's currently a quirk where if you don't toggle off to another projection, then it doesn't save when you click on **OK**.

9. Now, go to the map, open the projection manager and apply your new projection with OTF on to check whether it's right. You'll find your new projection in the third section, **User Defined Coordinate Systems**:

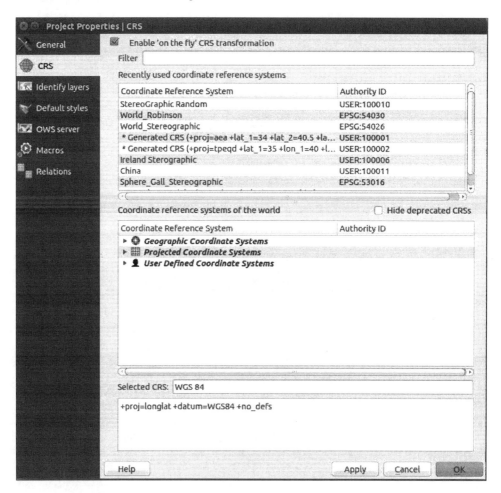

The following screenshot shows the projection:

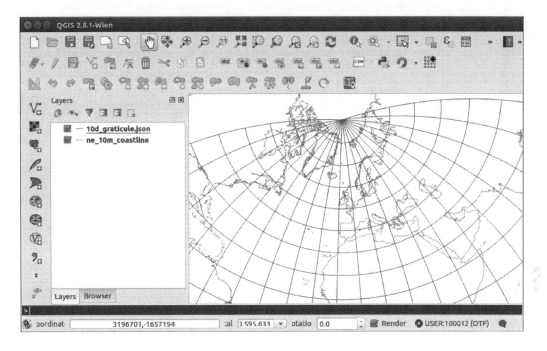

How it works...

Projection information (in this case, a `proj4` string) encodes the parameters that are needed by the computer to pick the correct math formula (projection type) and variables (various parameters, such as parallels and the center line) to convert the data into the desired flat map from whatever it currently is. This library of information includes approximations for the shape of the earth and differing manners to squash this into a flat visual.

You can really alter most of the parameters to change your map appearance, but generally, stick to known definitions so that your map matches other maps that are made the same way.

There's more...

QGIS only allows forward/backward transformation projections. Cartographic forward-only projections (for example, Natural Earth, Winkel Tripel (III), and Van der Grinten) aren't in the projection list currently; this is because these reprojections are not a pure math formula, but an approximate mapping from one to the other, and the inverse doesn't always exist. You can get around this by reprojecting your data with the `ogr2ogr` and `gdal_transform` command line to the desired projection, and then loading it into QGIS with **Projection-on-the-fly** disabled. While the `proj4` strings exist for these projections, QGIS will reject them if you try to enter them.

If you disable **Projection-on-the-fly**, make sure that all layers are in the same projection; otherwise, they won't line up. Also, perform all analysis steps before converting to a projection that is intended for cartography, as the units of measurement may become messy.

Geometries that cross the outer edge of projections don't always cut off nicely. You will often see this as an unexpected polygon band across your map. The easiest thing to do in this case is to remove data that is outside your intended mapping region. You can use a clip function or simply select what you want to keep and **Save Selection As** a new layer.

There are other common projection description formats (`prj`, `WKT`, and `proj4`) out there. Luckily, several websites help you translate. There are a couple of good websites to look up the existing Proj4 style projection information available at `http://spatialreference.org` and `http://epsg.io`.

See also

▶ Need more information on how to pick an appropriate projection for the type of map you are making? Refer to the USGS classic map projections poster available at `http://egsc.usgs.gov/isb/pubs/MapProjections/projections.html`. Much of this is also used in the Wikipedia article on the topic available at `http://en.wikipedia.org/wiki/Map_projection`. The `https://www.mapthematics.com/ProjectionsList.php` link also has a great list of projections, including unusual ones with pictures.

Working near the dateline

If you read the previous recipe about custom projections, you might have noticed the note about data that crosses the edge of projections and how it doesn't usually render properly. When working on data near -180 or 180 degrees longitude, you are going to have this issue. Maps showing far Eastern Russia, Fiji, New Zealand, and the South Pacific, to name a few places, will often contend with this issue.

The required solution really depends on what you're trying to do. If you just need a map of such areas, pick a locally suitable projection. If you have existing data from other sources, it may be cut along the edge and you might need to stitch it back together. As for worldwide maps, sometimes you have to trim .01 degrees of the edge of your data so that it doesn't display oddly.

Getting ready

To follow this recipe, you will need the `honolulu-flights.shp` layer and the SpatiaLite database `new-zealand.sqlite` from the sample data.

How to do it...

Load the `honolulu-flights.shp` layer in QGIS. This layer represents great circles flight lines from the Honolulu airport. As you can see, it is displayed in a very strange manner, as some flight lines cross the dateline meridian:

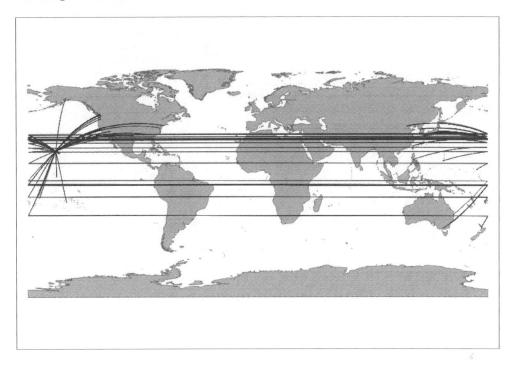

To display this layer correctly, we can select a suitable projection for your map. To do this, perform the following steps:

1. Open the **Project Properties** dialog by clicking on the *Ctrl + Shift + P* keyboard shortcut or navigating to **Project | Project Properties**.

2. Go to the **CRS** tab and activate the **Enable 'on the fly' CRS transformation** checkbox.

3. Select projection suitable for location. In our case, this is WGS84/PDC Mercator (EPSG:3832).

 Note that for different locations, different projections should be used.

4. Click on the **OK** button to save changes and close the dialog. Now, our data is displayed correctly:

Another option is to clip data to the dateline meridian. This can be done with the `ogr2ogr` tool from the GDAL toolset. To do this, perform the following steps:

1. Open the OSGeo4W command prompt if you are a Windows user, or the terminal window if you are a Linux or Mac OS user.

2. Change the directory to the folder where `honolulu-flights.shp` is located, for example, the following directory:

   cd c:\data

3. Enter the following command in the command prompt. Note that we first specify the output file and then the input file:

   ogr2ogr -wrapdateline honolulu-flights-wrapped.shp honolulu-flights.shp

4. After loading the newly-created `honolulu-flights-wrapped.shp` layer into QGIS, you will now see that flights wrapped on the dateline meridian are displayed correctly:

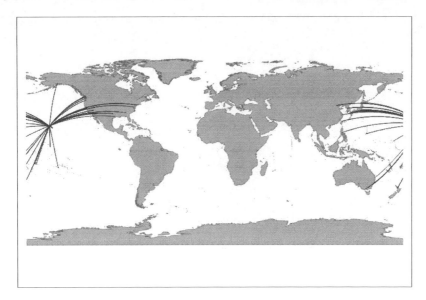

5. Now load the `nz-coastlines-and-islands` layer from the `new-zealand.sqlite` database. You should see two sets of polygons far from each other. This is New Zealand and Chatham islands, which should be located nearby:

To display them correctly, we can use the `ST_Shift_Longitude` function available in the SpatiaLite. To do this, perform the following steps:

1. Open the **DB Manager** plugin by clicking on its button on the toolbar or navigating to **Database | DB Manager | DB Manager**.

2. Expand the **SpatiaLite** group in the connections tree on the left-hand side of the dialog, and select the `new-zealand` database.

3. Open **SQL Window** and run the following query:

```
UPDATE "nz-coastlines-and-islands" SET
Geometry=ST_Shift_Longitude(Geometry)
```

4. Remove the `nz-coastlines-and-islands` layer from QGIS and add it again. Now, New Zealand and Chatham islands will be displayed correctly, as follows:

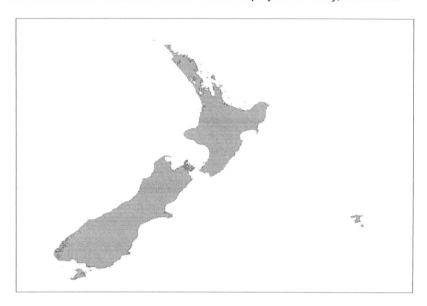

It is worth mentioning that the `ST_Shift_Longitude` function is also available in PostGIS.

How it works...

When we enable **'on the fly' CRS transformation**, every geometry is reprojected to the given CRS (in our case Pacific centered) so that coordinates now have the same sign.

The `ogr2ogr` tool with the `-wrapdateline` option splits all geometries that cross the dateline and write them to the output file. Geometries that do not cross the dateline are copied without changes.

The `ST_Shift_Longitude` function translates negative longitudes by 360 and as a result, all the data will be in the range of 0-360 degrees and displayed correctly.

See also

▶ http://docs.qgis.org/2.2/en/docs/user_manual/working_with_vector/supported_data.html#vector-layers-crossing-180-degrees-longitude

Working offline

The Internet is an awesome resource, but sometimes you just don't have access to it. For field work, in places with intermittent services, on an airplane, or even in a meeting room, you just might not be able to access all the stuff that you need. By stuff, we're referring to documentation (user and developer), but more importantly database layers (for example, PostGIS) and web service-based layers (for example, WMS, WFS, the OpenLayers plugin, and so on).

This recipe is about caching local copies of the files that you need on your computer before you leave for an unconnected place.

Getting ready

For this recipe, you will need to open a PostGIS database or WFS and enable the **Offline Editing** plugin that ships with QGIS.

How to do it...

1. Load your layer from PostGIS or WFS.
2. Make sure to activate the **Offline Editing** option.
3. In the **Database** menu, you should see **Offline Editing**, choose **Convert to offline project**:

4. Choose the local file to use to store the data.
5. Then, select all of the layers to convert (vector layers only):

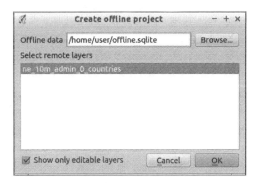

6. You can now use your PostGIS layers without a network connection to the online database. Go ahead and try to make some edits. (We recommend that you do this on a copy of database or table until you know what you're doing.)

7. When you come back to your network, you can now send your changes to the database by choosing the **Synchronize** option:

How it works...

The basics are straightforward, a copy of you data is saved into a SpatiaLite database locally on your computer. The project file records the change, and you are good to go as SpatiaLite can do anything any other vector data source in QGIS can do.

Be careful when working in a multiuser environment, this does not handle dealing with editing conflicts if multiple users have been modifying the same dataset independently.

There's more...

Also, there are all sorts of ways to create offline caches of Raster datasets (network files or web services) including `gdalwmscaching` or `mbtiles`. If you plan to need to work away from the Internet for periods of time, plan ahead, and test solutions before actually needing to go offline. No amount of plugins makes up for good planning.

Please remember to check the legality of caching web services (for example, Google and Bing) before doing so. OpenStreetMap is a reliable source of tiles for offline usage without restrictions.

See also

▶ GDAL WMS Cache options are available at `http://www.gdal.org/frmt_wms.html`

▶ A discussion of mbtiles usage is available at `http://blogs.terrorware.com/geoff/2012/11/17/offline-map-tiles-in-qgis/`

▶ A recent plugin to help you set this up is available at `https://plugins.qgis.org/plugins/MBTiles2img/`

Using the QspatiaLite plugin

Sometimes, you may not need to load a whole layer into QGIS, but only some subset of it, or perform some calculations on the fly. In such situations, the ability to run complex SQL queries and display their results in QGIS will be very useful.

This recipe shows you how to execute SQL code with the QspatiaLite plugin and load data in QGIS.

Getting ready

To follow this recipe, you need to create connection to the `cookbook.db` database created in the *Loading vector layers into SpatiaLite* recipe in *Chapter 1, Data Input and Output*. Alternatively, you can use your own SpatiaLite database, but be aware that you might have to alter some of the following SQL statements to match your tables.

Additionally, install the **QspatiaLite** plugin from **Plugin Manager**.

How to do it...

Make sure that you created a connection to `cookbook.db`. Start the **QspatiaLite** plugin by navigating to **Database | SpatiaLite | QspatiaLite**:

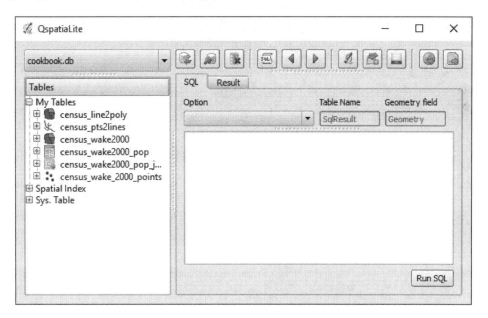

To execute the SQL query, perform the following steps:

1. Select database you want to use from the combobox in the top-left corner of the plugin dialog.

2. In the **SQL** tab, enter following query:

   ```
   SELECT "census_wake2000".'pk' AS id,
   "census_wake2000".'geom' AS Geometry,
   "census_wake2000".'area', "census_wake2000".'perimeter'
   FROM "census_wake2000" WHERE "census_wake2000".'perimeter' >
   100000;
   ```

   You can easily insert the table and column names by double-clicking on them in the **Tables** tree on the left-hand side of the dialog.

3. Click on the **Run** button at the bottom of the dialog to execute the query. The **Result** tab will open automatically and you can examine the query results in the table representation, as follows:

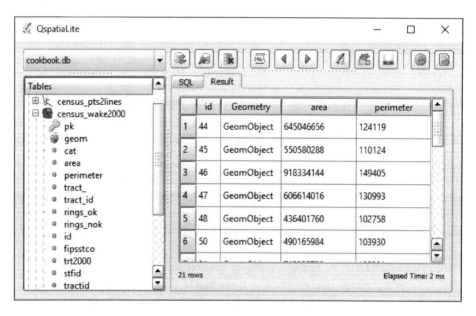

If the query results contain geometry information (the so-called geometry column), you can display them in QGIS. To do this, perform the following steps:

1. Switch back to the **SQL** tab.

2. In the **Option** combobox, select the action that you want to perform, for example, **Create Spatial View & Load in QGIS**.

3. In the **Table** field, enter name of the resulting view, for example, `above100k`.

4. Ensure that you entered the correct name of the geometry column in the **Geometry** field.

5. Click on the **Run** button at the bottom of the dialog.

6. A dialog will pop up asking for the source geometry table. Select table that you used in the query and click on **OK**.

7. A new view will be created and added to the QGIS as a new layer.

How it works...

When we click on the **Run** button, the query is passed to the SpatiaLite database engine for execution, and the results are returned to the plugin and displayed in the table. If you want to store results permanently, you can export them in a text file or in an OGR-compatible format using the corresponding buttons in the plugin dialog.

There's more...

You can also use the **DB Manager** plugin (which is bundled with QGIS) to execute SQL-queries directly and load them as layers.

See also

▸ A very good introduction to SpatiaLite and SQL can be found at `https://www.gaia-gis.it/fossil/libspatialite/wiki?name=misc-docs`. Also, a full list of the supported spatial SQL functions is available at `http://www.gaia-gis.it/gaia-sins/spatialite-sql-4.3.0.html`.

Adding plugins with Python dependencies

While the most common and widely-used Python packages are shipped with QGIS, and they can be used by plugins without any additional actions, some QGIS plugins need third-party Python packages, which are not available with the default QGIS installation.

This recipe shows you how to add missing Python packages to the QGIS installation.

Getting ready

To follow this recipe, you may need administrator rights if you are a Windows user, and QGIS is installed in the system drive.

How to do it...

This steps will install pip — a Python package management tool:

1. Download the `get-pip.py` file from `https://raw.githubusercontent.com/pypa/pip/master/contrib/get-pip.py` and save it somewhere on your hard drive, for example in `D:\Downloads`.

2. Open the OSGeo4W command prompt as administrator. Right-click on the **OSGeo4W Shell** shortcut on your Desktop and select **Run as Administrator** from the context menu. If you cannot find this shortcut on your Desktop, look for it in the Windows **Start** menu.

3. In the OSGeo4W command prompt, type `python D:\Downloads\get-pip.py`. Don't forget to replace `D:\Downloads` with the correct path to the `get-pip.py` file. Wait while the command execution completes.

Now, when pip is ready, you can easily download and install third-party Python packages. To do this, perform the following steps:

1. Open the OSGeo4W command prompt as administrator. Right-click on the **OSGeo4W Shell** shortcut on your desktop and select **Run as Administrator** from the context menu. If you cannot find this shortcut on the desktop, look for it in the Windows **Start** menu.

2. In the OSGeo4W command prompt, type `pip install package_name`. Don't forget to replace `package_name` with the name of the package that you want to install. For example, if you want to install the PySAL package, use this command: `pip install pysal`.

If you are a Linux user, use your package manager to install pip. For example, under Debian and Ubuntu, use the `sudo apt-get install python-pip` command to install pip. After doing this, you can use pip to download and install packages as described in the preceding paragraph.

Mac OS users can install pip via Homebrew using the `brew install pip` command.

Using pip, you also can view installed packages, update, and remove them. For more information please look at the pip documentation available at `https://pip.pypa.io/en/stable/`.

How it works...

pip downloads the requested package with all necessary dependencies from the Python Package Index (`https://pypi.python.org/`) and installs them into Python bundled with QGIS.

There's more...

You can also register Python bundled with QGIS in the Windows registry as the system default Python version. After this, you can use usual Windows installers to install the required packages. More information on this topic can be found at https://trac.osgeo.org/osgeo4w/ticket/114.

Using the Python console

QGIS has a built-in Python console, where you can enter commands in the Python programming language and get results. This is very useful for quick data processing.

Getting ready

To follow this recipe, you should be familiar with the Python programming language. You can find a small but detailed tutorial in the official Python documentation at https://docs.python.org/2.7/tutorial/index.html.

Also load the poi_names_wake.shp file from the sample data.

How to do it...

QGIS Python console can be opened by clicking on the **Python Console** button at toolbar or by navigating to **Plugins | Python Console**. The console opens as a non-modal floating window, as shown in the following screenshot:

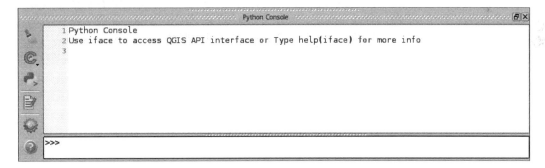

Let's take a look at how to perform some data exploration with the QGIS Python console:

1. First, it is necessary to get a reference to the active (selected in the layers tree) layer and store it in the variable for further use by running this command:

```
layer = iface.activeLayer()
```

2. After acquiring a reference to the layer, we can examine some of its properties. For example, to get the number of features in the layer, execute the following command:

```
layer.featureCount()
```

At any time, you can use the `dir()` function to list all the available methods of the object. Try to execute `dir(layer)` or `dir(QgsFeature)`.

3. You can also loop over layer features and print their attributes using the following code snippet:

```
for f in layer.getFeatures():
    print f["featurenam"], f["elev_m"]
```

Note that you need to press *Enter* twice after entering this code to exit the loop definition and start executing commands.

You can also use the Python console for more complex tasks, such as exporting features with some attributes to a text file. Here is how to do this:

1. Open the **Python Console** editor using the **Show editor** button on the left-hand side of the Python console.

2. Paste the following code into the editor (make sure to change path to file according to your system):

```
import csv
layer = iface.activeLayer()
with open('c:\\temp\\export.csv', 'wb') as outputFile:
    writer = csv.writer(outputFile)
    for feature in layer.getFeatures():
        geom = feature.geometry().exportToWkt()
        writer.writerow([geom, feature["featurenam"],
feature['elev_m"]])
```

3. If you are using your own vector layer instead of `poi_names_wake.shp`, which is provided with this book, adjust attribute names in line 8.

4. Change the file paths for the result file in line 4 depending on your operating system.

5. Save the script and run it. Don't forget to select the vector layer in the QGIS layer tree before running the script.

How it works...

In line 1, we imported the `csv` module from the standard Python library. This module provides a convenient way to read and write comma-separated files. In line 3, we obtained a reference to the currently selected layer, which will be used later to access layer features.

In line 3, an output file opened. Note that here we use the `with` statement so that later there is no need to close the file explicitly, context manager will do this work for us. In line 5, we set up the so-called writer—an object that will write data to the CSV file using specified format settings.

In line 6, we started iterating over features of the active layer. For each feature, we extracted its geometry and converted it into a **Well-Known Text** (**WKT**) format (line 7). We then wrote this text representation of the feature geometry with some attributes to the output file (line 8).

It is necessary to mention that our script is very simple and will work only with attributes that have ASCII encoding. To handle non-Latin characters, it is necessary to convert the output data to the unicode before writing it to file.

There's more...

Using the Python console, you also can invoke Processing algorithms to create complex scripts for automated analysis and/or data preparation.

To make the Python console even more useful, take a look at the Script Runner plugin. Detailed information about this plugin with some usage examples can be found at `http://spatialgalaxy.net/2012/01/29/script-runner-a-plugin-to-run-python-scripts-in-qgis/`.

See also

▸ If you are new to Python and QGIS API, don't forget to look at the following documentation:

- ❑ Official Python documentation and tutorial can be found at `https://docs.python.org/2/`
- ❑ *QGIS API Documentation* can be found at `http://qgis.org/api/2.8/`
- ❑ *PyQGIS Developer Cookbook* can be found at `http://docs.qgis.org/2.8/en/docs/pyqgis_developer_cookbook/`

- ▶ Another great resource to learn programming with QGIS is *QGIS Python Programming Cookbook, Joel Lawhead*, published by Packt Publishing

Writing Processing algorithms

You can extend the capabilities of QGIS by adding scripts that can be used within the Processing framework. This will allow you to create your own analysis algorithms and then run them efficiently from the toolbox or from any of the productivity tools, such as the batch processing interface or the graphical modeler.

This recipe covers basic ideas about how to create a Processing algorithm.

Getting ready

A basic knowledge of Python is needed to understand this recipe. Also, as it uses the Processing framework, you should be familiar with it before studying this recipe.

How to do it...

We are going to add a new process to filter the polygons of a layer, generating a new layer that just contains the ones with an area larger than a given value. Here's how to do this:

1. In the **Processing Toolbox** menu, go to the **Scripts/Tools** group and double-click on the **Create new script** item. You will see the following dialog:

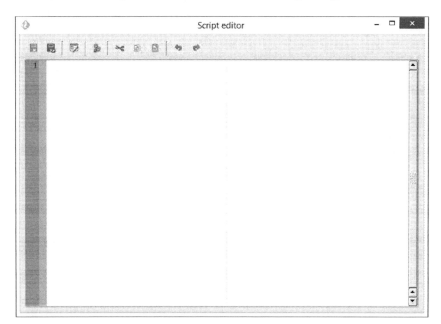

2. In the text editor of the dialog, paste the following code:

```
##Cookbook=group
##Filter polygons by size=name
##Vector_layer=vector
##Area=number 1
##Output=output vector

layer = processing.getObject(Vector_layer)
provider = layer.dataProvider()
writer = processing.VectorWriter(Output, None,
  provider.fields(), provider.geometryType(), layer.crs())
for feature in processing.features(layer):
  print feature.geometry().area()
  if feature.geometry().area() > Area:
    writer.addFeature(feature)
del writer
```

3. Select the **Save** button to save the script. In the file selector that will appear, enter a filename with the `.py` extension. Do not move this to a different folder. Make sure that you use the default folder that is selected when the file selector is opened.

4. Close the editor.

5. Go to the **Scripts** groups in the toolbox, and you will see a new group called **Cookbook** with an algorithm called `Filter polygons by size`.

6. Double-click on it to open it, and you will see the following parameters dialog, similar to what you can find for any of the other Processing algorithms:

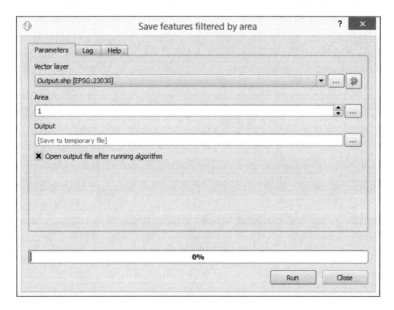

How it works...

The script contains mainly two parts:

▸ A part in which the characteristics of the algorithm are defined. This is used to define the semantics of the algorithm, along with some additional information, such as the name and group of the algorithm.

▸ A part that takes the inputs entered by the user and processes them to generate the outputs. This is where the algorithm itself is located.

In our example, the first part looks like the following:

```
##Cookbook=group
##Filter polygons by size=name
##Vector_layer=vector
##Area=number 1
##Output=output vector
```

We are defining two inputs (the layer and the area value) and declaring one output (the filtered layer). These elements are defined using the Python comments with a double Python comment sign (#).

The second part includes the code itself and looks like the following:

```
layer = processing.getObject(Vector_layer)
provider = layer.dataProvider()
writer = processing.VectorWriter(Output, None,
  provider.fields(), provider.geometryType(), layer.crs())
for feature in processing.features(layer):
  print feature.geometry().area()
  if feature.geometry().area() > Area:
    writer.addFeature(feature)
del writer
```

The inputs that we defined in the first part will be available here, and we can use them. In the case of the area, we will have a variable named `Area`, containing a number. In the case of the vector layer, we will have a `Layer` variable, containing a string with the source of the selected layer.

Using these values, we use the PyQGIS API to perform the calculations and create a new layer. The layer is saved in the file path contained in the `Output` variable, which is the one that the user will select when running the algorithm.

Apart from using regular Python and the PyQGIS interface, Processing includes some classes and functions because this makes it easier to create scripts, and that wrap some of the most common functionality of QGIS.

In particular, the `processing.features(layer)` method is important. This provides an iterator over the features in a layer, but only considering the selected ones. If no selection exists, it iterates over all the features in the layer. This is the expected behavior of any Processing algorithm, so this method has to be used to provide a consistent behavior in your script.

There's more...

Some of the core algorithms that are provided with Processing are actually scripts, such as the one we just created, but they do not appear in the scripts section. Instead, they appear in the **QGIS algorithms** section because they are a core part of Processing.

Other scripts are not part of processing itself but they can be installed easily from the toolbox using the **Tools/Get scripts from on-line collection** menu:

You will see a window like the following one:

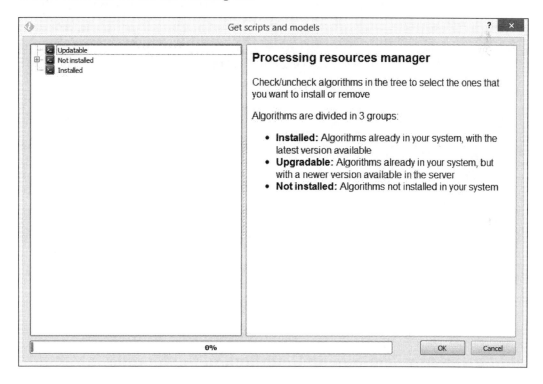

Just select the scripts that you want to install and then click on **OK**. The selected scripts will now appear in the toolbox. You can use it as you use any other Processing algorithm.

See also

▸   All the information about creating scripts and running Processing code from the QGIS Python console can be found in the corresponding section in the QGIS manual.

Writing QGIS plugins

One of the main reasons of the popularity of QGIS is its extensibility. Using the basic tools and features provided by the QGIS API, new functionality can be implemented and added as a new plugin that can be shared by contributing it to the QGIS plugins repository.

Getting ready

To be able to develop a new QGIS plugin, you should be familiar with the Python programming language. If the plugin has a graphical interface, you should have some knowledge of the Qt framework, as this is used for all UI elements, such as dialogs. To access the QGIS functionality, it is required that you know the QGIS API.

A very handy resource for all these (plus a few others) is the GeoAPIs website, which is created by SourcePole at `http://geoapis.sourcepole.com/`.

To simplify the creation of a plugin, we will use an additional plugin named Plugin Builder. It should be installed in your QGIS application.

How to do it...

The following steps create a new plugin that will print out detailed information about the layers currently loaded in your QGIS project:

1.   Open Plugin Builder by navigating to **Plugin | Plugin Builder**.

2.   Fill out the dialog that will appear, as shown in the following screenshot:

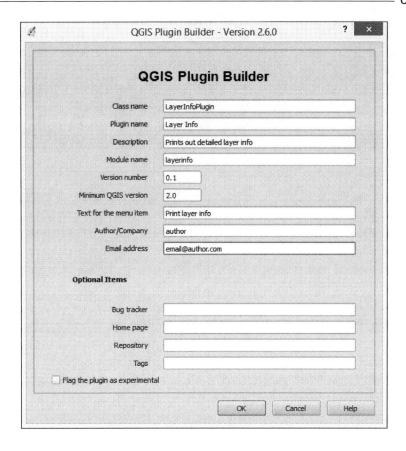

3. Click on **OK**.

4. In the folder selector dialog that will appear, select the folder where you want to store your plugin. Click on **OK** and the plugin skeleton will be created. In the selected folder, you will now have a subfolder named `LayerInfoPlugin`, with the following content (items in square brackets indicate folders):

```
[help]
[i18n]
[scripts]
[test]
icon.png
layerinfo.py
layerinfo_dialog.py
layerinfo_dialog_base.ui
Makefile
metadata.txt
pb_tool.cfg
```

```
plugin_upload.py
pylintrc
README.html
README.txt
resources.qrc
__init__.py
```

5. Open the `layerinfo.py` file in a text editor. At the end of it, you will find the `run()` method, with the following code:

```
def run(self):
    """Run method that performs all the real work"""
    # show the dialog
    self.dlg.show()
    # Run the dialog event loop
    result = self.dlg.exec_()
    # See if OK was pressed
    if result: pass
```

6. Replace the `run` method with the following code:

```
def run(self):
    layers = self.iface.legendInterface().layers()
    print "---LAYERS INFO---"
    for layer in layers:
        print "Layer name: " + layer.name()
        print "Layer source " + layer.source()
        print "Extent: " + layer.extent().asWktCoordinates()
        print
```

7. Install the `pb_tool` application by opening a terminal and running `easy_install pb_tool` (you can also use `pip install pb_tool` or any other way of installing a library from PyPI).

8. Open a terminal in the folder where you have the plugin code and run `pb_tool` and compile. Then, run `pb_tool deploy` to install the plugin in your local QGIS.

9. Open QGIS. Go to **Plugin Manager** and make sure that the new plugin we have created is there and is enabled:

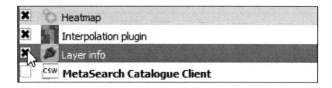

10. In the **Plugins** menu, you will now have the entry corresponding to the plugin:

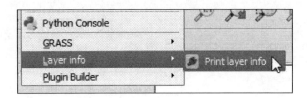

11. Populate your project with some layers so that the plugin can display information about them.

12. Open the QGIS Python console.

13. Run the plugin by selecting its menu entry. Information about the layers in the project will be shown in the console:

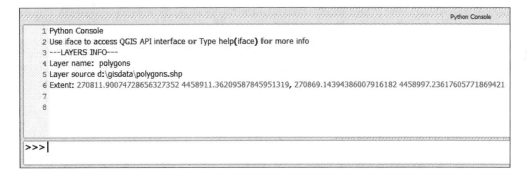

How it works...

The Plugin Builder plugin takes some basic information about the plugin to create it, and uses it to create its skeleton. By default, it includes a menu entry, which becomes the entry point to the plugin from the QGIS interface.

When the menu item is selected, the corresponding action in the plugin code is executed. In this case, it runs the `run()` method, where we have added our code.

The plugin will always have a reference to the QGIS instance (an object of class `QgsInterface`), which can be used to access the QGIS API and connect with the elements in the current QGIS session. In our case, this is used to access the legend, which contains a list of all the layers loaded in the current project. Calling the corresponding methods in each one of these layers, the information about them is retrieved and printed out.

The standard output is redirected to the QGIS Python console, so printing a text using the built-in Python print command will cause the text to appear in the console in case it is open.

QGIS stores its plugins in the `.qgis2/python/plugin` folder under the current user folder. For instance, this is when you download a new plugin using Plugin Manager. Each time you start QGIS, it will look for plugins there and load them. Copying the folder is done by the deploy task that we have run, and this allows QGIS to discover the plugin and add it to the list of available plugins when QGIS is started.

There's more...

The following are some ideas to create better plugins and manage them.

Creating plugins with more complex UI elements

The plugin that we have created has no UI elements. However, among the files created by the plugin builder, you can find a basic dialog file with the `.ui` extension. You can edit this to create a dialog that can later be used, by calling it from your plugin code. To know more about how to create and use UI elements from the Qt framework (QGIS is built on top of this framework), check out the PyQt documentation.

Documenting you plugin

Another thing that is created by the Plugin Builder is a Sphinx documentation project where you can write the usage documentation of your plugin using RestructuredText. To know more about Sphinx, you can visit the Sphinx official site at `http://www.sphinx-doc.org/en/stable/`.

The documentation project is built when the deploy task is run, and will create HTML files and place them in the plugin folder.

Releasing your plugin

Once your plugin is finished, it would be a good idea to share it and let other people use it. If you upload your plugin to the QGIS plugin server, it would be easy for all QGIS users to get it using Plugin Manager and also get the latest updates.

To upload the plugin, you first need to create a ZIP file containing all its code and resources. There is a `pb_tool` task for this, and you just have to run `pb_tool zip` in a terminal. With the resulting ZIP file, you can start the release process. More information about it can be found at `http://docs.qgis.org/2.6/en/docs/pyqgis_developer_cookbook/releasing.html`.

Using external tools

While QGIS itself is a great and functional program, sometimes it is better to use more suitable tools to perform some simple or complex actions. This recipe shows you how to use some of these third-party tools.

Getting ready

To follow this recipe, you will need a `btnmeatrack_2014-05-22_13-35-40.nmea` file from the book dataset. We will also use the `cookbook.db` SpatiaLite database that we created in the *Loading vector layers into SpatiaLite* recipe in *Chapter 1*, *Data Input and Output*, and the PostgreSQL database, which we developed in *Chapter 6*, *Network Analysis*.

Besides this, don't forget to install GPSBabel (usually this comes with QGIS), spatialite-gui, and pgAdmin (these should be installed manually).

How to do it...

First we will convert NMEA data to GPX format with GPSBabel, then learn how to use SpatiaLite GUI tools and pgAdmin to work with databases.

GPSBabel

GPSBabel is a command-line tool to manipulate, convert, and process GPS data (waypoints, tracks, and routes) in different formats.

To convert a file from the NMEA format to more common GPX, follows these steps:

1. Open the command prompt and go to the directory where the `btnmeatrack_2014-05-22_13-35-40.nmea` file is located. Usually, this can be done with the `cd` command, for example, if the file is located in the `data` directory on the `C:` drive, use this command:

   ```
   cd c:\data
   ```

2. In the command prompt, enter the following command to convert the NMEA file to the GPX file:

   ```
   gpsbabel -i nmea -f btnmeatrack_2014-05-22_13-35-40.nmea -o
   gpx -F 2014-05-22_13_35-40.gpx
   ```

spatialite-gui

spatialite-gui is a GUI tool supporting SpatiaLite. This is lightweight and very useful when you need to quickly perform some queries or just check contents of the SQLite/SpatiaLite database.

To explore spatial or nonspatial tables in the SpatiaLite database, perform these steps:

1. Start `spatialite-gui` by double-clicking on its executable file.

2. Connect to the database that you want to explore by navigating to **Files | Connecting an existing SQLite DB** or clicking on the corresponding button on the toolbar.

3. Select the table you want to explore in the table tree on the left-hand side of the **spatialite-gui** dialog, open its context menu by clicking on the right mouse button, and select the **Edit table rows** menu entry.

4. If your table contains spatial data, it is possible to view geometry in different representations. Select the field with the geometry information in the row, open the context menu by clicking the right mouse button and select the **BLOB Explore** menu entry:

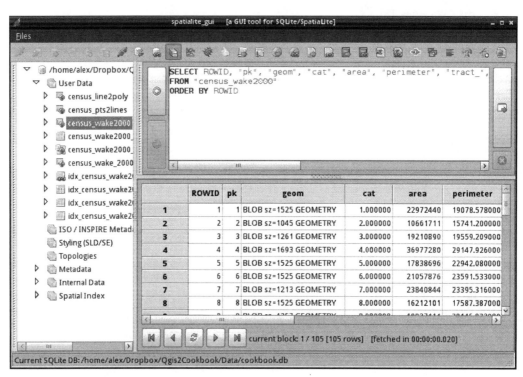

After massive edits, especially when tables were altered or deleted, it is recommended to run VACUUM command to rebuild the database. To do this, perform these steps:

1. Start `spatialite-gui` by double-clicking on its executable file.

2. Connect to the database that you want to explore by navigating to **Files | Connecting an existing SQLite DB** or clicking on the corresponding button on the toolbar.

3. Navigate to **Files | Optimizing current SQLite DB [VACUUM]** or click on the corresponding button on the toolbar.

pgAdmin

pgAdmin is an administration tool and development platform for PostgreSQL databases. It allows you to perform administrative tasks (such as backup and restore), run simple queries as well as develop new databases from scratch.

To create a backup of the database with pgAdmin, follow these steps:

1. Start pgAdmin by clicking on its desktop shortcut or by finding it in the **Start** menu.

2. Create a connection to your database server if it does not exist by navigating to **File | Add Server...** or clicking on the corresponding button on the toolbar.

3. Connect to the database server where your database is located by double-clicking on its name in **Object Browser** on the left-hand side of the **pgAdmin** window.

4. Select the database that you want to back up, open its context menu by clicking the right mouse button, and select **Backup**. A backup settings dialog will be opened, as shown in the following screenshot:

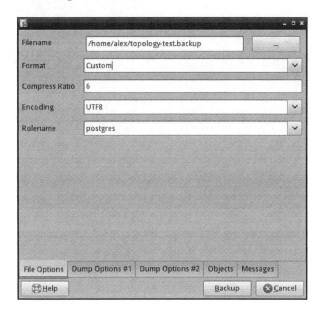

5. Choose a location where your backup will be saved, adjust the backup options according to your needs, and click on the **Backup** button to start the backup process. The progress will be displayed in the **Messages** tab.

To restore the database from the backup, perform the following steps:

1. Start pgAdmin by clicking on its desktop shortcut or by finding it in the **Start** menu.

2. Create a connection to your database server if it does not exist by navigating to **File | Add Server...** or clicking on the corresponding button on the toolbar.

3. Connect to the database server where you want to restore the backup and double-click on its name in **Object Browser** on the left-hand side of the **pgAdmin** window.

4. Select database that should be restored, open its context menu by clicking the right mouse button, and select **Restore**. A restore options dialog will be opened, as shown in the following screenshot:

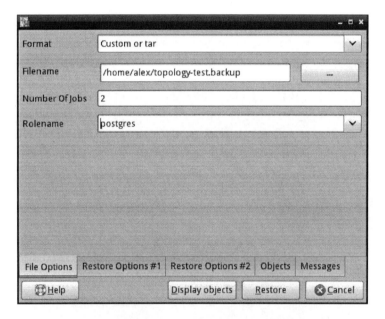

 It is worth mentioning that the pg_restore tool used by pgAdmin to restore cannot create the database that has to be restored. It is necessary to create a new empty database manually and then start the restoration with this freshly created database.

5. Select the location of the backup file and adjust the restore options according to your needs.

 Note that you can restore single table or schema, just click on the **Display objects** button after selecting the backup file and choose desired objects on the **Objects** tab.

6. Click on the **Restore** button to start restoring. The progress will be displayed in the **Messages** tab.

How it works...

All of the tools here work on the same file formats as QGIS. This allows for greater flexibility when working by being able to use the best tool at the right time.

There's more...

There are many other different tools that can be useful in various situations, for example, exiv2 can be used to manipulate the EXIF tags of the photos, ImageMagic to process rasters, and so on.

12
Up and Coming

In this chapter, we will cover the following topics:

- ▶ Preparing LiDAR data
- ▶ Opening File Geodatabases with the OpenFileGDB driver
- ▶ Using Geopackages
- ▶ The PostGIS Topology Editor plugin
- ▶ The Topology Checker plugin
- ▶ GRASS Topology tools
- ▶ Hunting for bugs
- ▶ Reporting bugs

Introduction

The software landscape is constantly changing and QGIS is no exception. There are new features added weekly, and a huge, growing library of plugins. This chapter highlights some of the newer features at the time of writing. These are features that we think will be around for some time due to their usefulness. Keep in mind, however, that they are still in development and can easily change at any moment; hopefully, this is for the better. Included in this chapter are the handling of some more recent and additional formats that were not covered earlier, such as LIDAR, File Geodatabases, and Geopackages. Also included are several recipes on topology usage, editing, and fixing. Finally, there are a few recipes on how you can become part of the community that helps evolve QGIS through bug hunting and reporting.

Preparing LiDAR data

LiDAR data is becoming more available, and it represents a fundamental source of detailed elevation data. This chapter will show you how to work with LiDAR data in QGIS.

Getting ready

We will use the Processing framework, so you should be familiar with it.

We will also use LASTools, which is not included with QGIS. Download LASTools binaries from `http://lastools.org/download/LAStools.zip` and install them on your computer.

Processing has to be configured so that it can find and execute LASTools. Open the Processing configuration by going to the **Processing | Options** menu and move to the **Tools for LiDAR data** section, as shown in the following screenshot:

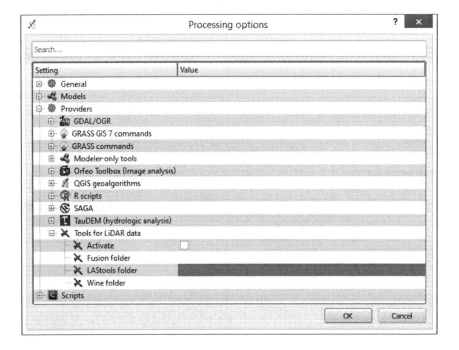

In the **LAStools folder** field, type the path to the folder where you have installed the LASTools executables.

How to do it...

In the data corresponding to this recipe, you will find a `las` file with LiDAR data. This cannot be opened in QGIS, but we will convert it so that it can be opened and rendered as part of a normal QGIS project.

Follow these steps:

1. Open the **Processing Toolbox** menu.
2. In the **Tools for LiDAR data/LASTools** branch, double-click on the **las2shp** algorithm. The parameters dialog of the algorithm looks like the following:

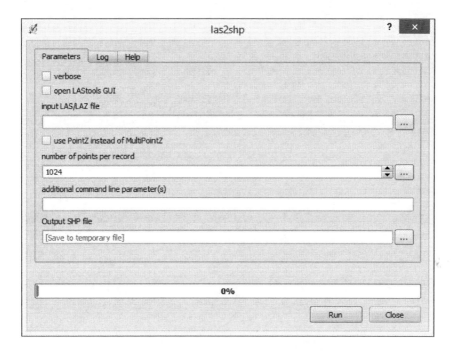

3. Enter the path to the sample LAS file provided with this recipe in the **Input LAS/LAZ file** field.
4. Enter the path to the output shapefile in the **Output SHP file** field.
5. Leave the remaining parameters as they are and click on **OK** to run the algorithm.
6. The resulting shapefile with the point cloud will be added to your QGIS project.

How it works...

The las2shp tool converts a LAS file into a SHP file. Processing calls las2shp using the provided parameters, and then loads the resulting layer into your QGIS project.

There's more...

You can also convert a LAS file into a raster layer using the las2dem algorithm instead.

In the **Tools for LiDAR data/LASTools** branch, double-click on the **las2dem** algorithm. The **Parameters** dialog of the algorithm looks like the following:

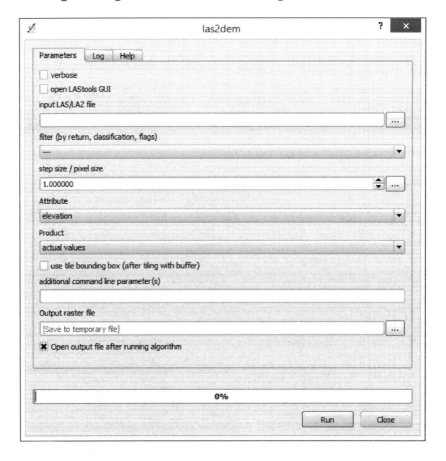

1. Enter the path to the sample LAS file that is provided with this recipe in the **Input LAS/LAZ file** field.

2. Enter the path to the output TIFF file in the **Output file** field.

3. Enter 0.005 in the **step size/pixel size** field.

4. Leave the remaining parameters as they are and click on **OK** to run the algorithm.

5. The resulting raster layer will be added to your QGIS project.

Opening File Geodatabases with the OpenFileGDB driver

File **Geodatabases** (**GDB**) are a relatively new format compared to shapefiles, and they were created by Esri for their Arc product line. They allow the storage of multiple vector and raster layers in a single database. Some government agencies release data officially in this format. However, only in the last few years has it been possible to open this data with open source tools.

Getting ready

For this recipe, you will need a File Geodatabase, naturalearthsample.gdb.zip, which is included in the sample data, and GDAL 1.11 or a newer version.

 Check your GDAL version by navigating to **Help | About | About**. If your GDAL is a lower number, upgrading your QGIS should get you a new enough version. Refer to http://qgis.org/en/site/forusers/download. html for more options, especially if on Linux where you may need third-party repositories for a newer version of GDAL.

File Geodatabases are actually folders full of all sorts of binary files. Typically, you will get them zipped and must extract the zip to a real system folder before you can use it.

How to do it...

1. Unzip the naturalearthsample.gdb.zip file so that you have a folder called naturalearthsample.gdb.

2. Select the **Add Vector** dialog.

3. Select **Directory** instead of **File** for the **Source type** option.

4. From the **Type** dropdown, pick **OpenFileGDB**.

5. Now, choose **Browse** and navigate to the naturalearthsample.gdb folder (if you haven't unzipped this already you need to do this first).

 Yes, it's a little odd to have .gdb on the end of a folder as this makes it look like a file. This just seems to be the standard convention.

6. Select the folder (not the contents), and then select **Open**.

7. Once back in the main dialog, choose **Open**, as shown in the following screenshot:

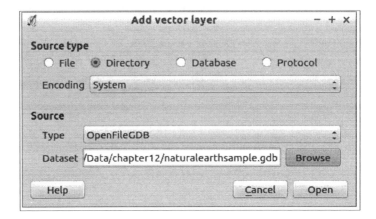

8. You should be prompted with a list of available layers. Select the ones that you want, and click **OK**. You can select multiple layers to add at the same time:

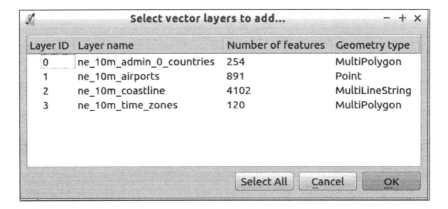

How it works...

This is fairly straightforward. You tell QGIS the root folder of the File Geodatabase, and it can figure out how to use all the files inside of the folder appropriately. As long as GDAL has a driver for a given format, then you should be able to open the data with QGIS. Support for additional formats is always ongoing and being refined.

There's more...

The key limitation to File Geodatabase drivers currently are that raster layers are not supported and that there is limited write ability for vectors. There are actually two different drivers. One is an open source project, which is built by the community, and is the default driver. The other is based on a development library, which is released publicly by ESRI that has specific license restrictions.

OpenFileGDB, the open source community-built driver, can open multiple versions of GDB (9 and 10), is read only, and comes with most versions of GDAL 1.11+.

The ESRIFileGDB driver can read and write vector layers (this has some limitations, which are discussed in the link in the *See also* section). However, it often can only open the version of GDB it was built for (the newest version only reads newer GDB formats, for example, 10). Sometimes, it requires you to build the GDAL driver from the SDK code provided by ESRI. (This is done for Windows users as part of osgeo4w; Linux, and Mac users at this time need to compile GDAL with the FileGDB SDK 1.4.)

To use this driver, pick a different type in the dialog as **ESRIFileGDB**. If you don't see it listed, you don't have a version of GDAL that includes this, and you will need to compile GDAL yourself.

If you get a database in this format, consider batch converting it to Spatialite, which will maintain most of the same information and give you full read, write, query, and edit capabilities in QGIS. You'll need the `ogr2ogr` command for now until someone writes a plugin (or you could load them one by one with the DB Manager):

```
ogr2ogr -f SQLite naturalearthsample.sqlite naturalearthsample.gdb -skip-
failures -
nlt PROMOTE_TO_MULTI -dsco SPATIALITE=YES
```

See also

▶ The GDAL/OGR information pages about the two formats can be found at http://gdal.org/drv_filegdb.html vs http://gdal.org/drv_openfilegdb.html

Using Geopackages

Geopackage is a new open standard for geospatial data exchange from the **Open Geospatial Consortium** (**OGC**), an industry standards organization. It is intended to allow users to bundle multiple layers of various types into a single file that can easily be passed to others. This recipe demonstrates how to utilize this new data format and what to expect in the future.

Getting ready

For this recipe, you will need a Geopackage file, often the extension is `.gpkg`. There should be a `naturalearthsample.gpkg` file in the provided sample data.

You'll also need GDAL 1.11 or newer; if you have QGIS 2.6 or newer, this probably came with a new enough GDAL. If you don't have a new enough GDAL, consider upgrading QGIS, which usually bundles newer versions.

 Want to check what versions you have? In QGIS, open **Help** | **About** | **About**.

How to do it...

1. Open the **Add Vector** dialog.

2. Click on the **Browse** button and select the `naturalearthsample.gpkg` file:

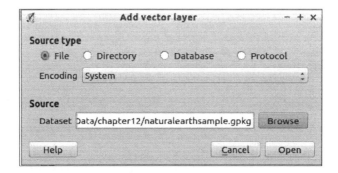

3. Now, back in the main dialog, click on **Open**.

4. This should prompt you, asking which layers you want to add from the database:

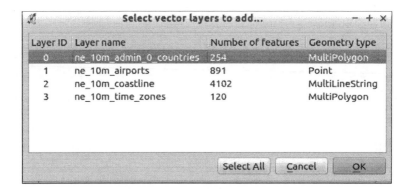

Note that the QGIS browser can detect and read Geopackage files. Just navigate to the file and double-click on it to get the same layer selector, as shown in the preceding screenshot.

How it works...

Consider Geopackage more of a read-only format. Even though it is not, its whole purpose is to exchange collections of data between systems with a single file, especially mobile systems. Due to this, once you have loaded layers, consider saving them to another format. Keep in mind that saving to Shapefiles may cause data loss in the attribute table. Spatialite or PostGIS are the recommend formats; refer to recipes *Loading vector layers into SpatiaLite and Loading vector layers into PostGIS* in *Chapter 1, Data Input and Output*.

There's more...

Geopackage is also a database that is based on SQLite and it is compatible with SpatiaLite. If you open it with SpatiaLite tools, you should be able to query the tables. Geopackage and SpatiaLite store geometries differently, so not all functions or spatial index methods are available to Geopackages, but they are very easy to convert.

QGIS 2.10 introduces the ability to write a single layer to a Geopackage. It's expected that QGIS 2.12 will add the ability to write multiple layers to the same Geopackage (as well as SpatiaLite). In the meantime, you can use `ogr2ogr` on the command line to manage layers in a Geopackage.

If you want to batch convert a Geopackage to SpatiaLite, this can be done on the command line (OSGeo4W Shell on Windows, and a Terminal on Mac or Linux), as follows:

```
ogr2ogr -f SQLite naturalearthsample.sqlite naturalearthsample.gpkg
-skip-failures -nlt
PROMOTE_TO_MULTI -dsco SPATIALITE=YES
```

You can also perform the reverse to create a Geopackage:

```
ogr2ogr -f GPKG naturalearthsample.gpkg naturalearthsample.sqlite
```

Keep your eyes out for future implementation of raster support. The Geopackage specification does include limited raster support, which is primarily targeted at including imagery or tiles in the database for use on mobile devices.

See also

▸ For more information about the format, visit `http://www.geopackage.org/`

The PostGIS Topology Editor plugin

Maintaining topology in the vector layers is very important; this results in greater data integrity and leads to more accurate analysis results. This recipe shows you how to edit PostGIS topology layers (in other words, layers with topology objects, such as edges, faces, and nodes) with QGIS.

> Installation of PostGIS with topology support won't be covered in detail here because instructions for the different operating systems can be found on the project website at `http://postgis.net/docs/manual-2.1/postgis_installation.html`. If you are using Windows, PostGIS can be installed directly from the Stack Builder application, which is provided by the standard PostgreSQL installation, as described at `http://www.bostongis.com/PrinterFriendly.aspx?content_name=postgis_tut01`.

Getting ready

To follow this exercise, you need a PostGIS database with topology enabled. In QGIS, you should set up the connection to the database using the **New** button in the **Add PostGIS Layers** dialog.

Also, it is necessary to install and activate the **PostGIS Topology Editor** plugin.

How to do it...

These steps will create a topology-enabled vector layer in your PostGIS database:

1. Open **DB Manager** by navigating to **Database | DB Manager**.
2. In the tree to the left-hand side of the dialog, select the database that you want to create the topology in.

3. Go to **Database | SQL window** to open SQL-editor, as shown into following screenshot:

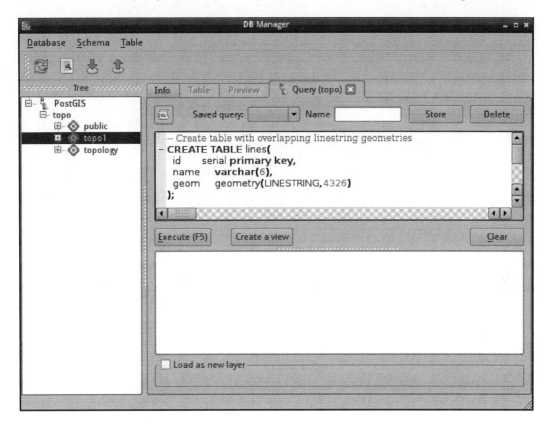

4. In the editor, paste the contents of the `topology.sql` file and click on **Execute (F5)** to run the queries.

5. After the topology has been created, click on the **Refresh** button on the **DB Manager** toolbar to reload the list of available tables. You should see a new `topo1` table in **Tree**.

6. Select the newly created `topo1` table in **Tree** and go to **Schema | TopoViewer** to load all the topology layers into QGIS. The result should look like the following:

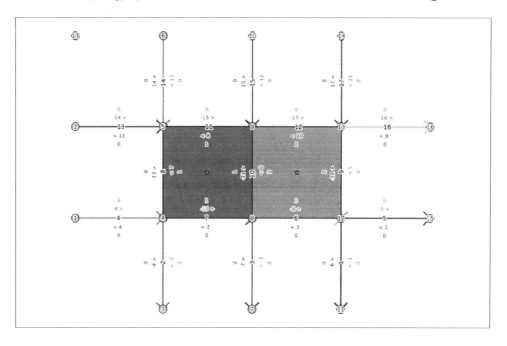

Once the topology is ready and loaded into QGIS, we can edit it with the **PostGIS Topology Editor** plugin. It is worth mentioning that, currently, the plugin allows us only to delete nodes and edges. Other editing operations are not supported.

To delete a node, perform the following steps:

1. In **Layers Panel**, expand the `Nodes` group and select the `topo1.node` layer.
2. Using the **Select features by area or single click** tool, select the QGIS canvas isolated node that you want to delete, for example node 17.
3. Click on the **Remove node** button, and the node will be deleted. In case of any error, you will see an error message with a possible reason.

> Remember that the **PostGIS Topology Editor** plugin operates on the database level and all actions performed by it can not be reverted.

To delete edges, perform the following steps:

1. In **Layers Panel**, expand the `Edges` group and select the edge layer that you want to edit, for example, the `topo1.edge` layer.

2. Using the **Select features by area or single click** tool, select the edges that you want to delete.

3. Click on the **Remove edge** button to remove the edges, and they will be deleted. In case of any error, you will see an error message with a possible reason.

As QGIS currently does not support dynamic updates of topology, it is necessary to reload topology layers with TopoViewer to reflect our edits:

1. Create a new project by clicking on the **New** button on the QGIS toolbar.

2. Open **DB Manager** by navigating to **Database | DB Manager**.

3. In the tree to the left-hand side of the dialog, find the database with your topology layers.

4. Select the `topo1` table in the tree, and go to **Schema | TopoViewer** to load all topology layers into QGIS:

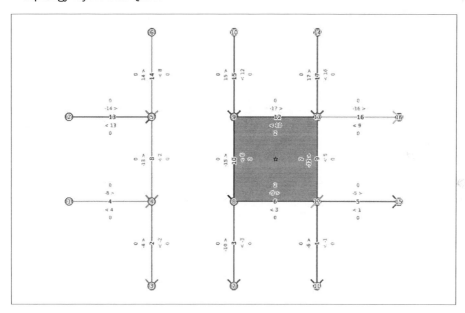

You will see that the previously deleted nodes and edges now disappear.

How it works...

The PostGIS Topology Editor plugin issues SQL queries directly to the corresponding topology tables in the PostGIS database to remove edges and nodes.

▸ More information about PostGIS topology support can be found in the official PostGIS documentation at `http://postgis.net/docs/manual-2.1/Topology.html`

The Topology Checker plugin

Topology is a set of rules that defines the spatial relationship between adjacent features, and it also defines and enforces data integrity and validity.

This recipe shows you how to use the built-in Topology Checker plugin to find topology errors in vector layers.

To follow this recipe, load the `census_wake2000_topology.shp` and `roadsmajor.shp` layers from the sample data. Additionally, make sure that the **Topology Checker** plugin is enabled in **Plugin Manager**.

The Topology Checker plugin allows us to test a vector layer or its part for different topology errors. Before we can use this, we should load all the layers that we want to test in QGIS and then configure topology rules:

1. Enable the **Topology Checker** panel in the **View | Panels** menu. This should add the plugin panel to the user interface, as shown in the following screenshot:

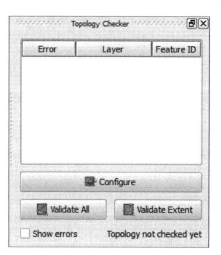

2. Click on the **Configure** button at the bottom of the plugin panel to open the **Topology Rule Settings** dialog:

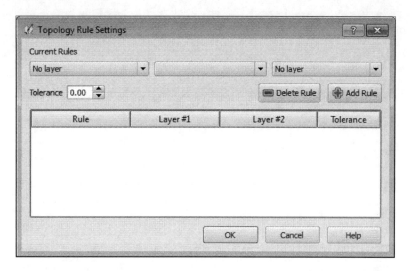

3. To set a rule, choose a layer that you want to check in the first combobox. Select the roadsmajor layer.

4. Then, select the rule from the second combobox, for example, **must not have dangles**. As this rule needs only one layer, the third combobox disappears.

5. Note that the list of available rules depends on the geometry type of the target layer; also, some rules allow the testing of the spatial relationship between two layers.

6. Click on the **Add Rule** button to add rule to the list of current rules:

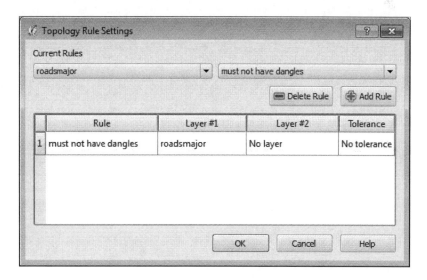

7. Let's add another rule, this time to check the polygonal layer. Select `census_wake2000_topology` as the target layer.

8. Select **must not overlap** as the rule and click on the **Add Rule** button to create a new rule.

9. Using the same approach, add another two rules to check this layer: **must not have gaps** and **must not have duplicates**:

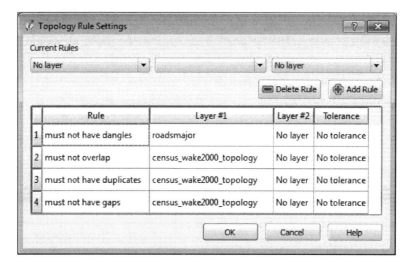

10. Click on the **OK** button to save your settings and close the dialog.

11. Now, when we have defined the rules, we can check topology of the whole layers by clicking on the **Validate All** button or only features within visible area by clicking on the **Validate Extent** button. For this recipe, we will validate all layers, so click on the **Validate All** button.

12. After some time (this depends on the number of the features in the layer and computer speed), all detected topology errors will be displayed in the plugin panel, as shown in the following screenshot:

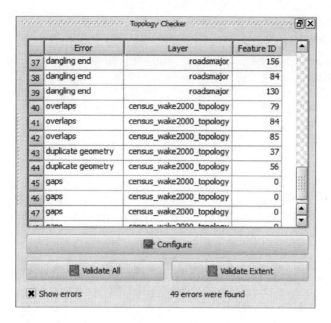

13. If the **Show errors** checkbox is activated (this is the default setting), topology errors that can be visualized will also be highlighted in red on the map:

14. Selecting the error in the plugin panel will center the QGIS map canvas on the problematic feature and highlight it in green if possible.

How it works...

The Topology Checker plugin uses the GEOS library as well as its own algorithms to check spatial relationships between features in the vector layer.

See also

▶ A short introduction to vector topology can be found in the Gentle GIS introduction at `https://docs.qgis.org/2.2/en/docs/gentle_gis_introduction/topology.html`

▶ More information about the available rules of the Topology Checker plugin can be found in the QGIS User Guide at `http://docs.qgis.org/2.8/en/docs/user_manual/plugins/plugins_topology_checker.html`

GRASS Topology tools

Having vector data without topology errors is important for further analysis, as these errors may lead to incorrect results.

This recipe shows you how to use the built-in GRASS tools to fix various topology errors in vector layers.

Getting ready

QGIS has very good integration with GRASS GIS; there is a **GRASS** plugin that provides access to the GRASS GIS database and functionality. GRASS algorithms are also available from the **Processing** plugin. The latter is simpler because you don't need to bother with setting up GRASS locations and mapsets and importing and exporting data.

To follow this recipe, load the `nonbreak.shp`, `dangles.shp`, and `nosnap.shp` layers from the sample data. Additionally, make sure that the **Processing** plugin is enabled in **Plugin Manager**.

How to do it...

The following steps show you how to fix various topology errors with the GRASS v.clean toolset using the Processing toolbox:

First, we will learn how to remove dangling lines. Dangling lines are lines that have no connection with other lines on one or either end nodes:

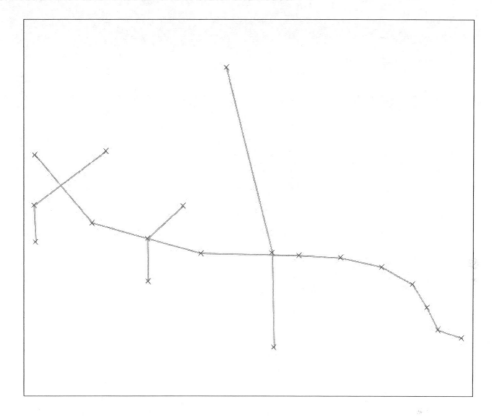

To remove them, perform the following steps:

1. In the **Processing Toolbox** menu, find the **v.clean** algorithm by typing its name in the **filter** field at the top of the toolbox. Double-click on the algorithm name to open its dialog.

2. In the **Layer to clean** combobox, select the dangling layer.

3. In the **Cleaning tool** combobox, select **rmdangle**—a tool for the removal of dangles.

4. The **Threshold** field is used to define the maximum length of the dangling line. For our example, enter **6.000000**:

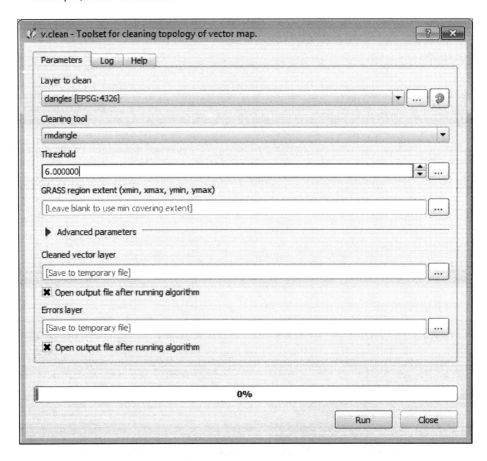

5. Click on the **Run** button to remove dangles. When the algorithm is finished, two new layers will be added to QGIS: the `Cleaned` layer contains cleaned geometries (shown in green) and the `Errors` layer contains dangles that were removed (shown in red):

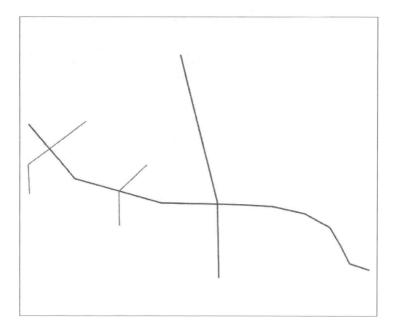

Another topology issue is missed line breaks in the intersection nodes. To add break at intersections, perform the following steps:

1. In the **Processing Toolbox** menu, find the **v.clean** algorithm by typing its name in the **filter** field at the top of the toolbox. Double-click on the algorithm name to open its dialog.

2. In the **Layer to clean** combobox, select the nobreaks layer.

3. In the **Cleaning tool** combobox, select **break**.

4. Leave all other parameters unchanged and click on the **Run** button to break lines on intersections. When the algorithm is finished, a new layer will be added to QGIS. You can easily verify that now lines are split at the intersection point.

Another very common topology issue is undershots, which happen when the line feature is not connected with another one at the intersection point and overshoots, which happens when the line ends beyond another line instead of connecting to it. Such errors often appear after inaccurate digitizing. To fix them, perform the following steps:

1. In the **Processing Toolbox** menu, find the **v.clean** algorithm by typing its name in the **filter** field at the top of the toolbox. Double-click on the algorithm name to open its dialog.

2. In the **Layer to clean** combobox, select the nosnap layer.

3. In the **Cleaning tool** combobox, select **snap**.

4. The **Threshold** field is used to define the snapping tolerance in map units. For our example, you can leave this unchanged.

5. Click on the **Run** button to remove overshoots and undershoots. When the algorithm is finished, two new layers will be added to QGIS: the `Cleaned` layer contains features with fixed errors and the `Errors` layer contains original invalid features.

How it works...

The rmdangle tool simply sequentially removes all dangling lines with length less than the given threshold. If the threshold is less than 0, then all dangles will be removed.

The break tool breaks lines at intersections, so all lines will have a common node. This tool does not need a threshold value to be specified.

The snap tool tries to snap vertices to another one within the given threshold, if no appropriate vertices are found, then no snapping is done. It is worth mentioning that large threshold values may break the topology of polygonal features.

There's more...

If you need more control over the topology cleaning process, try to use **v.clean.advanced** from the **Processing Toolbox** menu or consider using the GRASS plugin.

Also, there are other ways to clean vector topology, for example, using the lwgeom functions or external tools such as prepair and pprepair. Both tools are available as **Processing** plugins, and they can be installed via **Plugin Manager**.

See also

▶ More information about the GRASS v.clean toolset can be found at `http://grass.osgeo.org/grass64/manuals/v.clean.html`

Hunting for bugs

While QGIS developers do their best to make every QGIS release as stable as possible, sometimes you may encounter bugs or even crashes. To get them fixed in the future, it is necessary to inform the developers about issues.

This recipe shows you how to perform basic debugging and collect information that will help developers understand the problem better and help to fix it.

Getting ready

As the QGIS development process is very quick, bugs that are present in older versions are very likely already fixed in the latest version. So, it is necessary to ensure that you have the most recent QGIS version. If you use the development version of QGIS (so called "nightly" builds), upgrade to the last available build. If you prefer stable releases, then ensure that you have the latest stable version.

How to do it...

1. Repeat the same actions again using the same data and settings to ensure that this is not an accidental error.

2. Test your vector data (if any) with geometry checking tools to ensure that data is valid and has no geometry errors. If the data has geometry errors, then try to reproduce the bug with valid data.

3. Check whether the same error happens with other data to ensure that this is not related to the specific dataset.

4. If the error happens only on some specific features, extract them into a separate layer and make a small self-containing test dataset that allows you to reproduce bug. The same approach should be used if the dataset is large.

5. Sometimes, errors may be caused by third-party plugins. Disable all plugins and try to reproduce the error. If you cannot reproduce the bug with the disabled plugins, probably this bug is somehow related to some plugin. To find this problematic plugin, activate the plugins one by one and try to reproduce the error.

6. Look in the QGIS message log, it may contain useful debug and/or error messages that are related to your problem:

7. To open the **Log Messages** window, click on the **Messages** button located in the right corner of the QGIS status bar.

8. If QGIS crashes, try to create a backtrace and/or collect debug messages (refer to the following sections). This will be extremely useful if your bug is not reproducible on the developer's computer.

Creating a backtrace under Linux

Under Linux, QGIS automatically tries to use gdb to produce a backtrace when crashed.

 To see the backtrace, it is necessary to start QGIS from the terminal emulator.

If you see no backtrace after the crash, this may mean that the possibility to connect debugger to the running processes is disabled in your distribution (for example, Ubuntu after version 10.10). This behavior is controlled by the `ptrace_scope` sysctl value. If it equals to 1 ptrace calls from external processes are not allowed. A value that equals to 0 allows external processes to examine memory of the other process.

In such cases, to enable a backtrace creation, temporarily open the root shell and execute the following command:

```
echo 0 > /proc/sys/kernel/yama/ptrace_scope
```

If you want to enable a backtrace creation permanently, you need to edit the `/etc/sysctl.d/10-ptrace.conf` file as root, and set the value to 0. Then, run as root to reload sysctl settings, as follows:

```
sysctl -p
```

After this, repeat the steps to reproduce the crash, copy the backtrace, and attach it to your bug report or e-mail.

Capturing debug output with DebugView under Windows

DebugView is a small program for the Windows operating system that allows you to view and save the debug output of programs. With its help, you can easily get the QGIS debug output and add it to your bug report.

 Note that you will see no debug output if your QGIS compiled without debugging support. Official packages from the OSGeo4W installer and the QGIS standalone installer are built with the debugging output.

To get the debug output with DebugView, follow these steps:

1. Download DebugView from the Microsoft site at `https://technet.microsoft.com/en-us/sysinternals/bb896647.aspx`.

2. Extract the archive to some folder on your hard drive and launch `Dbgview.exe`.

3. Start QGIS and perform the actions that lead to a crash or an error:

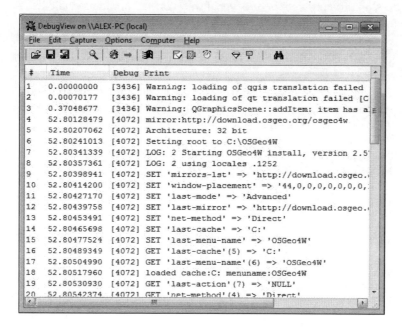

4. Save the log to a file using the **Save** button on the **DebugView** toolbar.

5. Attach the saved file to your bug report or e-mail.

   Also, if QGIS crashes, it produces a minidump file (usually these files are created in your Temp directory and have the tmp.mdmp extension), as shown in the following screenshot:

6. This file should also be attached to the bug report, as it allows developers to understand the problem better even if they cannot reproduce the crash on their computers.

How it works...

A backtrace is a summary of program functions that are still active. In other words, it shows all nested functions and calls from the program's start to the crash point. With the help of a backtrace, developers can isolate place where the bug is.

There's more...

If you have access to computers with different operating systems, it would be good to check whether this error is reproduced in different environments.

Almost all modern computers and laptops have enough performance to run virtual machines. The snapshots feature is available in the most popular virtual machines. You can have a clean and up-to-date system with recent QGIS for testing and debugging purposes.

See also

▶ More information about backtrace creation can be found on the QGIS site at `http://qgis.org/en/site/getinvolved/development/index.html#creating-a-backtrace`

Reporting bugs

Once you have found a bug and collected all the potentially useful information about its occurrence, it is time to create a bug report.

This recipe shows you how to file a bug report in a right way.

Getting ready

While QGIS project hosts its own bugtracker, you still need an OSGeo User ID to use it. If you don't have an OSGeo account, create one by filling in the form at `https://www.osgeo.org/cgi-bin/ldap_create_user.py`.

How to do it...

Go to the QGIS bugtracker at `http://hub.qgis.org/projects/quantum-gis/issues` and use your OSGeo User ID and password to log in. The **Login** link is located in the top-right corner of the page.

Before creating a new bug report, it is necessary to make sure this bug has not yet been reported. To do this, perform the following steps:

1. Go to the **Issues** tab.

2. In the **Filters** group, add and configure the necessary filters. For example, the following filters:

   ❑ **Status**: Configure this to find only open issues

   ❑ **Subject**: Configure this to find issues with the given substring in the **Subject** field

3. Click on the **Apply** link above the issues list to apply your filters:

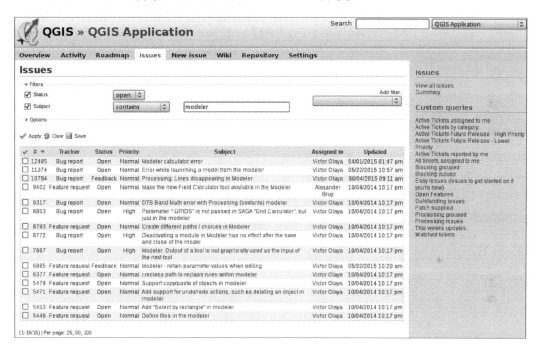

4. Check whether the resulting list contains issues that are similar to one that you found.

All tickets that match your criteria will be listed in the table.

Also, it makes sense to try to find similar issues with the ordinal search functionality:

1. Open the **Search** page at `https://hub.qgis.org/search/index/quantum-gis`.

2. Enter the keywords in the field.

3. Select **QGIS Application** from the combobox.

4. If necessary, perform the search only in ticket titles by activating the corresponding checkbox.

5. Deactivate all checkboxes under the search field except **Issues** to find only issues with given keywords.

6. Click on the **Submit** button to start the search.

Results will be displayed as a raw list of all existing tickets (open and closed), which contain keywords in their titles and description:

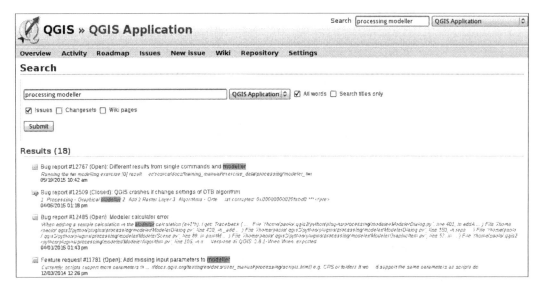

If your issue is already reported, add your observations to it. If you cannot find anything similar to your problem, it is time to submit a bug report. To do this, perform the following steps:

1. Log in to the QGIS bugtracker with your OSGeo user ID and password.

2. Go to the QGIS Application project at `http://hub.qgis.org/projects/quantum-gis`.

3. Open the **New issue** tab by clicking on the corresponding link in the menu and populate the form with the requested information:

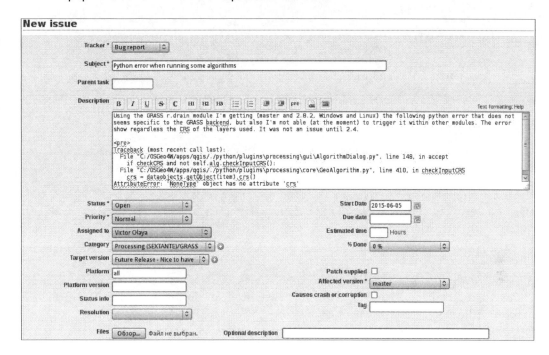

This form contains many fields, the most important ones are listed as follows:

▸ **Tracker**: This defines the ticket type. For bug reports, select **Bug Report**.

▸ **Subject**: This is a short and clear description of the problem. It will be used as the ticket title.

▸ **Description**: This is a full description of the issue. Describe your problem in detail and provide steps to reproduce it. If there are any debug messages in the console, backtraces, or minidumps, include or attach them, as well as the sample dataset. If you suspect that bug is related to the specific platform version or a specific version of the third-party dependency package (for example, GDAL, GEOS, SpatiaLite, and so on) provide this information too.

▸ **Priority**: This is where you set the anticipated importance of the bug. Currently, the following classification is used:

  ❑ **Low**: This is used for bugs that does not affect day-to-day usage of QGIS

  ❑ **Normal**: This is the default value for all new bug reports and feature requests

- ❑ **High**: This is used for bugs that have a significant impact on QGIS usability in some cases, but at the same time, they do not block QGIS usage in other tasks

- ❑ **Blocker**: This is used for bugs that make QGIS totally unusable, leads to data loss or corruption, or for regressions from previous QGIS versions

▸ **Component**: This chooses the most appropriate subsystem of QGIS, which is closely related to the issue.

▸ **Platform and Platform version**: This specifies the operating system and its version, respectively.

▸ **Causes crash or corruption**: This activates the checkbox if the bug causes a QGIS crash or data loss or corruption.

Check the formatting of the bug report by clicking on the **Preview** link at the bottom. To submit a bug report, click on the **Submit** button.

How it works...

Bug Tracker is a database with information about bugs. Developers look over bug queue and arrange them according to priorities, available resources, and fix them. Fixes usually go to the development version (the so-called "master"), but fixes for regressions and important bugs also go to the long-term release branch.

There's more...

Using the QGIS Bug Tracker, you also can leave feature requests and submit patches. However, for the latter, creating a pull-request at GitHub is preferable.

See also

▸ More information about OSGeo User ID can be found at `http://www.osgeo.org/osgeo_userid`.

▸ Additional information about using QGIS Bug Tracker can be found at the following wiki page `https://hub.qgis.org/wiki/17/Bugreports`.

▸ Also, the BUGS document in the QGIS source tree contains some useful tips. You can find it in the QGIS GitHub repository at `https://github.com/qgis/QGIS/blob/master/BUGS`.

Index

H

hillshade layer
  calculating 180, 181
  used, for enhancing map view 182, 183
hydrology
  analyzing 183-190
  workflow 188

I

Inkscape
  reference link 283
interpolation 139
Inverse Distance Weighted (IDW) 142

K

Keyhole Markup Language (KML) format 16
KML/KMZ files
  importing 16

L

LANDSAT data
  reference link 215
layer
  reprojecting 24, 25
layer blending modes
  about 269, 270
  feature blending modes, differences 271
  working 271, 272
layer data
  joining 40-42
LiDAR data
  preparing 334-336
links (edges) 144
Lizmap
  reference link 256

M

maps
  reference link 238
map series
  creating, Atlas used 295-298

Mapserver demo website
  reference link 226
mask
  used, for setting extents 207
mbtiles usage
  reference link 310
multiple route computation
  automating, batch processing used 158, 159
multispectral layers
  visualizing 212-215

N

NetCDF Browser plugin 20, 21
NetCDF file
  opening 19, 20
network analysis library
  reference link 155
network data
  obtaining, from OpenStreetMap
    (OSM) 168-170
network (graph) 144
nodes (vertices) 144
Normalized Differential Vegetation
    Index (NDVI)
  about 199
  bands, extracting 202, 203
  calculating 200, 201
null values
  distribution, exploring, in column 102-105
  handling 203-205
  null value rendering, controlling 206

O

OGC
  reference link 226
one-way streets
  reference link 152
  routing, Road graph plugin used 150-152
OpenFileGDB driver
  used, for opening File
    Geodatabases (GDB) 337-339
OpenGeo Geoserver Demo site
  reference link 236

Made in the USA
Middletown, DE
02 September 2016